D

The Art of World Team Tennis

The Art of World Team Tennis

Greg Hoffman

SAN FRANCISCO BOOK COMPANY   San Francisco   1977

Printed in the United States of America

Library of Congress Cataloging in Publication Data

Hoffman, Greg, 1946–
    The art of World Team Tennis.

    1. World Team Tennis (Organization) I. Title.
GV997.W67H63   796.34′228   77-70223
ISBN 0-913374-64-4
ISBN 0-913374-65-2 pbk.

10 9 8 7 6 5 4 3 2 1

The author is grateful to THE COCA-COLA COMPANY for permission to reprint on pages 105 – 115 excerpts from copyrighted material first published in a booklet entitled *Tennis Tips,* Copyright © 1976 by The Coca Cola Company Foods Division.

Contents

Introduction

From the beginning I was convinced that WTT would work and I was eager to do everything I could to make it happen. Of course, not everyone shared my enthusiasm. Negative reaction to the league poured in from all sides; from many of the players, from the media, and especially from the various ruling bodies of tennis who were alarmed at the prospect of having their long-standing authority over the game and the players eroded.

But WTT was an idea whose time had come and the substantial opposition was mostly ineffective.

First of all, the league was going to promote tennis as a spectator sport, something that had never been done on a large scale before. The tournament format wasn't able to guarantee that certain big name players would still be around after the early rounds. No player is immune to upsets. WTT, however, would have the advantage of being able to advertise a specific field of players every night and that was a big plus.

A definite country club image had greatly contributed to tennis's stagnation in terms of spectator appeal. For years tennis had been run by people who were generally well-intentioned, but unrealistic. They refused to accept the idea that the sport they controlled was something more than a game. And it *is* something more.

Tennis, like other professional sports, is a form of entertainment. Sure, I'm an athlete, but when I'm out on the court I'm also a performer and that court is my stage.

WTT recognized this aspect of the game and they provided the players with an extremely colorful stage and an audience unrestricted by a mass vow of silence. I admit that there have been times in my career when I've had to fight the temptation to grab the umpire's microphone and give the crowd a pep talk.

"Come on, you guys. We're out here busting our guts and you're sitting there giving us nothing in return." Obviously the crowd doesn't have an obligation to react to the match, but I can't stand indifference from spectators when I'm on the court; I need to feel *something* even if it's against me. That doesn't necessarily mean I expect or want a Fourth of July fireworks display. At Wimbledon, for instance, there is an incredible amount of drama and tension in the stands, but not much noise. I have never felt any indifference from either Wimbledon or WTT crowds, but it's a bit more boisterous in WTT. Another plus for WTT.

WTT gave the American sports fan a format he or she could relate to while horrifying many tennis purists in the process. The changes were designed for the masses though, not for the old-time country club crowd.

Although I have a reputation for being outspoken, I'm also a realist and I knew that something as different as WTT wasn't going to make it overnight. Few worthwhile things do. I felt that it would take three to five years of hard work to make it go. During the first year—1974—there were many times when I thought I'd guessed wrong. I was still convinced WTT would succeed if given enough time, but I wasn't sure it would be able to buy that time.

It would be a gross understatement to say that WTT had a few problems that year. Many of the players found it difficult to adjust to the idea of being part of a team effort after so many years of independent competition, and more than a few players were obviously in it just for the money. As player/coach of the Philadelphia Freedoms, I saw a lot of things I didn't like. I especially remember the night I actually went after a player on an opposing team because he refused to continue playing for some reason. He was being paid a lot of money to play tennis for his team and when I saw that he wasn't taking his obligation seriously, I completely flipped out. Fortunately, my husband Larry was in the stands. He saw what was happening and got to me before I got to the player.

Things weren't always super smooth on the court, and the owners were having their share of problems as well. They made quite a few mistakes, but that was to be expected. After all, they were trying to get a new business off the ground and they were doing it right out in public and not in a boardroom somewhere.

The second year, I'm happy to say, was much better. WTT lost a few teams after the first season, but adjustments were made and suddenly my three- to five-year timetable seemed realistic again. The owners were learning, the crowds were getting bigger, and I was having a ball with my new team, the New York Sets. Some of the frustrations of the previous year were gone.

The mid-season All-Star game in Los Angeles was WTT's big turning point as far as I'm concerned. It all came together that night and I knew we had turned the corner. I can't explain how or why I knew it, I just did It was a tremendous feeling. In fact, the only sour note for me personally in 1975 came when the Sets were eliminated from the post-season playoffs.

When we began the third season a lot of people didn't think I was being totally sincere when I kept saying that winning the WTT championship was my last big goal in tennis. I think they may have

construed my statements as a putdown of
Wimbledon and some of the other titles I had won,
but nothing could have been further from the truth.
It's just that there is an incredible sense of
accomplishment when a group of athletes work
towards a common goal for four months and then
achieve that goal. Coming close twice before, in
1974 with the Freedoms, and in 1975 with the Sets,
had taught me that, and I wanted the
championship as much as I've ever wanted
anything.

When I finally got to share in that feeling of
accomplishment after we beat the Golden Gaters in
the 1976 championship series, all the work,
waiting, and frustration seemed worthwhile.

The history of World Team Tennis is filled with
many amusing, frustrating, and triumphant
moments and that's what this book is all about.

But now we have to look to the future and the
view is spectacular. There's absolutely no doubt in
my mind that WTT will soon be a dominant
presence in tennis. The growth of the league, and
its acceptance, has been truly phenomenal and
that trend is going to continue. World Team Tennis
not only has arrived, it's here to stay.

BILLIE JEAN KING

Montreal
January 1977

A Short History of World Team Tennis

1 | I NEVER PROMISED YOU A ROSE GARDEN . . .

Once upon a time—in 1874 to be exact—a British officer of especially distinguished lineage stumbled upon a patch of soil that appeared to be exceedingly rich in commercial promise. Without a moment's hesitation Major Walter Clopton Wingfield began clearing the land with his bare hands. When he had finished sometime later, he proudly gazed upon a thoroughly denuded, rather small, hourglass-shaped piece of earth.

Major Wingfield was not without an advanced sense of territorial exclusivity and he decided that his parcel of land was in desperate need of a fence. He was also not lacking in eccentricity. Rather than enclose his creation with that fence, he elected to bisect it. Major Wingfield's Garden, as it came to be known among the locals, was formally unveiled a short time later. Some, of course, were unimpressed, but many who viewed the bizarre piece of turf found it charming.

Soon dozens of identical plots, all divided by an exact replica of Major Wingfield's strange fence, began to dot the countryside. Within a few years, however, the shapes of the gardens were modified from hourglasses to rectangles and the fences were replaced with new ones a full foot lower in height.

Within a few months a mysterious event occurred in Major Wingfield's original garden. Literally overnight, several beautiful rose bushes sprang from the fertile soil, apparently without benefit of seeding or tilling. The rose bushes grew up haphazardly around the garden, but they proved to be healthy, perpetually blooming specimens.

Populated thusly, Major Walter C. Wingfield's peculiar Garden greeted the dawning of the twentieth century and each of its pre-teen years. Then one day a rose bush that dwarfed all the others in size and beauty suddenly appeared on the very spot where the Major had turned the first handful of soil almost forty years earlier. Stronger and healthier than the other garden residents, the new arrival quickly assumed a position of authority. The massive late bloomer appeared to further strengthen the garden's seeming immunity from aphid attacks and other botanical annoyances. Several decades passed without consequence and the thriving garden approached its nonagenarian

seasons in pretty much the same condition it had always been in: self-perpetuating, staid, and quite content, thank you. Unfortunately, the 1960s were anything but staid and few corners of the globe went untouched by those turbulent times, including, of course, Major Wingfield's lovely rose garden.

Inevitably, the tiny paradise was infiltrated by several highly disruptive elements. Daisies, chrysanthemums, rhododendrons and even a Venus's-flytrap or two marched in and entrenched themselves amid the perpetually-blossoming splendor. The lush soil contained more than enough mineral content to adequately nourish the intruders, but the rose bushes, long the sole guardians of the garden, did not wish to share their domain with anyone, no matter how beautiful or exotic. Hostilities erupted. The garden was beset by

chaos, that at times, seemed to be on the verge of destroying it.

In that lamentable state, Major Wingfield's Garden approached its 100th anniversary. The prevailing gloom was deepened by persistent rumors that a particularly undesirable element was planning to put down roots in the garden. If true, the rumors signalled that the worst was yet to come.

It did.

On the very day of the garden's centennial, a new tenant arrived in the midst of the battling blossoms, and they looked in horror and disbelief at their very first, real, honest-to-God weed.

For a while, residents of the garden laid aside their personal differences and joined forces in an attempt to eliminate the despised newcomer. At least most of them did. There were a few plants who felt the weed was entitled to stay, but they were in the minority.

When the gutty little weed stood its ground the anti-weed forces decided to embark on a policy of calculated indifference and thinly-veiled contempt. They hoped the ugly, little thing would wilt and die of its own accord.

Well, the weed refused to shrivel and die. It grew noticeably stronger with each passing day. It even managed to gain the grudging acceptance of many of its early enemies. Against all odds, the weed had secured a place in Major Wingfield's Garden. Where, by the way, it plans to live happily ever after.

Ah, the wonders of Nature!

Those familiar with tennis history may recognize the strange saga of Major Wingfield's Garden as an allegory of the establishment and development of the modern version of that ancient sport.

Major Wingfield, was a real, living, breathing, bewhiskered Englishman. A member of the Honourable Corps of Gentlemen-at-Arms under Queen Victoria, he secured his niche in history by "inventing" lawn tennis, the precursor of modern-day tennis.

Variations of the sport, however, had been around since the 12th century and references to tennis can be found in French ecclesiastical manuscripts. Played indoors exclusively, tennis became the pastime of French royalty soon after it was introduced. There is also ample evidence indicating that the game quickly spread beyond the borders of France to the whole continent of Europe.

By the latter part of the 17th century, technological advances had resulted in the development of a ball that would bounce on a

surface other than flagstone and the ancient sport, somewhat modified, moved to the great outdoors. Thus began the modern game of lawn tennis.

Major Wingfield is generally credited with being the father of lawn tennis simply because he had the acumen to take out a patent on his court design and peddle it to interested buyers. Judging by the list of distinguished customers he published in 1875, he was quite successful. Calling his game "Sphairistike," a Greek word roughly translated as ball game, Major Wingfield applied for a patent in February 1874. The patent referred to "a new and improved portable court for playing the ancient game of tennis." Wingfield's skills as a salesman quickly resulted in the installment of hourglass-shaped tennis courts on the grounds of many of England's established croquet clubs.

The garden had been planted, but as we have seen, it was destined to undergo a number of modifications, both cosmetically and administratively. First, the dimensions of the court were altered to a rectangular shape. Subsequent changes in the court measurements and net height eventually stabilized at seventy-eight feet long by twenty-seven feet wide (thirty-six feet for doubles) and three feet high.

The rose bushes that appeared in Wingfield's garden represent the various Lawn Tennis Associations (LTAs) that were formed to administer the sport as it gained popularity. Many of these organizations were established before the turn of the century, but it wasn't until 1913, just a year after Major Wingfield's death, that a central controlling body was formed. The creation of the International Lawn Tennis Federation (ILTF) is symbolized by the arrival of the majestic rose bush.

For several decades, the various LTAs, operating under the ILTF umbrella, were charged with controlling the game of tennis in their particular jurisdictions, while encouraging as many people as possible to take up the sport. The ILTF and the LTAs also assiduously guarded the sport's strict code of amateurism, though not always effectively. It was an open secret that many amateur players were as adept at pocketing tightly-folded packets of surreptitiously passed cash as they were at putting away backhand volleys. Toward the end of the 1920s there were a few maverick excursions into professional tennis, but none that seriously threatened the sport's official policy of amateurism. Finally, in 1968, the long years of hypocrisy gave way when open tennis (amateurs and pros competing in the same events) became a reality at the British Hardcourt Championships.

The advent of open tennis paved the way for the emergence of several player organizations, formed as a direct result of the sport's move from under the kitchen table to the bank. These new organizations quickly became thorns in the sides of the rose bushes in Major Wingfield's Garden and a certain amount of friction occurred when the Association of Tennis Professionals (ATP), the World Championship of Tennis (WCT), the Independent Player's Association (IPA), and the Women's Tennis Association (WTA) put down roots.

And even as the sport was adjusting to this influx of newcomers, the brazen weed made its entrance. That weed was World Team Tennis, alias WTT.

2 | WELCOME TO THE MAJOR LEAGUES, KID

World Team Tennis, that sport's version of Rosemary's Baby; the moustache on the Mona Lisa; and, yes, the weed in Major Wingfield's Garden, put its crazy-quilt format and mixed bag of innovations on public display for the first time on May 6, 1974. Not since November 1, 1946, the date that marks the birth of the National Basketball Association (NBA), had a professional league been formed in a sport where no such league had previously existed.

The coming out party was staged at Philadelphia's massive sports arena, The Spectrum. Those who attended contended with a raging storm that was doing considerable damage to portions of the Eastern Seaboard. The storm succeeded in dampening the attire of the ten thousand-plus party-goers, but not their enthusiasm.

The opening night crowd probably contained a fair share of staunch tennis purists who braved the inclement weather to watch the upstart league double-fault its way to failure and ruin. Despite the

confident predictions that were flowing out of the league's southern California headquarters, many observers expected WTT's life span to approximate that of the average fruit fly.

After months of preparation, the league commenced operations with a match that featured two of WTT's most luminary attractions. The Philadelphia Freedoms, led by Mother Freedom herself, Billie Jean King, were going to kick things off against Evonne Goolagong, Ken Rosewall and their Pittsburgh Triangles' teammates.

The enthusiastic crowd began screaming during the opening ceremonies and player introductions. Then a massive replica of the Liberty Bell was

Evonne Goolagong of the Pittsburgh Triangles in action during the first WTT match, May 6, 1974.

rolled into the arena and rung in joyous anticipation of the. . . .

Wait a minute? Screaming spectators? A replica of the Liberty Bell? Wasn't this a tennis match, modified drastically perhaps, but a tennis match nonetheless? And aren't tennis matches notorious for drawing well-behaved galleries who oblige the players with church-like silence? Right on both counts. But this was World Team Tennis and whether the spectators were screaming in appreciation or sheer agony, they were not admonished to cool it. They were, in fact, officially encouraged.

The new breed of boisterous fans.

The policy of vocal participation at a tennis match, besides bordering on heresy, was an intregal part of WTT's "entertaining package." It also turned out to be one of the aspects of team tennis that attracted the most criticism, and not all of it from the outraged proponents of tennis's sanctification of silence. Quite a few players, especially those who had learned the game in the more sedate tennis atmospheres of Australia and Great Britain, thought it a bit much. Others, including Billie Jean, absolutely loved the commotion whether it was for or against them.

Audience participation was just one of many innovations that were unveiled on The Spectrum's center court that night. The traditional method of scoring had undergone radical surgery resulting in the removal of deuce and ad points. Gone also were the point designations, 15, 30, 40, game. Scoring the WTT way was as simple as one, two, three, four. In fact, it was 1, 2, 3, 4. The first player or players to win four points takes the game. Sweet, simple, and more important, eminently understandable to tennis neophytes. Other scoring advances introduced by the league included a nine-point, sudden death tiebreaker and that great match decider, the Super-Tiebreaker. (see p. 64)

Many hard-core purists were willing to rest their case against WTT on the basis of this single affront to their delicate sensibilities. In their view,

tampering with the traditional scoring system was a sacrilegious act that surpassed even the lack of vocal restraint imposed on the spectators. "At least when P. T. Barnum presented a circus," said the purists, "he said it was a circus."

Another controversial aspect of World Team Tennis was the actual format of competition. It consisted of six sets per match: two each of men's and women's singles and two sets of mixed doubles. Unlike tournament tennis, where the winner of a match is the player or players winning the most sets, the WTT match winner would be the team capturing the greatest number of total games during the six sets. This cumulative match scoring system made each game, each point, important. There would be no time to coast during a team tennis match.

On May 6th, it was the Philadelphia Freedoms who won the most games and the match. The Triangles grabbed 25 games and the hometowners accumulated 31. The Freedoms' victory, the first ever by a sexually integrated professional sports team, resulted in yet another innovation. The inaugural match put the Philly racqueteers on the top of the league's Atlantic Section team standings. Courtesy of World Team Tennis, the sport was suddenly entitled to take its place among those meticulously scanned sports page statistics: the baseball standings, box scores, etc. With the cooperation of tennis-oriented newspaper editors, it would be possible to check out the National League's RBI leader and WTT's top women's doubles team with a single glance.

Regulations on tennis attire, posted at the West Side Tennis Club. Another bit of tradition ignored by WTT.

And so WTT, with its boisterous spectators, streamlined scoring, odd format, player substitution rule, sexual equality, super-tiebreakers, bench jockeys, and box scores brought tennis to the major leagues in the spring of 1974.

3 | A CONSPIRACY OF CIRCUMSTANCES

Before the 1968 advent of open tennis—that is events where amateurs and professionals play together—defections from the amateur ranks were sporadic and often financially unsuccessful. There were, however, a few notable exceptions. In 1947, former amateur Jack Kramer embarked on an exhibition tour with future hustler Bobby Riggs. They drew an astounding crowd of over 15,000 to New York's Madison Square Garden. Even more amazing, the crowd showed up during one of the worst blizzards in New York history.

Kramer continued playing professionally until 1952 when he assumed an additional role of promoter. The following year, he put down his racquet and concentrated exclusively on promoting pro tennis. He organized exhibition tours and round-robin road shows featuring many of the fifties' top male players—Ken Rosewall, Lew Hoad, Pancho Gonzales, Pancho Segura, Butch Buchholz, and others. But Kramer retired from full-time promotions in 1962 and the pro game was in danger of disappearing entirely.

Fortunately, Ken Rosewall, then at the top of his career, and Lew Hoad succeeded in convincing the Grand Slammer himself, Rod Laver, to turn pro. Laver's decision turned out to be a lucrative one for him personally, and it helped keep the game from going under.

Though some of the best players in the world had abandoned amateurism, the established amateur playgrounds of Wimbledon and Forest Hills continued to thrive. But Wimbledon, the highly influential host of the world's premier tennis event, had long been lobbying for modernization of the antiquated amateur rules and the introduction of a limited number of open tournaments. The ILTF resisted the pressure because they were understandably afraid of losing their control.

Despite the certainty of incurring the wrath of the ILTF, the British LTA sanctioned a professional event at Wimbledon in August 1967. Laver, Rosewall, and six other pros came to play while the Old Guard of tennis cringed. The eight-man tournament, which was won by Laver, heralded the inevitability of open tennis. The British LTA was supported by several other nations and at an emergency meeting of the ILTF in the spring of 1968 an official policy allowing

open tennis was ratified. The pro game received a much-needed breath of new life.

Meanwhile, match point at the finals of Wimbledon's first professional event had barely left the strings of Rod Laver's racquet when two gentlemen in the United States made their respective moves into the hectic world of tennis promotion. Dave Dixon, a New Orleans businessman, had managed to convince well-known sportsman Lamar Hunt to invest in something called World Championship Tennis, Inc. (WCT). Hunt, who played a substantial role in the formation of the American Football League (AFL) and was that league's first president, brought in his nephew, Al Hill, Jr., and WCT was almost in business.

Having secured Hunt's backing, Dixon, went about the business of signing players for his proposed circuit, but he soon discovered he was not alone. George MacCall was after the same players for his organization, the National Tennis League (NTL). MacCall was no stranger to tennis. He had been a star player on the Bucknell team during his college days. He had also reached the finals of the Wimbledon men's 45-and-over doubles in 1964 and 1965. (Partnered with Pancho Segura, MacCall repeated that feat in 1970.)

Between Bucknell and Wimbledon, MacCall spent three years as captain of the US Davis Cup team. Unfortunately, his years at the helm of the Cup squad were less than notable ones. Under his guidance, the U.S. failed to survive the preliminary rounds of the competition in 1965, 1966, and 1967. In the summer of '67, George MacCall established the NTL, becoming WCT's chief competitor.

Almost immediately the fledgling NTL succeeded in signing established pros Rod Laver, Ken Rosewall, Pancho Gonzales, and Andre Gimeno, as well as amateurs Fred Stolle and Roy Emerson. MacCall also signed four leading women players: Billie Jean King, Ann Haydon Jones, promising newcomer Rosie Casals, and the possessor of tennis's most celebrated limp-wristed backhand, Francoise Durr.

Dixon meanwhile managed to secure pros Butch Buchholz, Dennis Ralston, and Pierre Barthes. They were joined by amateurs John Newcombe, Tony Roche, Cliff Drysdale, Nikki Pilic, and Roger Taylor.

Though it was by no means a league in the traditional sense, the National Tennis League was so named for a reason. MacCall and the others involved in the NTL had, as their ultimate aim, a full-fledged professional tennis league. There weren't enough professional tennis players available to support such a league in 1967, but MacCall was convinced there would be some day and he wanted to be ready.

WCT and the Hunt/Dixon/Hill triumverate had no such grandiose plans. Their ambitions lay somewhere between barnstorming exhibitions and traditional tournaments. The "Handsome Eight," as the original WCT players were dubbed, didn't exactly constitute an ideal tournament field, however, and the new organization was in trouble almost from the beginning.

Dave Dixon bailed out of WCT within a few months after its inception and Hunt took over his share of the action. He also brought in a man named Michael Davies whose experience as an amateur and professional player would prove to be an invaluable asset. Slowly, WCT was beginning to grow, both in the number of players participating and on the balance sheet.

Not so NTL. MacCall's group of six men and four women toured the country extensively, but the shoestring budget was unable to support the ambitious concept. It was a classic case of trying to do too much too fast and the NTL went out of business two years after it began.

WCT immediately absorbed 60 per cent of the NTL by purchasing the men's contracts from the defunct league but the other 40 per cent—the women—were cast adrift. Ironically, the frustrations encountered by the former NTL women over the next few years would lead directly to the formation of World Team Tennis.

4 | THE WOMEN'S GAME

Prior to the formation of the National Tennis League in 1967, the women's pro game in the United States was practically nonexistent. In 1947, Pauline Betz, the defending Wimbledon champion, and Sarah Palfrey Cooke, the 1945 U.S. Open titleholder, turned pro but went nowhere. A few years later, Betz and Gussie Moran, a young lady whose attire attracted considerably more attention than her playing ability, were signed by Bobby Riggs to accompany a men's exhibition tour he had organized.

Women's professional tennis was basically nothing more than a sideshow. In 1958 two-time Wimbledon and Forest Hills champ Althea Gibson turned pro and was joined by Karol Fageros as the opening act for the Harlem Globetrotters basketball team. By the end of the season, the women had become more disillusioned than wealthy, and the act was discontinued.

Women's pro tennis lay dormant until 1967 and the appearance of the short-lived NTL. For almost two years, Billie Jean King, Rosie Casals, Ann Haydon Jones, and Francoise Durr played alongside MacCall's six men. But when the league went under, they found themselves in the uncomfortable situation of being footloose, fancy free, and unwanted. They continued to play tournaments as independent pros, but far from being hailed as heroines by the other women, they were looked upon as pariahs who were only in tennis for the money.

In the bygone days of strict amateurism, men and women players had been treated as financial equals. Open tennis changed all that. Most of the tournaments were run by men and, not surprisingly, most of the prize money was earmarked for the men players. Publicly, the disparity in prize money did not appear to bother most of the women, who seemed content to tag along with the men. Women's tennis, even in 1969, was still basically a sideshow proposition.

But a few of the leading women players vociferously complained about the pecuniary imbalance, and at Wimbledon in 1969 there was an aborted attempt to form a women players association. Billie Jean King, who is not especially well known for her reticence, saw the handwriting on the wall and made up her mind to do something about it. She discussed the prize money situation with her husband Larry King, an attorney. The result of those discussions was a ten-page position paper regarding the current state of women's tennis, written by Larry in January 1970, and sent to the top eight women players, and to Gladys Heldman publisher/editor of *World Tennis* magazine.

The paper pointed out what everyone already knew: that the women's prize money in mixed events was far below the men's and that it was probably going to get worse before it got better, if in fact, it ever did get better. A fairly risky course of action was proposed; one that would really make or break the women's game. In Larry's and Billie Jean's view, the only real solution to the problem was to have the women set up a separate tour and go it alone, at least temporarily.

Larry suggested that a six-week series of three-day mini-tournaments involving the top eight players be organized. Unfortunately the response to his idea was negative. Billie Jean and Rosie Casals were all for it, but Gladys Heldman and the six other recipients of the proposal ignored it completely. Directionless, the women's game retained its second class citizenship.

Eight months passed before the situation reached crisis proportions. By then, most of the

Larry King, whose involvement in tennis went far beyond his marriage to Billie Jean.

women had seen the money lists for the Fall 1970 and Spring 1971 events. Finally they decided to take action. The turning point actually occurred when the players discovered that the Pacific Southwest Championships scheduled for August 1970 were offering $50,000 in total prize money for the men, but only $7,500 for the women.

At the U.S. Open in 1970 the women nominated Gladys Heldman to ask the Pacific Southwest's tournament director, Jack Kramer, to upgrade the women's prize money. Gladys agreed to negotiate with Kramer. She told him that offering a paltry $1,500 to the winner was unfair because the women would be risking out of pocket airfare and expences on a long shot. The $1,500 would allow the tournament winner to break even, but most of the women would end up losing money. In fact only the eight quarter-finalists would make any money at all.

Kramer refused to budge. Holding the traditional attitude that the men were superior players and that

no one came to see the distaff racqueteers anyway, he refused to raise the stakes.

The women were not pleased when Gladys relayed the bad news. Particularly outraged were the dynamic duo, Billie Jean and Rosie. They immediately asked Gladys to organize a boycott of the Pacific Southwest if their demands were not met. Additional negotiations with Kramer were arranged, but he was adamant. No increase.

Gladys called the women together in the locker room of the West Side Tennis Club, home of the U.S. Open, to discuss the situation. She advised against a boycott of the Pacific Southwest, proposing instead that they organize a concurrent event featuring the top eight women players. Putting on an alternative tournament would allow those women who were not at the top to compete in the Pacific Southwest and possibly pick up some prize money. Gladys volunteered to stage the protest tournament in Houston, if the women agreed to her plan. They did. Even Jack Kramer, who was fully informed of their intentions, promised not to put up a fight.

Gladys Heldman approached her contacts at Philip Morris and Virginia Slims. They agreed to put up the $7,500 prize money. The Houston Racquet Club, proposed sight of the renegade venture, applied for, and received, a regional sanction. So far, so good.

Then, just a few days before the Houston tournament was scheduled to begin, the USLTA overruled the Houston Tennis Association's regional sanction and said that if any of the eight women played in the event they would be suspended. Despite almost continuous negotiations between Gladys and the USLTA, the order rescinding the regional sanction stood.

Another player meeting was held to discuss this latest crisis and the eight players voted unanimously to sign $1 contracts with Gladys and play the Houston event as contract pros. The idea was almost as imaginative as it was ineffective. The women, Billie Jean King, Rosemary Casals, Nancy Gunter, Peaches Bartkowicz, Valerie Ziegenfuss, Kristy Pigeon, Judy Dalton and Kerry Melville were, as promised, immediately suspended by the USLTA. A ninth player quickly joined them in tennis limbo: Julie Heldman, Gladys's daughter. Unable to compete in Houston because of an injured arm, Julie nevertheless signed a contract and received a suspension for her efforts.

On the Tuesday of that first Virginia Slims tournament, Billie Jean called Larry in Berkeley to tell him that she had been officially suspended from all USLTA and ILTF-sanctioned events for life. Since the Houston affair was set up as a one-time shot, she figured that the time might be ripe to bring up Larry's January 1970 proposal for a women's exhibition tour. She asked him to come to Texas and meet with the suspended players.

Immediately, Larry contacted Dennis Van der Meer, his partner in a tennis camp venture called TennisAmerica, and they hastily put together a plan for staging several $10,000 tournaments beginning in 1971. Clutching the spur-of-the-moment tournament outline, Larry caught a plane for Houston. On Friday night, in Gladys Heldman's living room, he laid out his plan for the women: five $10,000 tournaments at first, with more to follow. The players were enthusiastic and they voted to hire Larry and Dennis Van der Meer to run the show in exchange for 10 per cent of the prize money.

No one was more surprised than Larry King when Gladys Heldman let it be known that he was stepping on her toes. He had assumed that her full-time duties at *World Tennis* would necessarily preclude her becoming a tennis promoter. But he was wrong.

Gladys indicated that she was willing to set up and run a women's circuit, so Larry graciously backed off. After all, she was perfect for the job. She already had a sponsor, a track record, and the trust of the nine women in her living room. Larry said he would assist her in whatever way he could, and Gladys Heldman emerged as the chief administrative officer of the Women's Pro Tour.

Within a few months, a series of contract pro tournaments were established for the 1971/72 winter and spring season and ten more players signed on, including the remaining ex-NTLers Ann Haydon Jones and Francoise Durr.

In January 1971, exactly one year after Larry King's original proposal, the first tournament of the Virginia Slims circuit, was held in San Francisco. It drew a total of only 4,000 spectators during a six-day period, but things slowly began to improve. Nearly two dozen tournaments were played prior to Wimbledon in 1971, offering total prize money of over $200,000. The Virginia Slims/Women's Pro Tour Circuit began to offer minimum prize money of $20,000 per event and it was open to all tournament players. The tournaments were also being played without USLTA sanction, although that august body did lift the player suspensions in February 1971.

The women's circuit was off the ground, but sadly, problems and discord abounded. At Forest Hills that summer, the USLTA issued an ultimatum to the growing Slims circuit, demanding, among other things, that minimum prize money standards be abandoned, that a sanction fee of 6 per cent of

the prize money be funneled into USLTA coffers, and that Mrs. Heldman relinquish her position of authority. Naturally, the players opposed USLTA's dictum. Virginia Slims also rejected the ultimatum and threatened to withdraw their television sponsorship funds from the U.S. Open and put them into the circuit. In addition, ten more women players approached Gladys Heldman and asked to sign up. In the face of such defiance, the USLTA backed down.

The Virginia Slims circuit began the 1972 season stronger than ever, but within a few months Gladys Heldman, apparently fed up with the constant and oppressive battles with the USLTA, announced that she was going to step out of the picture.

That unexpected announcement prompted Shari Barman, a Virginia Slims circuit player, to write her father, expressing doubts about the future of the tour. She solicited his help. Though Shari didn't know it at the time, her letter of August 20, 1972, was the seed of conception that resulted in the birth of World Team Tennis.

Shari Barman's letter.

VIRGINIA SLIMS
WOMEN'S TENNIS CIRCUIT
100 Park Avenue, New York, N.Y. 10017

NEWPORT 1972
AUG 20 — 12:45 PM

DEAR DAD:
THE CIRCUIT THIS SUMMER IS VERY BAD — DISORGANIZED AND IT LOOKS AS THOUGH IF SOMETHING DOESN'T HAPPEN SOON TO GET IT TOGETHER THERE WILL BE NO MORE VIRGINIA SLIMS CIRCUIT — WE NEED A NEW PROMOTER AND MANAGER NOW THAT GLADYS HELDMAN IS NO LONGER WITH THE GROUP ... ANYWAY, WE ARE IN QUITE A PREDICAMENT .... DO YOU HAVE ANY IDEAS ON THE SUBJECT ?? I'VE BEEN TALKING TO BILLIE JEAN A LOT AND I TOLD HER I WAS GOING TO TALK TO YOU ABOUT IT

WELL THAT'S ALL FOR NOW — WILL BE TALKING TO YOU SOON.

love FROM

Shari Barman

5 | THE FOUNDING FATHERS

Fred Barman was understandably distressed by his daughter's report concerning the unfortunate predicament of the women's circuit. A Beverly Hills business manager, Barman's stable of clients was comprised largely of movie and television people but he did represent one professional athlete: Mike Byers of the World Hockey Association's Los Angeles Sharks. That association was destined to play a pivotal role in the formation of World Team Tennis.

Immediately upon receiving Shari's plea for help, Barman called Dennis Murphy, the General Manager of the Sharks. Barman was fully aware of

Murphy's impressive sports background, including his role as co-founder of both the WHA and the ABA (American Basketball Association). Murphy listened to Barman's tale of woe and said he would talk to Gary Davidson, a fellow co-founder of the ABA.

A few days later, Murphy told Barman that both he and Davidson were interested in the fate of women's tennis and that the problem deserved further investigation. Barman and Murphy got in touch with Gladys Heldman, who personally assured them that she was indeed through with running the circuit. They then decided to solicit Larry King's advice.

Larry was not especially enthusiastic about their plans to assume control of the circuit. "There's no way Gladys Heldman's going to quit," King told them, "no way."

They said that she had told them she was definitely through, but King didn't buy it for a minute. "I don't care what she said. It's just a ploy to get out of some agreements she made with the USLTA. After disbanding the current circuit, she's going to organize a new one."

Since King didn't think Barman and Murphy stood a chance of replacing Gladys, he suggested that they set up a circuit that would operate when Gladys's didn't. At the time, the Virginia Slims circuit suspended operations before Wimbledon and resumed after Forest Hills, leaving the summer months wide open. King said that many of the women were tired of traveling to Europe for the summer and they might respond positively to an alternative circuit.

The two men asked King if he would be

Fred Barman, a WTT founder, who later became the first director of WTT Properties.

Dennis Murphy, WTT founder and first president.

interested in becoming a partner in such a venture. He turned the partnership offer down cold, but said he might be willing to have them *hire* him to run a summer circuit.

King explained his reluctance by running down the financial facts of tournament tennis. "Tournaments seldom make money," he said. "It generally costs between $100,000 and $150,000 to stage a seven-day event and a tournament always runs the risk of losing its top gate attractions in the early rounds. Also, the prime, revenue-producing days are the last two days, usually a Saturday and a Sunday. What happens if you go into the crucial days with no-name players and bad weather besides?"

Murphy and Barman were not dissuaded. On September 1, 1972, Shari Barman nervously addressed a group of women players who had gathered on one of the practice courts adjacent to the West Side Tennis Club's magnificent ivy-draped clubhouse. She announced that her father was on his way to New York to talk to them about taking over the management of their circuit.

Immediately after finishing her remarks, Shari went to one of the phone booths located in the darkly-panelled, narrow, main corridor of the clubhouse to call her father. Midway through the conversation she glanced into another phone booth across the way and was able to inform him that Julie Heldman was issuing a report of her own at that very moment.

The following day, Fred Barman and one of Dennis Murphy's associates arrived at Forest Hills and began lobbying for the women's support. Predictably, the players' reaction was mixed. It hardly mattered though because a few days later, Gladys Heldman announced that she was forming a new women's association. And the women said they were going to stay with her.

Barman, however, was far from discouraged. If anything, his desire to get involved in women's tennis had been intensified by his visit to Forest Hills. Shortly after returning to the West Coast, he and Murphy decided to get together with Larry King to discuss the situation further.

On September 20, 1972, the three men met in King's tiny, TennisAmerica offices located over a thriving massage parlor in Oakland. Murphy and Barman, said that they had decided on a summer tour and that they wanted Larry to supervise the tour as a paid employee.

A few months later, in January 1973, King, Barman, and Murphy met again, this time in Los Angeles. During their discussion about the proposed summer circuit, Murphy mentioned that he'd heard about a team tennis organization that

was currently trying to sell franchises. He was referring to a new National Tennis League formed in October 1972 by three Pittsburgh businessmen. (George MacCall, founder of the original National Tennis League way back in 1967, was not involved in any way with the new venture by the same name.) This NTL, was offering franchises for a mere $250,000 each.

"Maybe we should start a tennis league ourselves," suggested Murphy, ever the consummate sports entrepreneur.

"Now with *that* idea," said Larry King, "I'd be your partner."

Barman was also enthusiastic. They dropped the summer circuit idea immediately. Murphy said that Jordan Kaiser, one of his WHA buddies, would be the ideal person to direct the league's finances. Kaiser, a Windy City construction executive, was the owner of the WHA Chicago Cougars and he was currently the WHA treasurer.

A month later, on February 5, 1973, Murphy, Barman and King met with Kaiser at the Palm Springs Racquet Club. He agreed to join the venture as a partner and also agreed to put up some front money to get the idea off the ground.

Jordan Kaiser, WTT founder and second president.

It was decided that Murphy and King would join Kaiser as partners, with each man receiving a one-third share of the action. Barman, the catalyst who'd brought Murphy and King together, was handed the directorship of the league's properties. Their creation was called the International Professional Tennis League (IPTL).

6 | TEAM TENNIS, ANYONE?

The first order of business for the newly-formed IPTL was marketing. That particular task fell to Larry King, because he alone was familiar with the ins and outs of the tennis world. Within two weeks, he wrote the IPTL rules and regulations and devised a prototype for the league. An asking price of $50,000 per franchise was agreed upon, a promotional brochure was printed, and the International Professional Tennis League was ready to go public.

At the Los Angeles Sportscaster's Luncheon on March 14, 1973, it was announced that the IPTL would commence play the following April with twelve as yet unsold franchises. Each IPTL team would consist of two men and two women players competing in two men's and women's singles sets. When necessary, ties would be decided by a set of mixed doubles. The league also stated that a player draft would be held in the near future, and the names of such potential draftees as John Newcombe, Margaret Court, Rod Laver, and Billie Jean King were mentioned.

IPTL vice-president Larry King pointed out that the league's chances of signing players would hinge on the ability to successfully bid against the $30,000 to $40,000 top players might expect to win by playing the majority of the events on the traditional tournament circuit during the IPTL's proposed schedule. The press conference concluded with the announcement that an informational meeting for prospective franchise buyers would be held at Miami's Jockey Club on April 28.

The founders were somewhat disheartened to discover that the first public stirrings of the IPTL elicited the journalistic equivalent of a barely stifled yawn. They got about a half inch of ink in the *New York Times,* and not a lot more from anyone else. Even the ILTF and USLTA failed to acknowledge the existence of the fledgling league.

At least four people did sit up and take notice, (negative to be sure, but notice nonetheless). The Pittsburgh trio who had announced the formation of the NTL a few months earlier, in October 1972, viewed the IPTL as a blatant infringement of their idea, and they didn't like it one bit. Though they had been totally unsuccessful in selling their high-priced franchises, the NTL organizers decided to fight the West Coast group.

A lawsuit was prepared, but before it got off the ground, the IPTL requested and received a chance to discuss a possible settlement. The result of those negotiations was a merger of the NTL and the IPTL. In exchange for dropping the suit and agreeing to the merger, the Pittsburgh men were awarded a free franchise for their city. But it wasn't an IPTL franchise; it was a WTT franchise. The name change to World Team Tennis was a by-product of the merger.

That problem solved, WTT turned its attention to the fourth person who possessed a decidedly negative attitude about the league: good, 'ol Jack Kramer, the scourge of women's tennis and the director of the ATP, the men's player association. Kramer, alarmed by the WTT concept from the outset, decided to fight fire with fire. He contacted George MacCall and offered him the directorship of a six-week league-type concept to be owned by the players. Kramer, and player agent Donald Dell, knew that WTT, if successful, would greatly diminish the ATP's chances of controlling the men's professional game. They wanted to get rid of WTT and the sooner the better.

MacCall was still weighing Kramer's proposal when WTT stepped in and offered him the job of league commissioner. MacCall didn't accept the WTT offer, but he agreed to attend the informational meeting in Miami.

In the midst of all these maneuverings, Dennis Murphy, Jordan Kaiser, and Fred Barman were busy hustling WTT to anyone who would stand still for a minute and listen to them. The energetic Murphy proved to be an especially effective salesman and it was he who was primarily responsible for the rather spectacular turnout at the organizational meeting. It was attended by thirty-two groups, representing twenty-nine cities. Even WCT's Mike Davies, assuming the role of interested observer, showed up in Miami.

The overwhelming response, though gratifying, also presented a problem. Prior to the formal announcement of their intentions on March 14th, the four WTT founders were not in total agreement as to the number of franchises that should be awarded. Murphy was thinking in terms of two dozen or so, and King's feeling was that eighteen would suffice. Barman and Kaiser thought that eight would do it. Allowing for the normal loss that usually accompanies the launching of a new league, they finally decided to announce the availability of twelve franchises.

Looking over the number of prospective customers in Miami, however, it was clear that twelve might not be enough. The founders were concerned that the surprising display of interest might prompt some of those attending to walk away from WTT and establish a competing league. To combat that unspoken threat, which never materialized, the available franchise figure was raised from twelve to sixteen.

WTT then laid its cards on the table. The league structure, methods of operation, budgets, expected losses, all were presented to the gathering. WTT also offered a thorough analysis of the obstacles that were certain to be thrown in its path by the ILTF, the USLTA, and Jack Kramer's ATP. The league wanted potential customers to know exactly what they would be up against, and they wanted them to know it wouldn't be easy. But WTT also wanted to let them know it wouldn't be impossible either.

The two-day informational meeting convinced the founders to step up their timetable. Originally, they had calculated that they would have until the end of the year to organize, sell franchises, conduct a player draft, and still have a cushion of four months in which to sign players before the first season commenced in May 1974. If even half of those present in Miami weren't frightened off by the potential pitfalls, the frantic days of trying to sell the league were almost over. A second meeting was proposed. Billed as an organizational get-together, it was scheduled for May 22 in Chicago. Franchises would be awarded and checks would be accepted. Only the sincere need apply.

League officials had absolutely no idea of what to expect at Chicago. What if no one shows up?, they asked themselves. What then? At least they were able to derive a measure of comfort from the knowledge that if buyers *did* make an appearance, a duly-ordained WTT commissioner would be on hand to accept their franchise fees plus a $10,000 league assessment. The first WTT czar would be George MacCall. He had turned down Kramer's offer of running the ATP firewall and come to terms with WTT in Miami.

The fears of a "no-show" meeting turned out to be unfounded. Fourteen enthusiastic franchise seekers, representing a like number of cities, came to Chicago eager to sign on the dotted line. Since a Pittsburgh franchise had already been established by the NTL/IPTL merger, that brought the total number to fifteen.

This number posed a problem. A league usually strives to field an even number of teams to facilitate a balanced schedule. Commissioner MacCall and the founders found themselves with either one franchise too many or one too few. Since cutting back would be easier than adding on that's exactly what they decided to do.

They had endeavored to screen the applicants in an effort to determine whether or not their financial situations would support their entry into the arena

of professional sports, an arena in which money often disappears quickly. On the basis of their findings, they concentrated their efforts on trying to discourage the financially weakest candidate from buying in. The scheme failed. The man simply wouldn't allow himself to be talked out of a chance to own a professional tennis team.

At that point, Gary Davidson, the ABA co-founder who had expressed interest in getting into tennis, appeared and said he'd buy a franchise. End of problem. WTT immediately called a press conference and announced that sixteen franchises had been sold. World Team Tennis was officially in business.

New York, Boston, Philadelphia, Detroit, Florida, Pittsburgh, Cleveland, Toronto, Chicago, Houston, Denver, Minnesota, San Diego, Phoenix, Los Angeles, and San Francisco/Oakland were awarded franchises on May 22. Although the new owners included a number of people who were making their first plunge into professional sports, they were joined by Dr. Leonard Bloom, a successful San Diego dentist who already owned professional hockey and basketball teams and John Bassett, a former Canadian Davis Cup player and past Chairman of the Board of the National Hockey League's (NHL) Toronto Maple Leafs. Jerry Saperstein, once owner of the Harlem Globetrotters, had the New York WTT franchise, and Gary Davidson, the president of the WHA, headed the Phoenix entry.

The Minnesota franchise was awarded to another professional hockey team owner, Len Vannelli of the Minnesota Fighting Saints. The Cleveland team became the latest acquisition of Nick Mileti, whose portfolio already included three pro teams: the Cleveland Indians (baseball), the Cavaliers (basketball), and the Crusaders (hockey).

With all of that behind them, the league's co-founders affiliated themselves with individual teams. Larry King became a part owner of the San Francisco/Oakland team. Jordan Kaiser took the Chicago franchise, and Fred Barman and Dennis Murphy each took a piece of Los Angeles. Ironically, one person at the Chicago meeting who was among the most qualified candidates for franchise ownership left town empty-handed. Although his sports background, which included a fair amount of professional tennis experience, was impeccable and his financial situation positively legendary, Lamar Hunt never really considered picking up a franchise, probably because WCT was keeping him too busy. He did, however, come away from Chicago with a kind of grudging admiration of the league's reckless courage. Of course, his view was tempered by his memory of the early years

with the American Football League (AFL).

In an amazingly brief period of time, a revolutionary professional sports league had been conceived, a completely unique format had been devised, a potentially disastrous lawsuit had been circumvented, an organized counter-move had been thwarted, a commissioner had been hired, and, perhaps most important, sixteen franchises had been sold.

No doubt about it, World Team Tennis, the new kid on the block, had moved in and made itself right at home. There was, however, one small problem. The 16-team league had no tennis players.

7 | BLOWS AGAINST THE EMPIRE

Players or no players, Jack Kramer was not enchanted by WTT's almost spontaneous generation. Nor was he particularly overjoyed upon learning he had lost George MacCall to an upstart bunch of crazies who in his view were dedicated to the desecration of the traditional sport of tennis.

In April 1973, Kramer issued a call to arms to the ILTF, USLTA, foreign federations, and righteous thinking tennis players everywhere. Characterizing WTT as a blatant "attempt by rich American businessmen to take over the sport," he called for a united effort to quash the new league before it could get established. Failure to do so, Kramer hinted darkly, would be an open invitation to disaster.

But even as Kramer and ATP legal advisor Donald Dell were trying to mobilize anti-WTT forces, the despised "rich American businessmen" were preparing for the first WTT league meeting in Palm Springs on June 1–2. Held at the Occitillo Lodge, a classy establishment located on the fringe of that desert community, the WTT meeting commenced with the tedious but necessary chore of erecting a hierarchical structure. Founders Dennis Murphy, Jordan Kaiser, and Larry King were swept in as president, executive vice-president, and chief administrator, respectively. Next, the various committees that would deal with specific aspects of league operations—player conduct, officiating, rules, finances, etc.—were formed and staffed. The election of the Board of Directors completed the organizational chart.

The bylaws and constitution were presented and a $10,000 assessment was collected from each franchise. All in all, the first day of the first league meeting was the typical nuts and bolts beginning of a business venture that promised to be anything but typical.

The following day discussion centered on signing up players for the teams. Ah, yes, the players. Let's see. Sixteen teams with at least three men and three women each (the originally proposed rosters of two men and two women had been revised since the March press conference) meant that a minimum of ninety-six players would have to be hired, a fair number indeed. It would not be an easy task, but it was one the owners were anxious to tackle.

A player draft, much like the ones used by pro football, basketball and hockey teams, was scheduled for the first week of August, but the owners, fired with enthusiasm, said "What the hell, let's go out and try to sign a few biggies before the draft." They felt that if they were successful with a few big names, it would be easier to convince other players who still had reservations about team tennis to sign up. Perhaps. In any event, assembling sixteen well-balanced professional tennis teams loomed as a particularly difficult problem.

WTT didn't know what to expect from the players. Billie Jean, of course, was an enthusiastic supporter of the WTT concept and there was little doubt about her eventual signing. Among the men, John Newcombe was said to be favorably disposed toward the league. But in regard to most of the other players, the jury was still out.

Despite the air of uncertainty, WTT recognized that signing a number of certified, bankable draws was absolutely essential, and the sooner the better. To accomplish that mission, the owners organized a three-man recruiting committee, comprised of Commissioner MacCall, Larry King, and Director of Player Recruitment, Steve Arnold. They were dispatched with instructions to do whatever necessary to get players to sign WTT contracts.

The headhunters prepared a sales pitch. "World Team Tennis," they would say, "has more benefits than a Teamsters' contract. As you well know, in order to win a tournament you have to survive six or seven grueling matches. But with WTT, you will only play three or four matches a week, and they will be shorter and, therefore, less demanding physically. Besides tournaments produce only a single winner in each division; WTT will produce eight winning teams every night of league play. As a result, you, the player, will receive more recognition."

"You will also have the opportunity to play twenty-two matches in one city, and twenty-two matches on the road as a representative of that city. Besides building a home town following, the endorsement possibilities in that community are practically unlimited."

Other financial advantages offered by WTT included a guaranteed salary, a pension plan similar to those enjoyed by other major league athletes, medical insurance, and fully-paid travel expenses.

"If that's not enough, each team will have a full-time coach and trainer. Just sign here."

Who in his or her right mind could refuse such an attractive bag of goodies? That was the question weighing heavily on the minds of the WTT group as they winged over the Atlantic on their way to the wildest, weirdest Wimbledon ever.

Upon arrival the headhunters discovered that Jack Kramer had also been busy. The evidence was everywhere. Most of the men players, especially those who were ATP members, shrank from the WTT reps as if they had the plague or something.

"Well, at least the flight over was smooth," said Larry King. They were obviously in for a rough time, but Wimbledon '73 wasn't going to be a picnic for Kramer either.

Even a modicum of cooperation between Kramer's players' union and the ILTF might have severely lessened WTT's impact, but it was not to be. Instead the "Pilic Affair" reared its ugly head and shoved an ATP/ILTF donneybrook onto center stage, forcing the *WTT versus Everybody* battle into the background.

Nikki Pilic had originally been suspended by his Yugoslav federation for refusing to play a Davis Cup match, but Kramer and Dell appealed his three month suspension to the ILTF and it was reduced to one month. The ATP was still not satisfied because the suspension would still be in effect during the opening week of Wimbledon. Kramer and Dell then decided to go to court (civil, not tennis) and ask for an injunction forcing the ILTF to accept Pilic's entry at Wimbledon. Arguing that ATP members were beyond the control or disciplinary actions of national federations, and that the ILTF-upheld suspension of Pilic was aimed at breaking up the ATP, Kramer and Dell pleaded for the suspension to be dismissed. After due consideration, the British court turned them down. The suspension, said the court, was totally within the rights of the ILTF. As a result of that decision, seventy-nine ATP members walked away from Wimbledon and directly into the clutches of King, MacCall, and Arnold, who were waving lucrative contracts.

The WTT recruiters pounced on the striking players with the fervor of over-conscientious I.R.S. agents going after tax evaders. When the dust finally settled, they had signed Owen Davidson, Kerry Melville, Kerry Harris, and Clark Graebner. They had also received assurances from many other players that they were open to negotiations. Billie Jean King and John Newcombe were in fact already talking with the league and were expected to sign contracts at the August draft session.

Kramer didn't throw in the towel though. Instead he decided to increase his efforts to bury WTT once and for all. The league had applied for USLTA and ILTF sanctions even though they knew both organizations were adamantly opposed to the concept of team tennis. The USLTA must have realized that any overt move to block WTT would leave them open to anti-trust charges, so they apparently put the sanction request on the back burner while they worked on pushing through a special piece of legislation at the ILTF's annual meeting in Warsaw in July 1973. The proposed rule authorized the national federations to ban or fine players who signed contracts with promoters. It passed with flying colors. Obviously directed at WTT, the ruling supplied the USLTA with the legal ammunition to fight team tennis from behind the ILTF's billowing skirts.

Although the Warsaw rule wounded WTT, the most crushing blow to the league's chances of survival was delivered internally. It came from an unexpected source, the owners themselves.

As previously mentioned, the WTT owners had decided to test the waters by trying to sign a few major luminaries prior to the draft. As an added inducement, league officials had agreed to promise the chosen few the opportunity to choose the franchise for whom they wished to play.

Larry King told the owners that his spouse would come aboard for a five-year contract at $100,000 per year. He also stated that her first choices were New York, Los Angeles, and Philadelphia. New York immediately balked at the half-mill price tag. "Sure, we'd love to have her," they said, "but at 100 thou per year we feel a league subsidy might be in order."

King thought it over and agreed. The owners thought it over and disagreed. The shoot-from-the-wallet WTT bidding war had begun.

"I can't believe it," said the astonished Larry King. "You guys have just made Billie Jean rich."

The founders had always believed that WTT's financial health was dependent on keeping players salaries at a reasonable level. The hundred grand a year BJK wanted was high, but it wasn't unreasonable. The league desperately needed instant credibility and drawing power and Billie Jean was one of a handful of players who could provide both . . . but for a price. Well, she got a price alright, and because of it a lot of others did too. The owners apparently didn't want to wait three or more years to drop a bundle. They wanted

to do it right away!

As the bidding for BJK approached two million dollars, three teams were still involved: Minnesota, Philadelphia, and, incredible as it sounds, New York. That's right, the very same New York franchise that had yelled "subsidy" a mere million and a half dollars earlier.

Though the Big Apple would have been the ideal home base for a new league's top ink-getter, Billie Jean finally opted for Philadelphia's 1.8 million, five-year offer, primarily because of her personal friendship with Philly owner, Dick Butera.

Billie Jean had gotten rich alright, and WTT's financial forecast had been blown to smithereens in the process.

When the owners finally realized what had happened they went to great lengths to keep the terms of BJK's contract under wraps. They were afraid, and rightly so, that if the news leaked out the next big name player who took a seat at the bargaining table would demand an equal amount or possibly more.

Meanwhile, on Friday, August 3, 1973, the WTT owners, officers and staff members gathered in a stuffy auditorium located in Manhattan's Time-Life Building. Object: to draft approximately three hundred men and women tennis players. Since the draft session would only give the assembled sportsmen exclusive rights to negotiate WTT contracts with the players they selected, there was a very real possibility the league was embarking on an exercise in futility.

From the outset the WTT draft was more like a Monty Python spectacular than an orderly selection of tennis talent. Most of the drafters were embarrassingly unfamiliar with the intended draftees and such insightful questions as, "Is Zeljko Franulovic a man or a woman?" filled the air. A general lack of preparation was apparent, but there were a few owners who had brought along some qualified assistance. Joe Zingale of Cleveland, for instance, had retained Pancho Gonzales as his draft consultant and he secured the rights to an unknown 17-year-old Swedish youngster named Bjorn Borg in the first round.

Florida, by the luck of the draw, won the honor of picking first and their choice was a home-grown, two-fisted belter by the name of Christine Marie Evert. Since the culling order was reversed every other round, Florida also ended up with the draft's final selection. They grabbed Peru's Fiorella Bonicelli and it was all over.

Besides Evert and Bonicelli, 310 other tennis players were selected by the sixteen franchises during the twenty-round affair. A few teams managed to end up with less than twenty players though, usually because they named a player who had already been selected and were forced to pass. But every team had assembled a strong roster. Provided of course, they would be able to successfully negotiate with and sign some of the draftees.

A few surprises came out of the draft, and at least one very abrupt about-face. Stan Smith and Arthur Ashe, two particularly outspoken opponents of the team concept, were drafted by Minnesota and New York respectively, and Bobby Riggs, the chauvinist's main man, was drafted by Chicago in the ninth round.

The about-face was a consequence of Houston's negotiations with John Newcombe, their number one pick. Though light years away from Billie Jean's seven-figure deal, Newcombe was asking for a hefty amount. Houston desperately wanted him but they didn't feel comfortable with his salary demands. So the delegates from Texas asked for a league subsidy. The request was presented to WTT's Board of Directors who reversed their earlier stand on such matters. Newcombe signed with

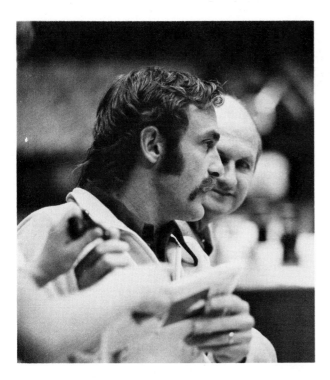

John Newcombe became the first big name male player to join WTT when he signed a $75,000 a year contract with the Houston EZ Riders. Here he signs an autograph for free.

Houston for $75,000 a year.

WTT officials felt that player interest was growing daily, but the biggest problem was that many players still feared being banned by the ILTF or their national federation.

But even before the owners had a chance to exercise the exclusive bargaining rights they had so recently acquired, Gary Davidson announced he had found a buyer for his Phoenix franchise. A Baltimore syndicate was willing to fork over $250,000 for his club, an amount five times the original $50,000 purchase price. WTT, of course, had no alternative but to approve the sale and Baltimore replaced Phoenix on the WTT map. Yet another franchise shift was to occur before the first season began. Dr. Leonard Bloom sold his San Diego franchise to a group from Hawaii for the princely sum of $300,000. At least someone was cleaning up.

But even as these internal shufflings were taking place, the league's status as the favorite target of the ATP, the ILTF, and the USLTA remained unchanged.

By early September Newcombe had already signed with WTT and it appeared that certain other ATP members were on the verge of doing the same. Jack Kramer responded by calling a meeting at Forest Hills and asking the ATP membership to boot Newk out of the organization. The players refused. After all, the ostensible reason for which the ATP had been formed was to protect players against such tactics, not to institute them. The players did, however, pass a resolution reiterating their preference for and support of the traditional tournament format that had been their bread and butter. WTT was not mentioned in the policy statement, but Kramer claimed it was a solid vote against the team tennis concept.

By the end of the year, WTT had not had much success in signing players and Kramer softened somewhat his tone of opposition. He even went so far as to say the ATP welcomed the team format, but in a different time period, say October, November and December, when it wouldn't conflict with any major tennis events. But during those particular months the league would be going up against basketball, hockey and football. In the summer, only baseball, primarily an outdoor activity, would be competing with WTT.

The final days of 1973 also saw Dennis Murphy's resignation as the league's first president. His six-month tenure ended when he accepted the presidency of the WHA. Jordan Kaiser became Murphy's Gerald Ford and Larry King stepped into the spot vacated by the vice-president.

Then WTT got a much needed break. Shortly

19

after the New Year, the league announced its intention of putting on a nationally televised mixed doubles tournament in Dallas, and Kramer and Dell quickly threatened to prohibit ATP players from participating. Their threat galvanized the WTT legal department into action. ''A clear case of anti-trust if ever there was one,'' said the league lawyers.

Lamar Hunt also took notice of Kramer's threat and indicated that WCT might be willing to come out in favor of WTT. Negotiations commenced and the result was an agreement between WTT and WCT to provide a joint pension plan for the athletes of both organizations. WTT agreed to fund the pension plan to the tune of $200,000 a year for five years. Besides the cool million, the league also agreed to put up an additional $125,000 over the five years to offset the WCT's administrative costs generated by the plan. The pension scheme was later abandoned when it was adjudged to be illegal because the intended recipients were technically considered to be independent contractors and, as separate entities, WCT and WTT would find themselves in violation of certain labor laws. Nevertheless, Jack Kramer surely was quite alarmed at the sudden display of coziness.

In January 1974, the same month WCT came out in support of the league, the ATP officially assumed a position of neutrality. The player's union modified its bylaws to enable members to sign WTT contracts without fear of reprisal from their union and an intolerable labor/management situation had run its course. Cliff Drysdale, president of the ATP quickly signed with the Florida franchise and others followed suit.

The ATP's conciliatory move also gave WTT's dormant sanction requests a boost. In March, the ILTF finally agreed to sanction WTT for $48,000 and a promise that players would be excused from league commitments to compete in the French and Italian Opens. Wimbledon, of course, had already been scheduled into the WTT season. The following month the USLTA also agreed to sanction the league for a mere $96,000.

On the surface at least, the major roadblocks had finally been removed from WTT's path.

Partially because of Kramer's influence, however, fourteen European federations still refused to accept WTT despite the ILTF sanction. The Europeans took an independent stand from the ILTF and dug in for a fight. Their refusal to capitulate would cause a number of problems during the summer of 1974, but for the time being their opposition to WTT remained firm.

Meanwhile back on the home front, the league, having successfully secured the official blessings of the ILTF, the USLTA, WCT, and the neutrality of the

ATP, suddenly began to fill its team rosters. By mid-March, WTT proudly announced that fifty-five players, including eleven of the sixteen first round draft choices, had signed league contracts. Evonne Goolagong and Jimmy Connors, after receiving assurances that they would be free to compete in the French and Italian championships, signed with Pittsburgh and Baltimore, respectively.

Other players, of course, had other reasons for affiliating themselves with WTT. Vic Edwards, Goolagong's coach, mentor, and surrogate father, hinted that he had brought her to WTT in an effort to improve her notorious and frequent lapses of concentration on the court, and there were several players who saw WTT as a means of prolonging a career or latching onto a bit of financial security.

But whatever the reason, the players, suddenly free from the threat of suspension (with the exception of certain Europeans), flocked to join such exotically named teams as the Aces (Chicago), Banners (Baltimore), Lobsters (Boston), Flamingoes (Florida), EZ Riders (Houston), Buckskins (Minnesota), Royals (Toronto/Buffalo), Freedoms (Philadelphia), Triangles (Pittsburgh), Sets (New York—not to be confused with the Mets, Jets, or Nets), Loves (Detroit), Nets (Cleveland), Racquets (Denver), Strings (Los Angeles), Leis (Hawaii) and Golden Gaters (San Francisco/Oakland).

These sixteen teams were divided into two divisions with each division containing two sections. The Atlantic Section (Baltimore, Boston, New York and Philadelphia) and the Central Section (Cleveland, Detroit, Pittsburgh, and Toronto/Buffalo) made up the league's Eastern Division. The Gulf Plains Section (Chicago, Houston, Minnesota, and Florida) and the Pacific Section (Los Angeles, Hawaii, San Francisco/Oakland, and Denver) formed the Western Division.

Each team would play a forty-four match season, twenty-two matches at home and twenty-two on the road. Those posting the best total won/loss records in each section would be eligible for the post-season playoffs that would determine the World Team Tennis champion. Any fan of professional team sports worth his or her six-pack, would doubtless feel comfortable with this familiar setup, but confirmed tennis purists could hardly be blamed for greeting the WTT master plan with unbridled skepticism.

World Team Tennis had confronted the powerful tennis establishment and, despite overwhelming odds, had won the right to exist. A little luck and a lot of hard work had brought WTT to the threshhold of its first season.

Phew!

WTT: The First Three Years

1 | 1974—THE FIRST SEASON

On May 6, 1974, nearly 11,000 people came to The Spectrum to see the new baby. Down on the arena floor Iggy Geneva and his Mummers' String Band provided some background music only slightly less frenetic than their appearance.

Various WTT functionaries, including Commissioner MacCall and president Jordan Kaiser, wandered around happily accepting congratulations while a full-scale replica of the Liberty Bell, the Freedoms' inanimate mascot that would ring in joyous celebration of each home town set victory, underwent a final clapper check.

Then Billie Jean King, the first female to coach a professional sports team that included male athletes, pranced onto the court for her warmup. A thunderous ovation momentarily drowned out the P.A. system which was now blaring Bread's song, *Mother Freedom,* as Billie Jean traded lazy groundstrokes with teammate Julie Anthony. Both players sparkled in their blue and white uniforms that prominently featured the Freedoms' Liberty Bell logo.

Over on the visitors' bench, the Pittsburgh Triangles, resplendent in bright yellow and green, gathered around coach Ken Rosewall for last minute instructions. Rosewall undoubtedly told his charges something they already knew, namely that the crowd would be their toughest opponent that night.

The festivities finally began a half-hour late as Billie Jean and Evonne Goolagong, a dream match under any circumstances, faced each other in the first regular season WTT match. Evonne flowed around the court like a fast-moving mountain stream. Completely outclassing the scrambling Billie Jean, she won 6–3. The two women repaired to the sidelines to watch Brian Fairlie hand Rosewall a 6–2 drubbing that gave the fans a good excuse to exercise their new-found right to participate vocally. Fairlie's victory over the 40-year-old Rosewall also unleashed the Freedoms' metal mascot which heralded the hometowners' first success of the evening by pealing with the exhuberance of a stripper who dearly loves her work. And the basketball scoreboard suspended from the apex of the arena's ceiling duly notified all present that the Freedoms led 9–8 in total games after the first two sets.

Mixed doubles was the next attraction and Philadelphia's Julie Anthony and Fred Stolle

An early WTT ad that appeared in the December 1973 issue of World Tennis.

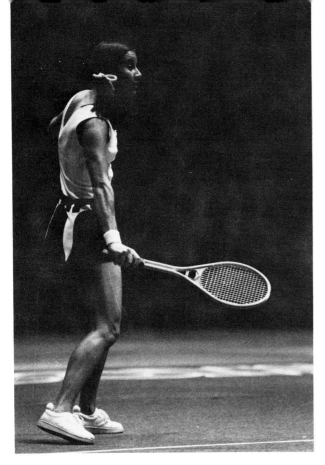

Julie Anthony of the Philadelphia Freedoms.

interview. ''Tennis has finally begun relating to the masses and people are really going to start getting turned on to the sport. It may take five years, but it's gonna happen.''

Over in the losers' dressing room, Coach Rosewall was a bit more subdued in his assessment of WTT's first outing. ''It's a completely new

Ken Rosewall, player/coach of the Pittsburgh Triangles.

managed a 7–6 win over Vitas Gerulaitis and Isabel Fernandez. Philadelphia 16, Pittsburgh 14, at the half.

Following a twenty-minute intermission that was enhanced by a succession of giveaways and the reappearance of The Iggy Geneva Band, Billie Jean got some sweet revenge against Goolagong, 6–2.

The reversal of the first half's pattern of play continued with Rosewall's fine performance against Fairlie, 6–3 and the Freedoms clung to a slim three-game lead going into the final set, mixed doubles. All Stolle and Anthony had to do was win four games. They did even better than that, clinching the Freedoms' first WTT match win with a 6–3 rout of Gerulaitis and his new partner, Peggy Michel.

Mother Freedom's coaching debut was an unqualified success and her team assumed possession of first place in the Atlantic Section of World Team Tennis' Eastern Division. Judging by the crowd's reaction, the league's debut was also an unqualified success. Though the vociferous displays of appreciation for particularly well-played points occasionally gave way to individual shouts of advice (''Attaway, Brian baby!''), or insults (''Face it, Rosewall, ya bum, you're old!''), the general tone was good-natured and not a single thin-skinned, hot-tempered tennis player had been moved to charge into the stands.

''We responded to the crowd in a positive manner,'' enthused Coach King at a post-match

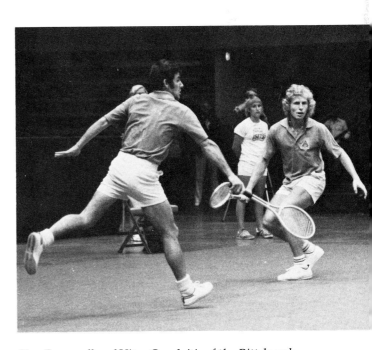

Ken Rosewall and Vitas Gerulaitis of the Pittsburgh Triangles, in doubles action.

format," he said. Then, perhaps with a nod towards his own inconsistent performance, he added, "The younger players will probably find it easier to adapt than some of the older ones."

The entire six-set match had lasted exactly two and a half hours, including the twenty-minute halftime, and though there were a few scattered complaints that the level of play was somewhat below the participants' known capabilities, most of those who attended went away happy. They had been exposed to something brand new and it had been entertaining and exciting.

But if the spectators were satisfied, the WTT brass was positively ecstatic. They were acting like proud fathers, and understandably so. After all, their baby was in good health and its future was extremely bright . . . or was it?

Flash forward to August 26, 1974. The Spectrum. The Freedoms are getting ready to meet the Denver Racquets in the second game of the WTT Championship playoffs. Denver, the Western Division pennant winner, has already won the first match in the best-of-three series that will determine the first league champ. The Freedoms face a must-win situation.

A few things have changed since opening day some four-and-a-half months earlier. The six-set format has been replaced by the more versatile five-set format featuring one set each of men's and women's singles and doubles, and mixed doubles. Another major change was that more often than not a typical WTT crowd could fit into a single Greyhound bus and still leave enough room for Iggy Geneva, his band, and their vast array of musical instruments.

An exaggeration? Sure, but not by much. Prior to the 1974 season, Commissioner MacCall had told the world that the break-even figure would be between 3,500 and 4,000 for each team's twenty-two home matches. Overall league attendance was averaging about half that by the end of the first season. There were a few bright spots though. The Freedoms were drawing an average of just over 4,100 at home, but a crowd that size can easily get lost in the cavernous Spectrum where seating capacity is 17,000. Despite leading the league in attendance, however, the Freedoms were racquet handle deep in red ink because of their heavy player payroll. The Minnesota Buckskins were also doing fairly well at the turnstiles but their bottom line was even bleaker than Philadelphia's. Jordan Kaiser's Chicago Aces averaged only 1,600 and had seen as few as 350 in the stands on some nights. And Houston, even with Newcombe on the roster, didn't do much better. The New York Sets,

operating out of Long Island's Nassau Coliseum, averaged 2,000. And if anyone even knew the Florida Flamingos existed they kept it a secret from that club's owners.

In fact only once during the entire 358-match WTT schedule was the opening night attendance surpassed. On June 1, Billie Jean and the Freedoms attracted 10,658 for a match at Minnesota.

The generally dismal attendance figures seemed to indicate that the individual stars were drawing the crowds, not the team tennis concept. The Philadelphia/Minnesota attendance was just one example of an out of town appearance by Mother Freedom that doubled, tripled, or even quadrupled the usual attendance figures. Proponents of the "star draw theory of spectatorial interest" were fond of pointing out that shortly after Baltimore's Jimmy Connors defeated Ken Rosewall in the 1974 Wimbledon finals 6,500 people showed up in Baltimore to watch an abbreviated replay of that

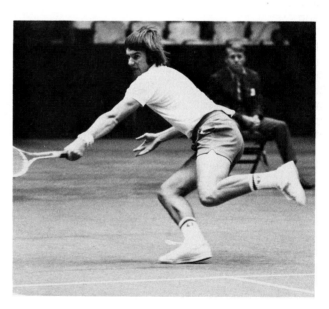

Jimmy Conners playing for the Baltimore Banners.

confrontation. But when those same two teams met again later in the season without the presence of Connors, whose WTT contract allowed him to skip a large percentage of his team's matches, only 300 of the faithful were on hand.

Nevertheless, WTT officials stolidly maintained that they were not overly distressed by the tepid attendance generated in the first year, preferring instead to point out that over 900,000 people saw the league in action.

The league acknowledged that the big names drew the crowds, but they felt that it was the only possible way to showcase the concept that would ultimately make or break the league. They also said they didn't expect it to happen overnight, but that acceptance of the concept might take as long as five years.

Maybe they were telling the truth, but it's hard to believe that they weren't a little discouraged when only 5,000 showed up for the second championship game, less than half the number present on opening night. The Liberty Bell mascot was still there, but its pealings seemed somehow less vibrant as they echoed through the Spectrum's mostly empty rows of seats. Throughout the whole season, in fact, much of the extraneous hoopla that had come to be associated with the individual WTT teams often ended up being more sad than inspiring.

But the Liberty Bell look-alike dutifully tolled as the Freedoms took the court. They were at the tail end of an immensely successful campaign, having lost only five matches all season, but they were fighting for their lives. Denver, the decided underdog, had brought a credible 30–14 record into the playoffs. The Racquets, a well-balanced, basically starless squad, were led by Tony Roche in their quest for the only certified non-stick trophy in professional sports: the Teflon Cup. That's right, the Teflon Cup.

Of course there was more at stake than a mere trophy. Money? Not really, unless the winning team voted to hock the trophy and split the proceeds. What was at stake was the pride and sense of accomplishment that is far more valuable than mere money or other tangible rewards. The World Team Tennis Championship was at stake and each player wanted a piece of it, bad.

The previous night in Denver, Billie Jean lost the opening set to the unorthodox but deadly strokes of Francois Durr, setting the tone for the Freedoms' uphill struggle. Philadelphia had lost each of the first four sets. The Racquets' Andrew Pattison knocked off Brian Fairlie in men's singles, Durr and Kristien Kemmer (Shaw) defeated Julie Anthony and Billie Jean in women's doubles, and Pattison and Roche teamed up to take Fairlie and Fred Stolle in men's doubles. Denver's men's doubles victory mathematically clinched the win for the Racquets because it put them ahead by ten games, 25–15, with only a single set remaining on the agenda. Though it didn't affect the outcome, Anthony and Stolle managed to salvage a bit of the Freedoms' pride with a 6–2 win over Kemmer and

Roche. The Philly mixed doubles victory also averted the WTT equivalent of a shutout.

The Racquet's easy victory was somewhat of a surprise, but nowhere near the one Coach King laid on the press after the match. "They were all over us," complained Mother Freedom, referring to

The Denver Racquets. Left to right: *Francoise Durr, Kristien Shaw, Stephanie Johnson, Pam Austin, Andrew Pattison, Jeff Austin, and player/coach Tony Roche.*

The Philadelphia Freedoms. Left to right: *Player/coach Billie Jean King, Fred Stolle, Brian Fairlie, Julie Anthony, Buster Mottram, and Tory Fretz.*

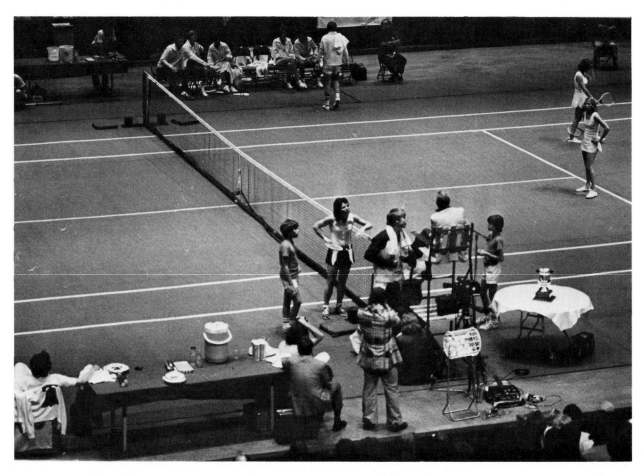

*In the heat of the battle. Billie Jean has a few words
with the referee during the championship match.*

the raunchy Denver fans. "There was no way we
could concentrate."

Hold it. Was this the same Billie Jean King who
for years had been preaching about the necessity
of taking tennis out of the stuffy country clubs and
giving it to the unwashed masses? The same Billie
Jean King who had enthusiastically applauded the
Freedoms fans' high decibel vocal displays? Was
she one of those people who could dish it out but
couldn't take it?

Not really. Her comments about the unruly,
hostile fans obviously were prompted by her deep
disappointment in her teams' performance.
Besides, Billie Jean didn't have a history of reacting
positively to losses of any kind.

In Philadelphia, however, it was the Racquets
turn to endure a healthy dose of verbal abuse. In
the first set, King grabbed a 4–0 lead over Durr
before things suddenly began to go Francoise's
way. King held on for a 6–4 win, but a two game

margin doesn't mean much in WTT, especially with
four sets remaining.

Since Brian Fairlie didn't have much luck against
Andrew Pattison in Denver, Coach King decided to
go with Buster Mottram in men's singles. Buster
might just as well have gone out without his
racquet because he won only one point while
allowing Pattison to coast to a 3–0 lead. King
hastily conferred with Stolle on the bench and they
agreed to yank Buster, pronto. Taking advantage of
the WTT rule that allows one substitution per set, a
cold Brian Fairlie was sent in to face the rampaging
Rhodesian. The sub, without benefit of a warmup,
had to serve the fourth game and his lack of
preparation showed. Fairlie lost his service and the
next two games as well. Pattison gave up only three
points in his 6–0 win and Denver was off and
running. King and Anthony picked up one game
during their 7–6 victory over Kemmer and Durr and
Stolle and Fairlie got back another in men's doubles,

but Denver led 22–20 going into the mixed doubles showdown.

Kristien Kemmer and Tony Roche clinched the final victory with a 6–4 win over Anthony and Stolle. The Denver Racquets, a team that had dropped eight of its first ten matches, became the first WTT championship team. Final score: 28–24.

The Racquets' locker room was lavishly stocked with champagne, the traditional thirst-quencher of championship teams, but Coach Tony Roche passed up the bubbly and popped a beer. Between generous slugs, Roche declared that the Denver victory was not unlike a Davis Cup win. "It was a team effort," he said. "A group of individuals working for a common goal."

Next door, the Freedoms were focusing their disappointment on the beleaguered Buster Mottram, the primary victim of Pattison's no-hitter in the men's singles. The Freedoms had won three

Denver emerges as the first WTT championship team.

Bud Fisher, owner of the Denver Racquets.

The Teflon Cup is awarded to the Denver Racquets.
From left to right: *Francoise Durr, Jeff Austin, Kristien Shaw, Pam Austin, and Tony Roche.*

26

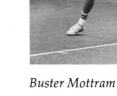

The victorious Racquets at rest. Left to right:
*Francoise Durr, Jeff Austin, Pam Austin, Tony Roche, Kristien
Shaw, Andrew Pattison, and Stephanie Johnson. Ms.
Durr's dog Topspin is the team mascot.*

Buster Mottram

of the five sets and had lost the mixed by only two games and it was their feeling that young Buster was directly responsible for the loss. Apparently forgetting that they represented the City of Brotherly Love, King, Stolle, and Fairlie loudly proclaimed that Mottram lacked a certain amount of intestinal fortitude and because of that deficiency their chance to tie the series had gone up in smoke. And on that rather unpleasant note, the curtain was brought down on the first World Team Tennis season.

And what a season it had been. Between the opening day's optimism and the final day's bickering WTT had made many mistakes, especially financial ones. But there were also a number of triumphs and at least one major controversy.

You will recall that well before the season began, WTT had secured a peace settlement with its organized opposition. WCT had come out in favor of the league, the ATP had grudgingly taken a neutral stance, and the ILTF and USLTA had given WTT their official blessings in the form of expensive sanctions.

Unfortunately, the ILTF sanction turned out to be as worthless as a broken racquet string, thanks in part to the ATP's Jack Kramer and Donald Dell. They had used their substantial influence to persuade fourteen European tennis federations to take a stand independent of the ILTF by honoring the anti-contract pro agreement passed the previous summer, several months before the ILTF backed down and gave the league a sanction.

Technically, that sanction should have removed the Europeans' official opposition to WTT, but it didn't. As a result, WTT players were not allowed to play in the French and Italian Opens in the summer of 1974. Among those blacklisted were Jimmy Connors of the Baltimore Banners and Evonne Goolagong of the Pittsburgh Triangles. Their banishment from the French Open led directly to a fresh flurry of million-dollar lawsuits.

Both players had begun the 1974 tennis year with wins at the Australian Open, the first leg of the Grand Slam. When their entries were refused by the second leg of the Slam, the French Open, they protested and directed the French federation's attention to the ILTF sanction. The Europeans, even in the face of certain legal action, held firm.

The ban may have prevented Connors from joining the select company of Don Budge and Rod Laver, the only players to win the tennis Grand Slam. Though he went on to win at Wimbledon and Forest Hills, we'll never know what would have happened had Connors been allowed to play on the Parisian clay.

We do know that Connors, with the backing of

the WTT, proceeded to sue the daylights out of everyone in sight. He and Goolagong jointly sued the French federation for a million francs each, and Connors filed against the Commercial Union Assurance Company, who sponsored the French Open as part of the Commercial Union Grand Prix series, the ILTF, and, of course, Kramer and Dell of the ATP.

Ironically, just one year earlier, the ATP membership, with only two exceptions—Ilie Nastase and Roger Taylor—had boycotted Wimbledon to protest the suspension of one player. Yet when a couple of dozen players, including a few ATP members, were banned from the French Open, the union didn't lift a finger. In fact, it supported the French federation's action. Kramer said that he was merely following the wishes of the majority of the ATP membership who remained loyal to the tournament circuit when he threatened not to cooperate with those tournaments if WTT-affiliated players were allowed to compete.

But when he found himself faced with another hefty lawsuit, Kramer gave in and persuaded the Europeans to lift the foolish ban. They did, and it appeared that the last vestige of opposition, overt or otherwise, had been removed once and for all. That's when the ILTF decided to collect its fat franchise fee from WTT. But the league was not about to fork over a check to the ILTF because its sanction had turned out to be totally ineffectual.

"Let me put it this way," said Larry King, "If you buy a car and the car is delivered without an engine, tires, seats, or a steering wheel, are you obliged to pay for it?"

Based on that principle, WTT has not, as of this writing, paid off the ILTF. Conversely, the ILTF, as of this writing, has not let more than six months go by without trying to collect. WTT did, however, pay the $96,000 USLTA sanction fee with $96,000 worth of tickets. The USLTA undoubtedly would have preferred cash, but they accepted the freebies. It's safe to assume that they didn't think at the time that WTT would be around long enough for them to use them.

While off-court problems were being settled, WTT was attempting to bring tennis to the masses. The rnasses, however, were not responding in the numbers that had been anticipated, but the league was still optimistic.

In its premier season of 1974 Billie Jean King dominated WTT's women's singles statistics with forty-eight victories and only eight losses. Her games-won percentage of .637, coupled with her success in coaching the Freedoms to the best finish in the league, earned her the Most Valuable Player award. (It didn't earn her the Coach of the

Year award though. That particular honor went to Tony Roche.)

Connors, with fifteen singles victories and only three defeats, led the men, but Newcombe, 27–5 and .593 in games won, played almost twice as many matches. Ken Rosewall, the grizzled veteran who lost the finals at Wimbledon and Forest Hills to Connors, established himself as the workhorse of the men's singles. He played fifty-one matches, winning thirty, and losing twenty-one.

Tom Okker, The Flying Dutchman, playing for the lowly Toronto/Buffalo Royals, who won only thirteen times all year, finished third in the men's singles category. He won thirty and lost only eleven while posting a respectable .592 games-won percentage.

In doubles, King and Anthony were the top women's team and Newcombe and Dick Stockton led the men. A grand total of 160 mixed doubles combinations saw action and Cleveland's Peaches Bartkowicz and Clark Graebner grabbed the top spot with a 7–3 record and a .632 games-won percentage.

With the exception of the Eastern Division's Atlantic Section where the Freedoms (39–5) finished twenty games ahead of runner-up Boston (19–25), the final team standings reflected WTT's tough competitive balance.

Originally, eight of the sixteen teams, the first and second place finishers in each Section, were slated for post-season playoff spots but the final standings caused that plan to be altered slightly. In the Central Section, third-place Cleveland had posted a better regular season record than Boston, runner-up in the Atlantic Section. As a result, the Nets were allowed to replace the Lobsters in the first round of the playoffs.

Besides the back-door Nets, Pittsburgh, Minnesota, Houston, San Francisco/Oakland, Detroit, Denver, and Philadelphia entered the race for the Teflon Cup.

The sectional titles would be decided by a two-match series between the qualifiers from each Section, and the Division crowns would hinge on the outcome of a similar series played by the first-round survivors. In both cases, the team winning the most games during the two-match series would advance. The championship series, featuring the respective divisional winners, would consist of a best-of-three series.

Out West, Houston fell to Minnesota and the Golden Gaters were eliminated by the Denver Racquets. Denver then knocked off Houston for the Western Division title.

In the East, Philadelphia disposed of the Cleveland Nets while the Pittsburgh Triangles were

taking care of the Detroit Loves. The Freedoms then dispatched Pittsburgh and won the right to meet Denver in the finals, to their ultimate chagrin.

This recap, however, does not expose the moments of high drama and low comedy that occurred during WTT's first season, and there were plenty of both.

For example, there was the time Jimmy Connors took offense at a particularly indelicate remark concerning his well-publicized social relationship with Chris Evert. Connors immediately put aside what he was doing at the time—which was trying to hold his service during a close set—and headed for the bleachers with the obvious intention of using his racquet in a manner never intended by the manufacturer. Fortunately, a security guard had sufficient presence of mind and enough physical bulk to restrain the irate player.

Then there was the time the New York Sets' Manuel Santana elevated the art of tennis court clowning to new heights. Mr. Santana accomplished that amazing feat merely by gripping his racquet by the strings and swatting at the fuzzy yellow sphere with his skinny racquet handle.

Not long after that incident, Santana and Rosie Casals, Detroit's number one female player, were singled out by Cleveland Nets owner Joe Zingale for responding to hostile fans with ''obscene gestures.'' Of course, Casals and Santana weren't the only WTT players who occasionally communicated with the fans, but they were the ones who prompted Zingale to demand an emergency owner's meeting to put a halt to such displays. Commissioner MacCall agreed with Zingale.

''The umpire has to control players who use obscene gestures on the court,'' said MacCall, ''and if he can't handle it, we'll get a 300-pound orangutan and put him in the umpire's chair.''

Putting an orangutan in the umpire's chair probably wouldn't have bothered either Billie Jean or the Boston Lobsters' equally volatile coach, Ion Tiriac. They would argue with anybody or anything when they felt their team had been wronged by a bad call.

The first season also witnessed an amazing acrobatic display by the Triangles' Vitas Gerulaitis. Pittsburgh was playing the Golden Gaters in the Oakland Coliseum late in the season when Gerulaitis, playing at the net in men's doubles, saw a Frew McMillan lob sail over his head. He turned and sprinted towards the baseline to intercept the lob but McMillan had applied enough topspin to remove the fuzz from the ball. The object of Gerulaitis's frantic pursuit touched down near the baseline and arced towards the press table some

Billie Jean King with a unique racquet press given to her by Ion Tiriac of the Boston Lobsters.

The Lobsters' mascot.

Manuel Santana of the New York Sets, 1974.

forty feet away. No matter. Like a centerfielder chasing a long fly, he checked the ball's trajectory and turned on his afterburner. As the assembled press recoiled in horror and dove for the cement floor, Gerulaitis leaped onto the notebook-covered table and dove through the large blue curtain that functioned as a portable backdrop. Point to the Gaters. A Red Badge of Courage to Vitas Gerulaitis.

And who can forget Virginia Wade's late season defeat of the high-flying Billie Jean King? The normally reserved Britisher had joined the New York Sets in mid-season. At first she was upset by the constant racket during play. But when she defeated arch rival King, Wade responded to the ear-splitting ovation with completely uncharacteristic theatrical gestures of appreciation.

Even Elton John, the bespectacled singer and frustrated athlete who had once been quoted as saying that he would gladly give up his musical fame and exotic outfits for the chance to become the men's singles champ at Wimbledon got into the act. He played a half-time exhibition match at the Spectrum and demonstrated that although he's not a bad tennis player, he's a better musician. He also drew attention to WTT by donning a Freedoms' uniform and serving tennis balls into the crowd during one of his Philadelphia concerts. Elton's close friendship with Billie Jean also inspired him to write and record a song called ''Philadelphia Freedom.''

The first WTT campaign also saw a husband trade his wife to another team, a player get mugged in the parking lot after a match, a low attendance record of 168 people, and a team that needed financial assistance from the league so they could participate in the playoffs.

But the first season had its share of positive moments as well. Wimbledon, for instance. For months, WTT's detractors had suggested that league players would find that their games had been ruined by the innovative format and the lack of tournament competition. It didn't happen. In fact seven of the eight Wimbledon titles went to WTT-affiliated players in 1974. Jimmy Connors (Banners) won the men's singles; John Newcombe (EZ Riders) and Tony Roche (Racquets) won the men's doubles; Evonne Goolagong and Peggy Michel (both Triangles) took the women's doubles; and Owen Davidson (Buckskins) and Billie Jean King (Freedoms) captured the mixed doubles title.

There were those who said WTT would never get organized and they were proven wrong. There were those who said WTT would never get off the ground and they were proven wrong. There were those who said WTT would never complete its first season and *they* were proven wrong. But skeptics are not easily convinced. Now they were saying that WTT would not live to see a second season. Jimmy the Greek, in fact, was laying 2–1 odds against it. Maybe he'd gotten a look at the financial statements.

Seasonal Standings

1974
Eastern Division

Atlantic Section	W	L	Pct.	GB
Philadelphia	39	5	.886	—
Boston	19	25	.432	20
Baltimore	16	28	.364	23
New York	15	29	.341	24
Central Section	W	L	Pct.	GB
Detroit	30	14	.682	—
Pittsburgh	30	14	.682	—
Cleveland	21	23	.477	8
Toronto-Buffalo	13	31	.295	17

Western Division

Gulf Plains Section	W	L	Pct.	GB
Minnesota	27	17	.614	—
Houston	24	19	.558	2½
Florida	19	25	.432	8
Chicago	15	29	.341	12
Pacific Section	W	L	Pct.	GB
Denver	30	14	.682	—
Golden Gaters	23	21	.523	7
Los Angeles	16	28	.364	14
Hawaii	14	29	.326	15½

Playoff Standings

1974	W	L	Pct.	GW	GL
Denver	5	1	.833	170	130
Pittsburgh	3	1	.750	108	79
Philadelphia	3	3	.500	146	144
Minnesota	2	2	.500	92	101
Houston	1	1	.500	47	48
Cleveland	0	2	.000	44	49
Detroit	0	2	.000	27	63
Golden Gaters	0	2	.000	41	61
Totals	**14**	**14**		**675**	**675**

2 | 1974—EPILOGUE

To say that WTT took a financial beating during the first season would be an understatement. Collectively, the sixteen franchises had dropped nearly eight million dolars, more than three times the amount originally projected, and several teams were in serious trouble.

"We're just like every other WTT team," said Bob Love, General Manager of the Detroit Loves, confirming the rumors. "We're for sale. And if we can't find a buyer there won't be a team next year."

Betty Jones, co-owner of the Houston EZ Riders, was slightly more optimistic. "I'm sure we'll go one more year," she said, "but I'm very disappointed that WTT hasn't grown faster." Part of her disappointment was based on the fact that only 1,500 fans showed up to watch her team's first playoff game against Minnesota.

But while Detroit was looking for a buyer and Houston was cautious about another go-round, Jerry Fine of the Los Angeles Strings was actually looking forward to WTT's sophomore year. "Sure, I had a few periods of depression, but we're anxious for next year because it will give us an opportunity to do some of the things we should have done this year."

"The honeymoon is definitely over," said Ray Ciccolo, an economy-minded Volvo dealer whose Boston Lobsters had lost a paltry $300,000. "We

The Freedoms and the Lobsters square off at the Boston University Arena.

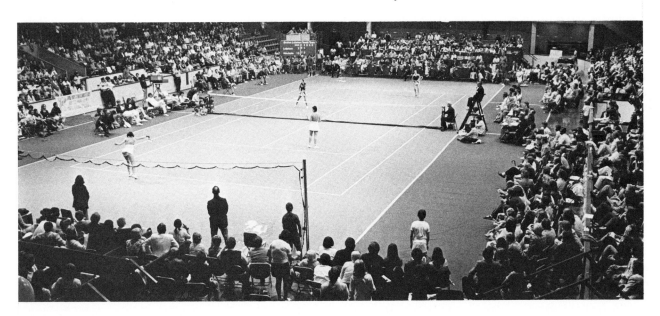

paid WTT players more than they ever made and a lot of them had a take-the-money-and-run attitude. That really bothered me.''

The players weren't entirely to blame, however. Many of the owners were more than willing to shell out big money in the hopes of buying a winner. John Bassett of the Toronto/Buffalo Royals signed Tom Okker for five years at $135,000 a year, for example. Deals like that were bound to affect team budgets.

Lee Meade, owner of the Minnesota Buckskins, summed up WTT's financial predicament nicely when he said, ''We're in a contest to see who's going to lose the least money because nobody's going to make any, that's for damn sure.''

He was, of course, correct. Every team lost money the first year, a lot of money. The Minnesota Buckskins ran out of money towards the end of the season and had to ask for $30,000 to meet their payroll.

Other WTT players weren't quite so fortunate and as late as December 1974, four months after the first season had ended, nearly two dozen athletes were still waiting for their final paychecks. Besides Minnesota, whose disappearance from the WTT lineup was almost assured, four other franchises had not been able to pay a portion of their players' salaries: the Baltimore Banners, the Florida Flamingoes, the Hawaii Leis, and the Chicago Aces.

The latter team's inability to meet its obligations presented a particularly thorny problem because the Aces' owner, Jordan Kaiser, was also the president of the league, and it just didn't look right to have the president in debt to his employees. Exit Jordan Kaiser, league president number two.

Kaiser wasn't the only WTT executive to find himself out of a job in September 1974. Commissioner George MacCall was also dismissed by the owners. Policy differences were given as the reason for MacCall's hasty departure and the league suddenly found itself without a leader, a less than ideal situation for such a troubled enterprise.

On September 29th, Frank Fuhrer, an insurance executive who had picked up controlling interest in the Pittsburgh Triangles, was voted in as WTT's third president. Fuhrer's tenure promised to be an interesting one because he was known to be temperamental and quite outspoken.

Witness the following remarks that appeared in a *Sports Illustrated* profile:

Frank Fuhrer on owning a WTT franchise: ''I'm engulfed in an ego trip with the rest of the idiots who own clubs.''

Frank Fuhrer on what owning a WTT franchise

has exposed him to: ''The total greed of the players and the general cheapness of the sporting public.''

Frank Fuhrer on his right to advise his team's coach: ''I don't know a tennis ball from a pile of manure, but I do know how to keep people organized, motivated, and disciplined.''

This was the man whose first league assignment was to find at least four qualified candidates to fill the vacant commissionership. The plan was to have the owners interview each of the contenders and pick one.

Frank Fuhrer, third president of WTT.

Fuhrer accepted the assignment but failed to complete it. After an intensive two-month search, he presented one candidate to the owners. Not surprisingly, there were a few protests. Fuhrer stubbornly stood by his single choice and refused to continue the search.

Larry King led the palace revolt that resulted in Fuhrer's removal and became the fourth WTT president and the third founder to hold that job. However, he told the owners that he would accept the presidency only on the condition that a replacement be found before the second season began.

A number of people, including the deposed Frank Fuhrer, felt that King was an unwise choice to head the league because of his obvious conflicts of interest. The critics feared that the husband and wife team of Billie Jean and Larry would completely dominate the league.

''Nonsense,'' said President King, ''I don't have any conflicts of interest. If anything, I have a consolidation of interests.''

Maybe. But he also had the unenviable task of stabilizing a shaky league that had just lost one of its franchises. As expected, the Minnesota Buckskins dropped out after the first season. As a result only fifteen franchises showed up at the Americana Hotel in New York for the second annual WTT draft in November. Though their numbers had been diminished, not much else had changed. Names were still being mispronounced all over the place and the gender of some of the players was still confusing many of the owners. They muddled through the draft and immediately plunged into the business of redistributing the former Buckskins' players.

Since the WTT draft system did not bind draftees to a contract, the owners often made unusual draft choices to enliven the proceedings. Bobby Riggs was drafted again, this time by Billie Jean's Philadelphia Freedoms, and the rights to Elton John were grabbed by the same franchise. At least if they signed Elton the Freedoms would be able to throw some terrific team parties.

Come to think of it, so could the Hawaii Leis and Los Angeles Strings if they managed to sign their respective draftees, Bill Cosby and Johnny Carson.

"How they ever passed up Henny Youngman, I'll never know," said one observer, and all over Hollywood theatrical agents were getting calls from

Bill Cosby, a WTT draftee who didn't sign.

their clients asking why they hadn't been offered a WTT gig like Carson and Cosby.

Another unusual draft choice was Stan Malless, president of the USLTA. His selection by the Loves led to the conjecture that his appearance in a WTT uniform was part of the price the league had to pay for the USLTA sanction.

At the conclusion of the draft proceedings president King went forth to meet the press. "It's always possible for a new league to lose some teams," he said, "but we don't expect WTT to lose any more." After the laughter subsided, he went on to announce that the Detroit Loves had been sold to a group in Indianapolis. Some of the "new money" everyone had been talking about had actually materialized.

King also said the owners had voted to extend the Wimbledon break from two weeks to three and that January 15, 1975 had been set as the date on which each team would be required to produce a $50,000 letter of credit if they wanted to stay in the league.

The hefty bond would act as WTT's in-house insurance policy against non-payment of salaries and other financial transgressions. Something was obviously needed to sooth the apprehensions of the players, especially those who had been unfortunate enough to have played for a troubled franchise and the bond was a step in the right direction. Even so, at least one owner argued that the amount was insufficient.

League president and incurable optimist Larry King confidently predicted that each franchise would show up on January 15 with the required fifty grand. "At this point," he said, "every franchise is looking forward to participating in the 1975 WTT season." The owners had six weeks to settle their outstanding debts and raise the protection money.

Unfortunately, five teams came up short. The Baltimore Banners, the Chicago Aces, the Florida Flamingoes, the Toronto/Buffalo Royals, and the Boston Lobsters joined the Minnesota Buckskins in the WTT graveyard. The league champ Denver Racquets lucked out and came into some of the "new money," becoming the Phoenix Racquets in the process.

Of the remaining ten WTT franchises, only Philadelphia was still on the edge of collapse. The Freedoms' precarious position made the other owners nervous so they decided to add an eleventh franchise as a hedge against Philly's possible disappearance. The owners reasoned that if eleven teams were scheduled for the 1975 season one team would always have an open date and it would be a simple matter to plug the idle team into the vacancies that would result from an untimely drop out.

The creation of the San Diego Friars seemed to be a brilliant stroke of planning. Billie Jean was suddenly traded to New York and Philadelphia's chances of survival looked dim. But the league's crazy square dance of realignment wasn't over yet. Shortly after Billie Jean's departure, the Philadelphia Freedoms were sold to a group in Boston and renamed the Boston Lobsters, just like the original Boston Lobsters. If the whole thing sounds a bit confusing, bear in mind that this was World Team Tennis, the league in which the bizarre is the norm.

With six franchises folding, three relocations, and one brand new team, it should come as no surprise that there were several player shuffles as well. A redistribution draft was held to find employment for many of the players who had contracts with teams that no longer existed, and other players became free agents or trade booty.

Rosie Casals moved from the Detroit (Indianapolis) Loves to the L.A. Strings, Tom Okker went from the defunct Royals to the Golden Gaters, and the Gaters traded Margaret Court to the Hawaii Leis. Marty Riessen signed with Cleveland and Jimmy Connors decided to jump ship and didn't sign with anybody. Raz Reid and Ion Tiriac, both of whom played for the original Boston Lobsters, joined the new Boston Lobsters, late of Philadelphia. Kathy Kuykendall gained the peculiar distinction of becoming the first WTTer to play for three teams when she signed with Hawaii for 1975. During the first season she had been a Philadelphia Freedom before moving over to the Baltimore Banners.

Out of the sixty-seven women and sixty-six men who had played in WTT in 1974, sixty-two signed on for the second season. Those sixty-two vets were joined by twenty-six rookies and the new eleven-team lineup geared up for the second annual opening day. The missing franchises had necessitated a consolidation of WTT's basic structure, and the four Sections were gone. Only the two Divisions remained: Eastern and Western. The San Diego Friars, Los Angeles Strings, Golden Gaters, Phoenix Racquets, Houston EZ Riders, and Hawaii Leis represented the West, while the New York Sets, Pittsburgh Triangles, Cleveland Nets, Indiana Loves, and Boston Lobsters made up the Eastern division.

All systems were go as eight teams traveled to Texas to participate in a pre-season exhibition spectacular. The two-day tune up was won by the powerful New York Sets who defeated the Indiana Loves in the finals, but the big news was that the

Houston EZ Riders had suspended operations. And then there were ten.

Houston's swan dive less than a week before the start of the regular season made the WTT officials look like master planners. Their decision to add a franchise back in January, averted a disaster of immense proportions in April. But they had come up with the correct solution to the wrong problem. Philadelphia was supposed to fold, not Houston.

Billie Jean, at least, escaped to New York when the Freedoms started to look shaky, but what about Newk? Here it was just a few days before the season and he was out of a job. So for that matter were his Houston teammates. No problem. Newcombe went over to Hawaii, joining his countrywoman Margaret Court, and most of the other EZ Riders were picked up by other franchises.

Of course, it wasn't quite as easy as it sounds. Larry King admits to having an unusual recurring nightmare around the time Houston went under. "We were re-distributing so many players," King said, "that I started to dream that we'd end up with one ninety-player team."

About the only thing that remained stable during the first few months in 1975 was the one that shouldn't have: the league presidency. A successor hadn't been found, and King, against his personal wishes and promises, was still at the helm.

3 | 1975—THE SECOND SEASON

When WTT's reluctant monarch promised that the league's sophomore year would be one of experimentation, he wasn't lying. The compact, streamlined 1975 World Team Tennis model wasn't going to be content with a logical, sensible schedule that called for each team to play twenty-two matches at home and twenty-two away. Nosireee! They were going to try something new. They were going to experiment with the league schedule.

Besides redistributing players and shuffling franchises the owners had spent a considerable amount of time in the off-season plotting new methods of showcasing the league and they came up with . . . The Spectacular. Or, as Mike Lupica of *World Tennis* magazine called it, "The Marquis de Sade Invitational."

The basic idea of the Spectacular was to get a group of WTT teams together for a three-day orgy of tennis. WTT, the arch enemy of the tournament format, was going to try something that closely resembled a tournament format. Never mind the fact that one of the major selling points of the league had been that a loyal home following would be built by a team over the course of the season, WTT was going to keep the teams moving. Strings' owner Jerry Buss had convinced the other owners that the idea of having the Cleveland Nets play the Pittsburgh Triangles in, say San Diego, would be the thing to do.

A typical Spectacular, for instance, was held over Memorial Day weekend. The glorious event began in Boston on a Thursday night with the Los Angeles Strings going against the Cleveland Nets. After the Cleveland—L.A. match, the New York Sets took the court against the home team in the evening's feature match. New York remained undefeated as they cake-walked all over the winless Boston club. The day ended with the players packing for a trip to Providence, Rhode Island. At least the Lobsters and Sets were heading for Providence. Cleveland and Los Angeles had already departed for Springfield, Massachusetts, where they would meet up with San Diego and Phoenix for a doubleheader involving any or all of the above.

Meanwhile the Indiana Loves were waiting for the Sets and Lobsters down in Providence.

While the Nets, Strings, Friars and Racquets were doing whatever they were doing in Springfield, a few dozen curious passers-by wandered in to watch the Loves knock off the Lobsters in Providence. They also saw the Loves' Ray Ruffels try to knock off Bob Hewitt. Or vice versa. In any event, the irate players had to be separated by Tiriac, Larry King, and Loves' owner, Bill Bereman. The umpire patiently listened to the players accuse each other of every high crime and misdemeanor known to man before he did Ray Ruffels the favor of booting him out of the match. The umpire also awarded Boston one game as recompense for Ruffel's indiscretionary actions which included hurdling the net and confronting Hewitt somewhere near the Lobster's service line.

It didn't help a bit. Not only did the fading Lobsters lose to Indiana, they had to return immediately to the site of the defeat and play the high-flying New York Sets for the second time in less than 24 hours. And once again the Sets triumphed.

The seven teams then converged on Boston for Saturday's grand finale which was scheduled to begin at noon with Phoenix facing Indiana. At the appointed hour, however, only 400 fans were in the stands.

Mike Lupica wasn't the only veteran WTT-watcher who pointed out that the exceedingly dismal turnout shouldn't have been unexpected. "It

was like having the Chicago Cubs play the San Diego Padres in Fenway Park," he wrote.

The day's second match pitted the home town Lobsters against the Cleveland Nets and that thriller was followed by San Diego versus Los Angeles, a natural geographic rivalry that was only three thousand miles out of its element. In the fourth and final match, the weary Boston Lobsters

Lobster teammates Raz Reid and Kerry Melville tie the knot while player/coach Ion Tiriac looks on.

went against New York for the third time in three days. And for the third time in three days. . . . etc. The Lobsters had played one match on Thursday, two on Friday, and two more on Saturday. Understandably the players tended to froth at the mouth at the mere mention of the word "Spectacular," and Ion Tiriac said that the idea "was the worst thing that ever happened in sports."

Tiriac's comment notwithstanding, the WTT Spectaculars did provide at least one memorably bizarre match that ended up being contested in front of exactly zero spectators. It all started when a Los Angeles/Indiana match was included as part of an Hawaii-hosted Spectacular. For reasons far more confusing than important, the match never came off and all concerned agreed to make it up at a later date. Some time later, it was decided that the make-up match would be played following a Spectacular in San Diego, but there was one tiny, little problem. There wasn't enough time to print up the tickets or promote it. As a result, Los Angeles beat the Loves 21–10 in a ghost match. Or so the league claims.

The grossly unpopular Spectaculars and doubleheaders weren't the only experiments dreamed up by WTT's mad scientists during Year Two. On July 12, the league made its long awaited national television debut with the WTT All-Star game. They chose that occasion to unveil the latest radical innovation: a multi-hued, no-line tennis court. To the uninitiated it must have looked like a cross between one of Grandma's patchwork quilts and a Jackson Pollock painting. If the casual tennis fan was shocked by the garish court, the purists must have been outraged.

"What's all the fuss about?" said Larry King. "It's still a tennis court. Where's it written that it has to be one color?"

The court of many colors was just one of the stars of WTT's Saturday night TV show. The Eastern All-Stars, led by Marty Riessen, player/ coach of the Cleveland Nets, easily defeated their western counterparts, 28–21. Riessen was named

The 1975 Western Division All-Star team. **Left to right:** *Tony Roche, Racquets; Vijay Amritraj, Friars; Betty Stove and Frew McMillan, Golden Gaters; Francoise Durr and Andrew Pattison, Racquets; Tom Okker, Golden Gaters; Rosie Casals, Strings; and John Newcombe, Leis, who was injured and could not play.*

the All-Star game's Male Most Valuable Player, the first WTT award he was to win in 1975. At the conclusion of the season, the 37-year-old player was named Male Rookie of The Year, the oldest rookie of the year in professional sports history. The All-Star Female MVP award went to Francoise Durr of the Phoenix Racquets for her 6–4 win over Billie Jean King, WTT's First Lady and the reigning women's singles Wimbledon champ.

Just a week before the All-Star match in Los Angeles, Billie Jean had annihilated Evonne Goolagong in the Wimbledon finals and then announced that she was retiring from tournament singles play. It was a storybook ending to one of the greatest tournament career's in tennis history, but her victory also went a long way towards proving that the WTT players' amazing performance at Wimbledon the previous year was no fluke.

In 1975, WTT-affiliated players occupied twelve of the final sixteen positions at Wimbledon and were shut out in only one event: men's singles. Besides the King/Goolagong women's singles final, WTT players Sandy Mayer (Sets) and Vitas Gerulaitis (Triangles) took the men's doubles from Allan Stone (Loves) and non-WTTer Colin Dowdswell. In the women's doubles event, Ann Kiyomura (Gaters) and Kazuko Sawamatsu teamed up to defeat Betty Stove (Gaters) and Francoise Durr (Racquets), and Margaret Court (Leis) and

The Eastern Division All-Star team. Left to right:
Billie Jean King, Sets; Mark Cox, Triangles; Bob
Hewitt, Lobsters; Ann Haydon Jones, Nets; Allan
Stone, Loves; Virginia Wade, Sets; Marty Riessen,
Nets; Evonne Goolagong, Triangles; and Fred Stolle,
Sets.

Marty Riessen, the Male Most Valuable Player in the
1975 All-Star game.

Francoise Durr, the Female Most Valuable Player in
the 1975 All-Star game.

Marty Riessen (Nets), beat Stone and Stove in the all-WTT mixed doubles final.

If Wimbledon was a success for the league in general, the first half of the second WTT season was a great success for the New York Sets in particular. The New Yorkers had won their first sixteen matches before they were finally unstrung by the Strings, thirty-three days into the season. The Sets' winning streak allowed them to build a substantial lead over the second place Triangles in the 1975 Eastern Division race. The post-season playoff structure had been modified somewhat from the first year and the respective Division winners would have to face the winner of a one-match qualifying round between the second and third place teams in a best-of-three series to determine who would play for the league championship. Out West, the Racquets, Strings, and Golden Gaters were involved in a close race for the pennant at the halfway point, but New York appeared to have a lock on the title even before the Wimbledon break rolled around.

The Triangles, however, came back from England and started a winning streak of their own. Vic Edwards, the only non-playing coach in the league, suddenly could do absolutely nothing wrong. The Triangles lost only twice in their last twenty-two matches, both times to the New York Sets. Slowly the Pittsburgh squad narrowed the gap until finally they emerged as the Eastern Division front-runner.

On the last day of the regular season, the Triangles (35–8) were one game ahead of the Sets (34–9) with one game left. And guess who was going to play whom? That's right. If there was an award for fortuitous scheduling, it would have gone to the WTT schedule makers by a unanimous vote.

Out West, the Golden Gaters had put together a late season surge to finish seven games ahead of runnerup Phoenix and L.A. had grabbed third place. Boston took third in the East and the only unknown finish would be decided in Pittsburgh.

A record WTT crowd of 10,589 jammed into the Pittsburgh Civic Center to watch the monumental battle for first place. A New York win would give each team an identical record of 35–9 and a playoff for the Division pennant would become necessary. It didn't happen. The Triangles won the match and assumed possession of first place. They then sat back to await the outcome of the New York/Boston playoff match. Nearly everyone viewed the Sets loss to Pittsburgh as a temporary setback. They would merely walk over the Lobsters (20–24) and catch the next flight to Pittsburgh for the *real* playoffs. After all, the Sets had beaten the Lobsters seven times during the regular season, and why should the playoffs be any different? Why indeed?

The only thing was, nobody ever considered the tenacity of the Boston team. Apparently believing they had the match sewed up, the Sets built an 18–12 lead after the first three sets. But Sandy Mayer went down to Battlin' Bob Hewitt in men's singles, 6–2, and New York's lead dwindled to two, 20–18. Player/coach, Ion Tiriac and WTT's Female Rookie-of-the-Year, Greer "Cat" Stevens then went out and promptly trimmed Fred Stolle and Billie Jean in mixed doubles, 6–4. After five full sets the score was tied, 24-all and both teams prepared for the nine-point "Super-Tiebreaker" that would decide the match and, more important, Pittsburgh's next opponent. Tiriac was bushed, so he inserted Hewitt in his place. New York elected to stay with the King/Stolle duo. Seven points later it was all over and the lowly Boston Lobsters, had eliminated the powerful New York Sets. For the second year in a row, Billie Jean King saw the WTT Championship slip from her team's grasp.

Boston's highly commendable performance, however, turned out to be a one-night stand and they promptly dropped two in a row to the Triangles, 26–16, and 23–14.

On the other side of the continent, the Los Angeles Strings were almost run off the court by Phoenix in their qualifying match, 20–8. (That strange score is not a misprint. Unlike regular season play, WTT officials decreed that once a playoff contest became mathematically out of reach, the match would be declared officially over.) The Racquets' victory set up a Gaters/Phoenix series and the first meeting went to the Gaters, 25–24. The following day the results were the same and the score was Gaters 26, Phoenix 20.

Fittingly, the respective Division winners had survived the playoffs and would meet in the best-of-three championship series. With the league's almost pathological penchant for the bizarre it would have surprised no one if the Strings and Lobsters had emerged as the championship contenders, but it just didn't quite work out.

After dropping their first match to the Gaters, the Triangles had beaten the westerners four straight during the regular season. They fully intended to continue that streak for at least two more matches. The Gaters, however, would not be pushovers by any means. Not with player/coach Frew McMillan, 1975's Coach-of-the-Year, Tom Okker, 1975's Male Most Valuable Player, Betty Stove, the Dutch Treat, and Wimbledon doubles titleholder, Ann Kiyomura.

The Triangles would counter with Evonne Goolagong, 1975's Female Most Valuable Player, veteran Mark Cox, Peggy Michel, and Vitas Gerulaitis.

Both teams presented well-balanced units and

38

WTT president Larry King presents the 1975 Female Rookie of the Year Award to Greer Stevens of the Boston Lobsters.

Sandy Mayer of the Sets during the 1975 playoffs.

the series was rated as a tossup when they finally got down to business in San Francisco's massive Cow Palace. The Gaters normally operated out of the Oakland Coliseum directly across the Bay, but Ringling Bros. and Barnum and Bailey's menagerie preempted them at championship time. As a result, neither team really enjoyed a home court advantage.

Regardless of the location, the Triangles stepped right up and made themselves at home, for four sets. Leading the Gaters 24–20 going into the mixed doubles, however, the gang from Pittsburgh suddenly saw their lead, and ultimately the match, go to the Golden Gaters. Betty Stove and Frew McMillan, "The Mad Hatter" with a two-fisted grip on everything but his serve, decimated Peggy Michel and Kim Warwick, 6–1.

Match one to the Gaters, 26–25. After a three-day intermission, the action resumed at Pittsburgh's Civic Center and the home town fans saw their team even the series with a 28–25

victory. The second match also marked WTT's second exposure on national television and the contestants put on a good show for the cameras.

The deciding match was set for Monday, August 25. That very same evening, the United States' other major league summer sport, baseball, was competing for the area's sports dollars a few short miles away. So what would it be, sports fans? The Pirates and the Reds, the Golden Gaters and the Triangles, or a *Medical Center* rerun?

Well, 6,882 fans attended the World Team Tennis Championships, including the full membership of the wildest, loudest, and self-proclaimed rudest fan club, the G-men. All season long, the uninhibited G-men had been loudly screaming their allegiance to their hero, young Vitas Gerulaitis. They had also made no attempt to conceal their contempt for any player who challenged their idol on the court. As a result of their leather-lunged displays, the G-men had gotten used to seeing some of their cruder members being escorted from the arena at the behest of Frank Fuhrer, no shrinking violet himself. It was a surprise, therefore, to see Fuhrer wearing a shirt emblazoned with the legend *G-men,* at the August 25th match. It was as if Richard Nixon had suddenly joined the Weathermen.

"I've been tossing these guys outta here all year," said Frank. "I don't know, maybe the shirt will help."

The G-men were certainly up for the occasion and so were the less obnoxious Triangles' rooters. The Pittsburgh Steelers had won the Super Bowl in January and the Pittsburgh Pirates were on their way to the National League Playoffs and the fans were kind of getting used to winners.

The Gaters charged out of the chute and took the women's doubles, 6–2, but Goolagong got it all back with an identical victory over Betty Stove. With the match tied at eight games apiece, McMillan and Okker, the league's premier doubles team, lost to Gerulatis and Cox 7–5, giving the Triangles a 15–13 edge. The G-men, including new member Frank Fuhrer, went crazy. Down on the bench, Coach Edwards had decided to go with Gerulaitis in the men's singles, even though Vitas had been beaten by Okker the previous day, 6–4. Edward's decision proved to be the right one, and Gerulaitis crushed the more experienced Okker 6–1. The seven game lead put the match out of the Gaters reach and the mixed doubles went unplayed as a result. The Pittsburgh Triangles were the 1975 World Team Tennis Champions, a fact that didn't escape the attention of the G-men.

As they say, "To the victor goes the spoils," so, in the midst of a high-decibel, impromptu celebration, the Pittsburghers gathered around Larry King to receive theirs. Each player received a Championship medal and then King presented the Bancroft Cup, the Teflon Cup's replacement, to coach Vic Edwards and owner Frank Fuhrer.

For his part in the Triangles' victory, Vitas Gerulaitis was awarded the Playoff Most Valuable Player trophy. Giving credit where credit was due, Gerulaitis promptly dedicated his award "to the G-men, for making it all possible."

There was also a lot of talk about the "honor and prestige" that went with the Bancroft Cup and the discussion of filthy lucre was kept to a bare minimum. For good reason. There wasn't much to talk about. Since the players' share of playoff money was directly related to the gate receipts, they would be lucky if they each got enough to buy a morning paper and a cup of coffee. Only 11,000 spectators had attended the three-game championship series.

"Besides," said Frank Fuhrer, "we pay them more than enough in regular season salaries."

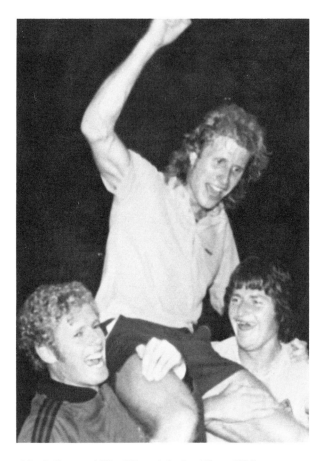

Mark Cox and Kim Warwick give Playoff Most Valuable Player, Vitas Gerulaitis a lift.

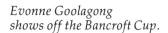

Evonne Goolagong shows off the Bancroft Cup.

Evonne celebrates the Triangles' win with a fully clothed shower.

The final words were left to Larry King. "This," he said, "is the greatest night in World Team Tennis history."

Final Standings

1975	Eastern Division			
	W	L	Pct.	GB
Pittsburgh	36	8	.818	—
New York	34	10	.773	2
Boston	20	24	.455	17
Indiana	18	26	.409	18
Cleveland	16	28	.364	20

	Western Division			
	W	L	Pct.	GB
Golden Gaters	29	15	.659	—
Phoenix	22	22	.500	7
Los Angeles	20	24	.455	9
Hawaii	14	30	.318	15
San Diego	12	34	.272	17

Playoff Standings

1975	W	L	Pct.	GW	GL
Pittsburgh	4	1	.800	122	95
Golden Gaters	3	2	.600	116	118
Boston	1	2	.333	55	72
Phoenix	1	2	.333	64	59
Los Angeles	0	1	.000	8	20
New York	0	1	.000	24	25
Totals	**9**	**9**		**389**	**389**

4 | 1975—EPILOGUE

Upon hearing that his obituary had been published somewhat prematurely, Mark Twain sent a telegram to the erring newspaper. "The report of my death," it said, "is greatly exaggerated."

So it was with World Team Tennis.

Even as the Pittsburgh Triangles were toasting their championship with slugs of champagne from the Bancroft Cup, *Tennis Illustrated,* a Los Angeles-based monthly magazine, was proclaiming the death of the league. Adorning the cover of that publication's August 1975 issue was a photograph of a graveyard that prominently featured a very authentic appearing tombstone bearing the legend, "World Team Tennis, 1974–1975. R.I.P."

The cover was graphically pleasing and extremely clever. It was also wrong. Dead wrong. WTT's health had never been better and all its vital signs were strong. By August each franchise had successfully completed the 1975 league schedule, and all of the players had been paid in full and on time.

Though the Spectaculars and doubleheaders had diminished the number of playing dates to 165, WTT's attendance had registered a phenomenal 28 per cent increase over Year One. Over half a million people had turned out in 1975, raising the average match attendance to 3,050. Not exactly spectacular, but it was respectable.

Of course none of the teams had made any money the second season, but then again none of them had suffered great losses either. And none of the owners seemed particularly distressed. Perhaps losing money had become a habit with them. Or, more likely, the owners merely subscribed to Larry King's pet theory of economics which went something like this:

"Suppose you buy a house or piece of property and make mortgage payments of two hundred dollars a month. That's twenty-four hundred dollars a year, right? O.K. Now, did you lose that twenty-

A premature obituary on the cover of the August 1975 issue of Tennis Illustrated.

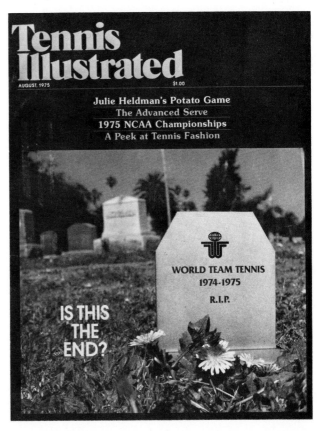

four hundred dollars, or did you make a twenty-four hundred dollar *investment?* You're out of pocket two thousand four hundred bucks, but the value of your property is increasing, right? Well, that's basically the situation the owners are in. They are looking at their teams as properties in which they're investing.''

As if to add a measure of validity to Larry King's economic analysis of the league's financial status, WTT announced, in November 1975, that the assessed value of the franchises had risen to the grand sum of $750,000. One owner, in fact, reported that he'd recently rejected a bid of a cool million for his club. If nothing else, WTT was in the major leagues inflation-wise.

Though things were going fairly well for WTT, a few other sports leagues were discovering that the world of professional athletics wasn't all sunshine, roses and lollipops. The World Football League (WFL) had quickly gone down the tubes, baseball attendance was on the decline, and the ABA was rumored to have several financially troubled franchises.

Why then had WTT not only survived but grown? Why was the radical little league still around when a flagging economy was wreaking havoc with spin-offs from such established spectator draws as football and basketball? One of the most important reasons for WTT's survival was a phenomenon known as "The Tennis Boom." Tennis was enjoying a period of growth unparalleled in American sports history. A 1975 survey indicated that more than 33 million people in this country had taken up the sport and their numbers were increasing daily. Tennis had established itself as the sport of the 70s: an industry that was generating a billion dollars a year. It now ranked fourth in the spectator popularity contest, right behind baseball, football, and basketball.

Over 17 million videoland viewers had tuned in to watch Jimmy Connors beat Rod Laver in a Challenge Match held in Las Vegas. Instead of the traditional weekend visit to Grandma's house, whole families were heading for the local public courts. And why not? Chances were Grandma was already there, chasing lobs instead of baking toll house cookies in her stuffy kitchen.

Quite naturally, the Tennis Boom resulted in the desire of many of the participants to improve their skills, and what better way then to spend an evening watching a dozen of the top men and women players competing in a World Team Tennis match. Want to improve a terminally-ill backhand? Come on down and watch Evonne Goolagong. Get confused about where to position yourself in a hot doubles match? Frew McMillan and Tom Okker will show you how to do it. Got a second serve that bounces twice before it clears the net? No problem. Just check out Francoise Durr. On second thought, maybe you could watch how Sandy Mayer or Betty Stove accomplishes that minor miracle.

Besides offering its spectators a chance to have some fun and possibly pick up a few pointers, WTT was a professional sporting event that attracted many female fans. Surveys had shown that women usually comprised 20–30% of the audience at football games. WTT, however, often attracted a male-female ratio that was closer to 50–50, and occasionally women spectators clearly outnumbered the men. World Team Tennis, the league that offered something for everyone, was slowly but surely carving out its niche in the sports world.

It was true enough that each of WTT's ten franchises were located in a single country, and that the league's single brief encounter with foreign soil (the Toronto/Buffalo Royals) had ended ignominiously, but in December 1975, WTT truly went international.

On December 27, team tennis detente took its place alongside Ping Pong diplomacy when the Soviet Union agreed to field a team of its top players for a five-match series against a group of WTT All-Stars. The event, officially billed as the Wiesman-Toyota Cup, would be held in March 1976 and would alternate between Moscow and three American cities.

The idea for such a series originally occurred to WTT officials at Wimbledon the previous summer and they approached a prominent Russian tennis official with the plan. The Soviets were immediately receptive to the idea. They, in fact, were in the midst of a tennis boom themselves and they saw the series as an opportunity to give some of their top-flight players another healthy dose of international competition.

WTT believed that a Team America/Team Russia confrontation would be an ideal means of emphasizing and publicizing World Team Tennis. It would also be a terrific lead-in to the third season which would begin in late April.

Larry King put together a written proposal and sent it off to Moscow. Several weeks went by with no reply, so he approached another Russian tennis honcho at Forest Hills in September. King was amazed to discover that the gentleman from the USSR had never heard of the plan, so he explained the whole thing once more. A second written proposal was requested and King complied. Still no word. King finally placed a call to Moscow and was invited over to discuss the idea in detail. His frustrations continued when he landed in the Russian capital. Everyone he met said it was a grand plan but no one seemed either willing or able to commit to the series. A few days after his arrival, the Russians invited King to a meeting and he thought his hosts were finally ready to get down to business. No such luck.

The meeting turned out to be a civic get-together of some sort and Larry King spent the day listening to endless speeches about "housing, wildflowers, and brown bears, I think." Eventually, however, WTT's proposal was discussed and approved. The belated Christmas present stipulated that each country would keep its own gate receipts and pay its own expenses. The ground rules further stated that WTT's five-set format would be used in the three U.S. matches, but the first two matches, which were scheduled for Moscow, would blend conventional scoring with the WTT single-set formula. It was further agreed that the team

Team America in Moscow, accepting flowers from the ballgirls and ballboys. **Left to right:** *Sandy Mayer, Sets; Vitas Gerulaitis, Triangles; Marty Riessen, Nets; Mona Guerrant, Loves; Rosie Casals, Strings; Billie Jean King, Sets; and coach Butch Buchholz, Leis.*

capturing the most games during the series would be the overall winner.

With the signed contract in hand, Larry King returned to the United States and began to assemble Team America. Billie Jean King (Sets), Rosie Casals (Strings), Mona Guerrant (Loves), Sandy Mayer (Sets), Vitas Gerulaitis (Triangles), Marty Riessen (Nets), and their coach, Butch Buchholz (Leis), prepared for a Midnight Flight to Moscow where they would meet an impressive Russian squad. Olga Morozova, Alex Metreveli, and Natasha Chmyreva would lead the Soviet charge with the able assistance of Marina Kroshina, Tiemuraz KaKulia, and Vadim Borisov.

Several weeks before the opening match of the series, nearly 26,000 tickets for the first two matches had been sold in Moscow in less than three hours. *Pravda,* the official Soviet newspaper was moved to gush that tennis had joined basketball in box-office drawing power.

Clutching the hottest ticket in town, 13,000 people, jammed into the Central Lenin Stadium Ice Palace on March 8th for the historic first major coed team confrontation between the two countries. Billie Jean and Rosie Casals, however, came close to missing the whole thing. Less than two days earlier, they had reached the doubles finals at the San Francisco Virginia Slims

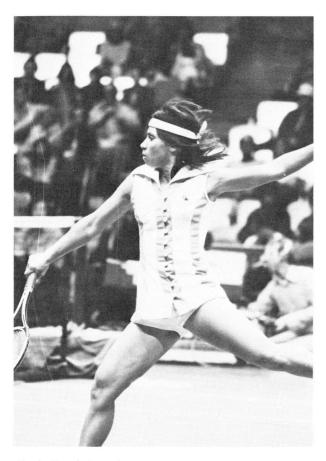

Rosie Casals in action.

After a shaky start, the Soviets settled down and put on a fine show, winning three out of five sets, but Team America came out on top in the one statistic that really mattered: games won, 26–21. Nevertheless, the Moscow papers spoke of a dramatic upset and had the USSR winning the first match.

Any confusion about the Wiesman-Toyota Cup results was cleared up the next evening though as Team America increased its cumulative games won lead to 52–40 while winning each of the four sets played the second match.

Regardless of the score, the Russian leg of the series was adjudged a smashing success by all concerned. Though only a handful of Americans, mostly U.S. embassy employees, were present at the Moscow matches, the crowd had consistently and lustily applauded noteworthy shots by both teams with equal gusto. The decidedly non-partisan display of enthusiasm was due in part to

In November 1975, WTT announces that Chris Evert, the number one female player in the world, has signed with the Phoenix Racquets.

tournament and only a lot of hustle and an assist from Aeroflot, the Soviet airline, enabled them to arrive at the Ice Palace only moments prior to the opening ceremonies. As it was, they were still struggling with their uniforms when they were introduced to the enthusiastic Russian tennis crowd. They stumbled onto the court just in time to hear the stirring musical tribute their hosts had composed in honor of the occasion. "The March of The Tennis Players," a functionally named piece, was played along with the respective national anthems.

Despite the fact they were thousands of miles from the nearest WTT city, Team America enjoyed a definite home court advantage. There were only about 3,500 hundred tennis courts in the USSR at the time, and not a single one that was multi-colored and lineless, so WTT shipped one of theirs over to Moscow. The Soviet players were able to practice on the garish piece of carpet for a few weeks, but their nervousness at playing in front of the home town folks offset their familiarity with the court.

Ilie Nastase joins the Hawaii Leis.

international competition, and, for the first time, America's top men and women players had represented their country on an equal basis.

WTT didn't concentrate all of its off season energies on the Russian series though. In November 1975, Chris Evert, a young lady with few tennis worlds left to conquer, decided to give World Team Tennis a try. She signed with the Phoenix Racquets.

"I may not get a second serve in all year," Chris said referring to the possibility that her cool court demeanor might not be able to withstand the heat of a hostile crowd.

Then a month later, the original court jester himself, Ilie Nastase, became a member of the Hawaii Leis shortly after capturing his fourth Masters title. Nastase's presence would undoubtedly give that club a lift since Margaret Court and John Newcombe had decided to sit out the 1976 season.

Evert and Nasty weren't the only big-name newcomers, however. In February, the San Diego

Rod Laver joins the San Diego Friars.

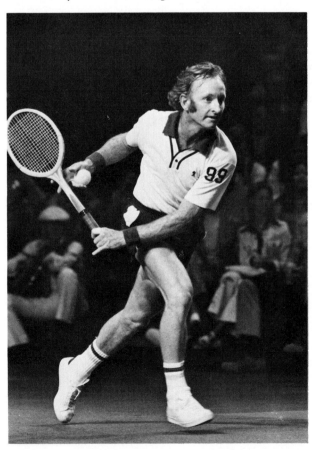

the fact that many of the spectators were tennis coaches and students.

"The crowds were extremely sophisticated and very receptive, very appreciative," said Marty Riessen. "It was a pleasure to play in Moscow and I look forward to going back." The other U.S. players shared that view.

The series then moved to Philadelphia, Cleveland, and Indianapolis for the next three matches. The crowds were smaller in the States, but the level of tennis was superb. Team America won the series 136–95, but the event proved the Soviets are catching up quickly.

And WTT scored a few more firsts. The team tennis series had given the Soviet people a rare opportunity to watch their players compete in

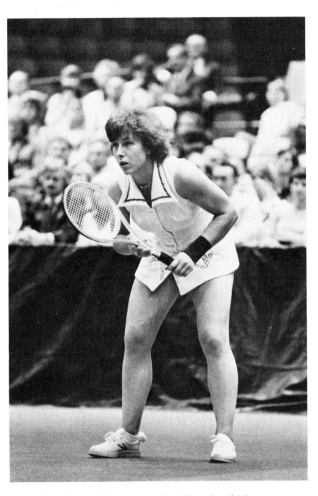

Martina Navratilova joins the Cleveland Nets.

Friars announced that they had added Rod Laver to their roster, and shortly thereafter, Martina Navratilova signed with the Cleveland Nets. Martina, of course, had recently made headlines by defecting from her native Czechoslovakia. Besides the four well-known rookies, the league was going to present a few other new things in 1976. WTT had decided to use their attention-getting surface for every match and they were going to introduce a revolutionary new system of officiating in Year Three. A series of training schools had been held in the spring and the graduates were expected to add another element of big-league professionalism to WTT. The umpires and linesmen would be paid by the league and many of them would travel from city to city at least part of the season. Additionally, the new system reduced the number of match officials from eleven to five. The system had been tested during the Russian series with favorable results and each linesman and umpire had taken and passed an eye test.

The eagle-eyed officials would be keeping their peepers on WTT's official tennis ball which was manufactured by Pennsylvania Tire and Rubber Company, Penn for short. The league was also attracting several other national advertisers. Besides Penn, the Coca-Cola people had made a deal with WTT and Tab became the league's official soft drink. American Airlines was the official airline, and Tred 2, a rapidly growing tennis shoe resoling outfit climbed aboard as the official shoe. Home Box Office, Inc., a subscription cable television

Evonne Goolagong combines graceful motion with intense concentration.

network, announced that WTT would be one of their regular Wednesday night features, and a major network deal was being discussed as a real possibility.

World Team Tennis's third regular season of play was scheduled to commence on Saturday, May 1, 1976.

Larry King was still president and the league was in great shape.

5 | 1976—The Third Season

Though the second season was far more successful than the first both campaigns had demonstrated WTT's amazing instinct for survival. As the league prepared to begin its third season, the main question was whether or not it could capitalize on that ability to survive.

There were, of course, several indications that it could and would. "If we can't make it now, it's because we're too stupid to run a league," was the way Frank Fuhrer put it.

WTT would at least enjoy a previously missing element of operational stability. Each of the ten teams participating in the 1975 season would be returning, each under the same ownership. Maybe the WTT owners foresaw an end to the red ink in 1976, but if they did, they weren't admitting it.

"There's no way in hell we're going to make money this year," said the New York Sets' owner, Sol Berg, "but we'll cut our losses even further. In the long run we'll make it, but not this year."

New York was definitely the least likely franchise to break even. They had the highest payroll in the league. Billie Jean, Virginia Wade, Sandy Mayer, Phil Dent and Fred Stolle didn't work cheap, a fact that would be reflected in the Sets' post-season balance sheet. And to further depress New York's financial outlook, the Sets were not exactly turning people away from the Nassau Coliseum when they played at home. Although the Sets' attendance figures had gone up in Year Two, the increase was well behind that of the other teams.

The one franchise that stood the best chance of breaking even in 1976 was the Indiana Loves. Loves' owner Bill Bereman possessed the smallest payroll in the league. To the other owners' dismay, Bereman steadfastly clung to the belief that signing and promoting superstars was not the way to go. Instead, he concentrated on putting together a team of competent individuals who would work well as a team but whose collective drawing power was less than dramatic.

A common joke around the league was that the Loves' total payroll was less than the monthly payments on a used Porsche. That was the joke but the other owners weren't laughing. Since there was no gate-sharing in WTT, the Loves obviously benefited greatly from the visit of a team laden with big names. Conversely a visit from the Loves did little to enhance the home team's gate receipts.

If the WTT owners weren't spending a lot of time wondering how they were going to spend excess profits, they were comforted by growing signs of acceptance of the league. Along with the increased corporation sponsorship, season ticket sales were on the rise. Phoenix reported they had sold nearly 3,000 tickets and Hawaii's figure was well over 1,000, double the number sold the previous season. Advance ticket sales were also climbing. The Gaters increased their advance ticket sales by nearly 20,000 over the 1975 season. WTT was finally beginning to realize its potential in establishing the broadest fan base in professional sports.

There still wasn't a national television contract, but league officials said that was no big thing. NBC was going to televise the All-Star game for the second year in a row, and several teams had made arrangements to have some of their matches televised by local, independent stations.

Fully aware that the third season would be crucial to the league's continued growth, the WTT braintrust decided to make a few cosmetic changes. The exclusive use of the color court for all league matches would be the most obvious change. Season three would also see a return to a schedule that was simple and logical. The Spectaculars and doubleheaders of the previous year had been eliminated. But the big news in 1976 was that WTT had added four more big names—Evert, Laver, Nastase, and Navratilova—to its already impressive roster of players.

One of the four, Chris Evert, wasted no time in making her presence known. Two weeks into the season, the Evert-powered Phoenix Racquets were dominating the league, both on the court and at the box office. They were undefeated and occupied the top spot in the Western Division with a two-and-a-half game lead over second place San Diego. Chris had contributed to the Racquets' success by winning all of her first seven singles matches while losing only nine games. Her games-won percentage, WTT's most important measure of player effectiveness, was an astounding .824.

It was obvious that the league record for singles play was in danger if Chris was able to maintain her torrid pace for the full season. In 1975, Billie Jean had established a .641 percentage, nearly

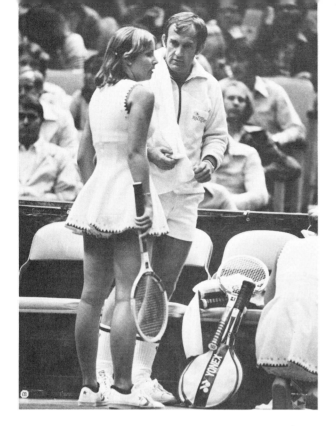

Chris Evert gets some advice from coach Tony Roche.

Kristien Shaw, Chris Evert's doubles partner.

Chris and Kristien discuss strategy.

two hundred percentage points behind Evert's early season pace.

But while Chris Evert was tearing up the league, another highly-touted rookie was having problems. Ilie Nastase's name is synonymous with problems, but he was really outdoing himself this time. Like the Racquets, Nastase's Hawaii Leis had also posted a perfect record during the early going. Only it was perfect in the wrong way. The Leis were 0–6 on May 17 and Nasty ranked 13th in the men's singles statistics. His mediocre performance, however, was overshadowed by his absences from the team. Every Nastase no-show was a direct violation of WTT's new contract ruling that stipulated that every player was committed to the full schedule. The only exceptions to that ruling were players who had previously signed multi-year contracts that allowed them to miss certain matches. Yet Nastase had somehow managed to sign an outside contract that conflicted with his WTT obligations. On June 4, the Leis were scheduled to play the Golden Gaters, but Nastase was not in Oakland. He was in—of all places— Hawaii where he was scheduled to play in an Avis Challenge Cup match the following morning at seven. The Rumanian's absence did not escape the attention of Gaters' owner, Dave Peterson, who threatened to do everything but call out the National Guard.

It wasn't the first time Peterson had been burned by Nastase. Several weeks earlier the Leis had appeared without their main box office draw, who it was said, had been summoned to Rumania by government authorities. But whether Nastase was in Eastern Europe or not, his behavior wasn't going over very well with WTT officials.

While the league and several individual teams, including Hawaii, were preparing legal action, King met with Nastase at Wimbledon during the league's halftime break. The result of their lengthy discussions was that the errant player promised to return to the Leis and complete the second half of the season. He was also relieved of about one-fourth of his salary in the form of a substantial fine.

"WTT has reached a point in its growth where it can no longer afford to tolerate actions such as Nastase's," said Larry King, announcing the return of the prodigal player. "We wanted him back, and we want other players to join WTT, but we want them to know that we have rules and that contracts cannot be broken or violated on a whim."

Ilie "Nasty" Nastase in a cheerful mood shows off his birthday cake.

A pensive Nastase.

King's strong words reflected the league's emerging strength in dealing with players. It was a far cry from only two years earlier when the owners were offering everything but a Cabinet post to players of Nastase's stature if they would consent to play a WTT match every now and again.

Fortunately, however, Nastase's situation was unique. Evonne Goolagong also missed several matches during the first half of the season, but her absence was due to a leg injury. While she was out, however, the Triangles fell to last place in the Eastern Division. At the Wimbledon break, they

were far behind the Division leading New York Sets who had won seventeen matches and lost only four. In the West, only Hawaii appeared to be out of contention at the halfway point. Phoenix (15–4) led the charging Golden Gaters by only two games.

In individual statistics Chris Evert's games-won percentage had slipped to .787, but it was still well ahead of Goolagong's second place mark of .659. Evert had won 18 sets and lost only one during the first half. On the men's side, Sandy Mayer's led with .609. Rod Laver was second with .550 and Marty Riessen, the 1975 men's singles leader, was entrenched in third place at .529.

In doubles, it was all Gaters. Betty Stove and Francoise Durr led the women's doubles and Frew McMillan and Tom Okker did likewise in the men's standings. In mixed doubles, Stove and McMillan were slightly ahead of New York's Billie Jean King and Phil Dent.

The fans, of course, were keeping an eye on the players, but WTT officials were keeping an eye on the gate. Both liked what they saw. The league drew over 350,000 people for 103 dates during the first half of the season, for an average of almost 3,500. The previous year, less than 200,000 had attended pre-Wimbledon WTT matches.

Phoenix was averaging over 6,500 for each of their ten home matches, an increase of 61.8 per cent over 1975. The L.A. Strings had a 126 per cent attendance increase and the Friars attendance went up 92.6 per cent.

In the East, the No-Name Loves registered the largest increase: 79.9 per cent. An average of 2,100 Hoosiers had turned out for each of their nine home dates.

Naturally, optimism ran high. "We've traditionally been stronger in the second half of the season," enthused Larry King, "when the championship races tighten."

Wimbledon '76 would also provide a terrific advertisement for WTT, especially as far as the women were concerned. In the all-WTT women's singles final, Chris Evert disposed of Evonne Goolagong, before teaming with the Nets' Martina Navratilova to take the women's doubles title from WTT players Betty Stove and Billie Jean King. Francoise Durr, Betty's doubles partner during the

The L.A. Strings at play in The Forum.

Kristien Shaw of the Phoenix Racquets.

In 1976 attendance was up and the crowds were less boisterous.

Andrew Pattison of the Phoenix Racquets

Coach Tony Roche in action.

The Gators' Tom Okker serves one up during the men's doubles.

WTT season, was reunited with her old Denver Racquets coach, Tony Roche, and they triumphed in mixed doubles over Rosie Casals and Dick Stockton.

In the men's singles event, Sandy Mayer and the Triangles' Vitas Gerulaitis scored some points for WTT and themselves by dumping Jimmy Connors and Arthur Ashe, respectively. Ilie Nastase, occasionally a member of the Leis, worked his way into the finals but was defeated by Bjorn Borg. WTT-affiliated players had once again shown the world that competing within the WTT framework did not diminish their effectiveness during tournament play.

They also proved that tennis fans in the United States read the papers because when league action resumed in early July, a record crowd of 13,492 showed up in Pittsburgh to watch a replay of the Wimbledon women's singles final.

Evert and Goolagong, both of whom had lost only one set in WTT events, squared off in a match that saw the Australian win 6–4. Goolagong's victory, her 15th in a row and 16th in 17 outings, provided the necessary margin for a Pittsburgh win, 24–23.

Bud Collins introduces the 1976 WTT All-Star squads to a crowd of 12,581 in the Oakland Coliseum and NBC's television audience.

The Strings' Bob Lutz was down 0-4 in men's singles, but came back to force a tiebreaker in the set.

Then, two nights later, they met again. The occasion was the second annual WTT All-Star bash. A sell-out crowd of 12,581 jammed into the Oakland Coliseum and were treated to a match whose suspense and drama would have made Alfred Hitchcock turn green with envy.

Bud Collins and his video sidekick, Julie

Heldman, were joined by John Newcombe in the broadcast booth as a dazzling array of tennis talent took their bows. The star-studded cast included Rod Laver, Bob Lutz, Billie Jean King, Vitas Gerualitis, Tony Roche, Martina Navratilova, Virginia Wade, Tom Okker, Francoise Durr, Betty Stove, Dianne Fromholtz, Marty Riessen, Phil Dent, John Alexander, Sandy Mayer, and, of course, Chris Evert and Evonne Goolagong.

The match opened with Okker and Laver coasting to an easy 6–2 victory in men's doubles over the East's Phil Dent and John Alexander. Then came the one event everyone was waiting for: women's singles. Goolagong glided through the set and brought the East into range with a 6–3 win. Mixed doubles was next. Billie Jean and her Sets teammate, Sandy Mayer, went out to tackle the reigning Wimbledon mixed doubles' champs, Tony Roche and Francoise Durr.

Billie Jean, inspired by the vociferous crowd and the NBC cameras, put on a great performance as she and Mayer gave the lead to the East, with a 6–

Vitas Gerulaitis gives theatrical thanks after defeating Bob Lutz, 7-6.

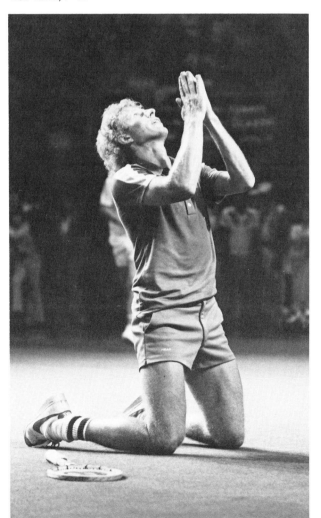

2 win. After three sets the score was: Eastern All-Stars 14, Western All-Stars 11.

Men's singles looked like a runaway for the East's Gerualitis as he jumped off to a four–zip lead over the Strings' Bob Lutz. But Lutz wasn't going to let himself be humiliated in front of a national television audience. Slowly at first, he began to come back. Then, after surviving several set points, he tied the set at six apiece. Gerulaitis recovered in time to win the tiebreaker, and the set, but his 7–6 victory didn't put the match out of reach.

Going into the last set, women's doubles, the East had a four-game lead, 21–17, which was quickly increased to 24–17 when Martina Navratilova and Virginia Wade grabbed a 3–0 lead over Betty Stove and the Strings' Dianne Fromholtz. The previous year, a seven-game lead during the final set of a WTT match would have made it mathematically impossible for the trailing team to win. This flaw in the scoring system had been criticized endlessly, and it had been eliminated in 1976. WTT had added a new wrinkle to the scoring format during the off-season and it was called "Overtime." Overtime by WTT definition simply meant that if the trailing team happened to win the final set of a WTT match, the competition would continue until the trailing team either lost a game, or tied the match. If the trailing team did manage to tie the match, a Super-Tiebreaker would be played to settle the matter.

But it didn't seem very likely that the All-Star match would go into overtime the way Wade and Navratilova were playing. However, it was the West's night for dramatic comebacks, and Stove and Fromholtz did just that. Wade and Navratilova (not to mention Coach Stolle) watched in horror as their lead dwindled, then disappeared. Somehow, the West pulled out a 7–6 victory and the match headed into overtime. All the East had to do was win one game before the West won three and the match was theirs. With the crowd roaring on every point, Stove and Fromholtz tied the match at 27–all. Since it was fairly obvious that the momentum had gone out of Wade and Navratilova, East Coach Fred Stolle yanked them and put in King and Goolagong to play the nine-point Super-Tiebreaker. And although Fromholtz had played exceedingly well, West Coach McMillan decided to replace her with the rested Chris Evert. Stove stayed in.

Fittingly, the match went down to the very last point. The crowd was on the verge of hysteria as Evert prepared to serve to King at 4–all in the Super-Tiebreaker. Chris followed her serve to the net and met Billie Jean's return with a forehand volley to Evonne's backhand. But Evonne's

Martina Navratilova takes a break during the women's doubles.

attempted passing shot barely made it to the net and it was all over. The West's dramatic come-from-behind 28–27 victory avenged the loss they had suffered the previous year. It also showed a national television audience that the WTT brand of tennis is exciting sports entertainment.

Besides winning the match, the West also swept the individual awards at the All-Star confrontation. Tom Okker and Dianne Fromholtz were named as the event's Male and Female Most Valuable Players. Chris Evert, who played the winning point in the match, wasn't singled out for a league award that night, but a few days later she was honored by an entire state. July 12, 1976, according to an official proclamation from the Arizona governor, was designated "Chris Evert Day." Not bad for a kid whose ties to the state only went back to the previous November.

Chris, of course, responded to that particular honor by continuing to win practically every time she laced up her tennies. She had to win because

Virginia Wade and Martina Navratilova try to figure out what happened to their 3-0 lead.

Betty Stove and Dianne Fromholtz play a winning doubles set, sending the All-Star match into overtime.

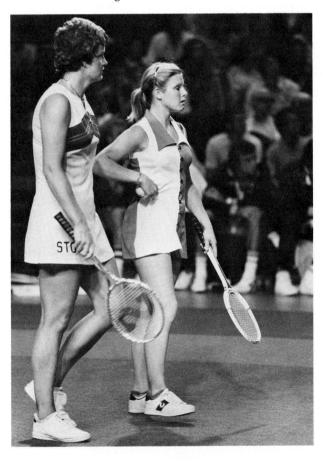

the Racquets were being pressed by the Golden Gaters in the race for the Western Division title. By August 1st, only a single game separated the two teams in the league standings.

It was a different story at the other end of the country. The Sets had easily clinched the top spot so the real battle was for second place. The Triangles were making another post-Wimbledon run for the playoffs and found themselves only one game out of second place with six matches left to play. The Cleveland Nets, who had played well all season, couldn't hold on at the end and won only two of their final eight matches. The Triangles, meanwhile, won all six of theirs and moved four games ahead of the Nets to within nine of New York.

On July 19, the Triangles were in the Eastern Division cellar. By August 8, they were in second place. Concurrent with the Triangles' climb from the basement, the league office released some new attendance figures. During the week following the televised All-Star game, six of the twenty WTT matches drew over 7,000 people each, including 11,742 in Pittsburgh to watch a Nets/Triangles duel. And the Triangles were then in last place! Perhaps even more amazing though, was that with four full weeks remaining on the schedule, the 1976 attendance had surpassed total attendance records for the previous year.

Meanwhile Nastase had returned to the Hawaii Leis for the second half of the season, but he wasn't very happy about it. Most of his disenchantment seemed to focus on the fans, who were branded as "animals" by no less an authority than Mr. Congeniality himself. Nastase had some problems with a few players as well. In New York, he balked at playing a doubles match against a Sets' duo that included Sandy Mayer because he was upset by Mayer's alleged stalling tactics during their singles match earlier in the program. Later, Nastase almost got into a display of fisticuffs with Pittsburgh's Mark Cox, and once he slammed a ball at Frew McMillan during a doubles match against the Gaters in Hawaii.

Nastase did, however, finally make it to Oakland, raising his attendance record in that city to .333. After watching the Gaters hand his team another loss that further cemented the Leis' last place finish, Nastase had a few words to say about WTT, most of them unkind.

"The tennis is mostly good," he said, "but the rest of it is too much like a circus. Too much noise, and too many people moving around." Too bad.

Nastase and his Lei teammates weren't going to the playoffs, but the Phoenix Racquets were and that led directly to a rather unfortunate occurrence.

The Racquets were scheduled to play the Nets in Cleveland on Sunday night, August 15th, before meeting the Golden Gaters in the first playoff game in Phoenix the following night. A cross-country flight to play a match that wouldn't affect the standings, but just might affect the Racquets playoff performance, was not looked upon favorably by the Phoenix officials. On the other hand, the Nets' officials always looked forward to a visit from Evert and Company, as did the concessionaires at

Tom Okker helps broadcast a televised Gator-Phoenix match.

the Nets' home arena. Joe Zingale, owner of the Cleveland club, was therefore extremely disturbed when he received word from Phoenix owner James Walker, that Chris Evert, Kristien Kemmer Shaw, Andrew Pattison, and player/coach, Tony Roche were physically unable to play in Cleveland on August 15th. Zingale immediately protested to the league office and threatened to cancel the match, which ironically, had been scheduled for that date as a favor to Phoenix.

Originally, that Sunday was going to be free day so the playoff teams would have a breather before the post-season play commenced. Evert, however, had a previous commitment to play in The Family Circle Cup during the first week of the season, so Phoenix's matches were rescheduled and they didn't play that first week. Four months later the favor had come back to haunt the Racquets.

Even though he faced a certain $10,000 fine plus an assessment for damages, Walker refused to send his team to Cleveland. Roche, Shaw, Evert and Pattison were "recovering" in Phoenix while subs Stephanie Tolleson and Butch Walts, along with three temporary additions to the Racquets' roster were being annihilated by the Nets, 31–14.

54

Though the Cleveland match was the third loss in a row for the Racquets, they still finished two games ahead of the runnerup Golden Gaters in the final standings. More important, the match concluded the third straight regular season in which all the WTT teams completed the entire schedule. (Actually, that's not entirely true. Hurricane Belle forced the cancellation of a late-season Sets/Lobsters match. It was not made up.)

For the third straight year the post-season playoff structure was brand new. In 1976, the first and second place finishers in each Division would be playing a best-of-three series with the survivors going on to the best-of-five championship series.

In the West, the doubles-oriented Golden Gaters geared up to face the Phoenix Racquets and the league's premier women's singles player, Chris Evert. In the opening match at Phoenix it was the Gaters' doubles strength that prevailed. The defending Western Division champs opened with a strong 6–2 win in men's doubles thanks to WTT's top male duo, Frew McMillan and Tom Okker.

Betty Stove, who had lost to Chris in each of their six regular season meetings, then took Evert to a tiebreaker in the women's singles. Stove held on to win the tiebreaker 5–3, as 5,848 Phoenix fans in Veterans Coliseum looked on in disbelief. The rout continued with a 6–0 whitewash of Evert and Kristien Shaw by Stove and Francoise Durr and the Gaters held 19–8 lead at the intermission. When Play resumed, Okker beat Andrew Pattison 7–6 in men's singles and Gater sub John Lucas and Durr crafted a 6–2 win over Tony Roche and Kris Shaw in mixed doubles. The Gaters had taken the first confrontation, 32–16, and both teams headed for Oakland for match two.

The following night the Racquets came back to win both singles events, Evert over Stove, 6–1 and Pattison over Okker, 7–5, but the Gaters again demonstrated their dominance in doubles, winning all three sets. In fact, the final total games tally for the six sets of doubles played during the Western Division playoffs was 36–9, Gaters. Though the Gaters' back-to-back wins quickly settled matters in the West, their championship series opponent had not yet emerged from the battle back East.

Billie Jean, making her third straight run at the elusive WTT Championship, surely must have experienced a sense of *déjà vu* when the Sets lost the first playoff match to the late-blooming Pittsburgh Triangles, 26–25. Following the mid-season break, she had returned to singles play on a fairly regular basis and had posted a 14–2 record with both losses coming at the hands of Evonne Goolagong. In the second playoff match, however, Billie Jean got one of those losses back, 6–4, and

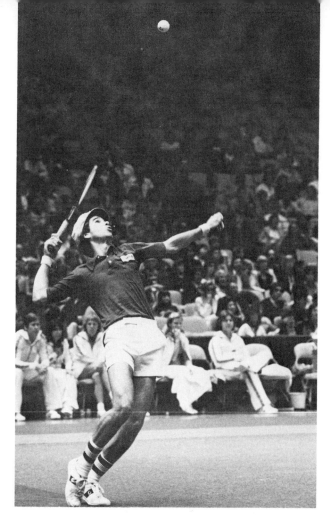
Coach Frew McMillan led the Gators into the playoffs.

the Sets evened the series at one apiece, 29–21. Match three saw her get back the other one by an identical score and the Sets, the team with the best regular season record in 1976, captured the best-of-three playoff series. They would meet the Gaters for the WTT championship.

"We nearly won the WTT championship when I coached the Philadelphia Freedoms in 1974," said a determined Mother Freedom after the Sets eliminated Pittsburgh, "but we missed out. Then last year we (the Sets) missed out again. I want this one bad."

And she wasn't kidding, folks. Billie Jean & Company shoved the Gaters all over the Oakland Coliseum in the opening match. The Sets won everything but women's doubles, and they didn't lose that one by much. Final score: 31–23. Probably the main surprise of that first meeting was the ease with which Sandy Mayer handled Okker in the men's singles. Mayer wasn't even breathing hard as he came off the court after his 6–3 victory over the usually tenacious Flying Dutchman.

Match number two was scheduled for a Saturday afternoon at the Coliseum. Billie Jean and Virginia Wade came out running and approximately thirty seconds after it had begun the women's doubles ended. Stove and Durr, the Gaters' formidable

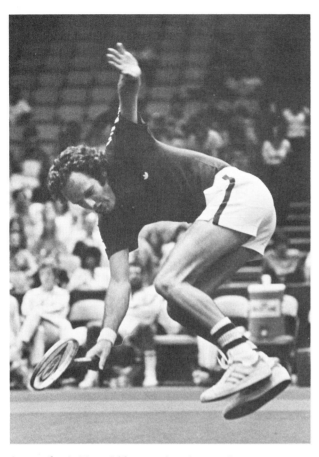

An acrobatic Tom Okker at play during the championships.

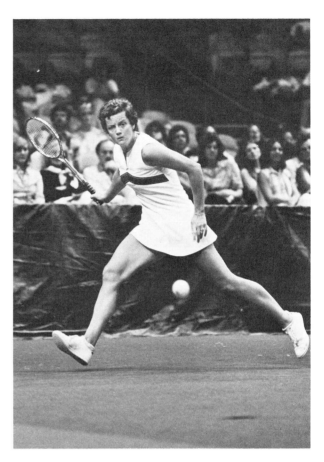

Betty Stove beat Chris Evert in the Western Division playoffs, but couldn't handle Virginia Wade in the Championships.

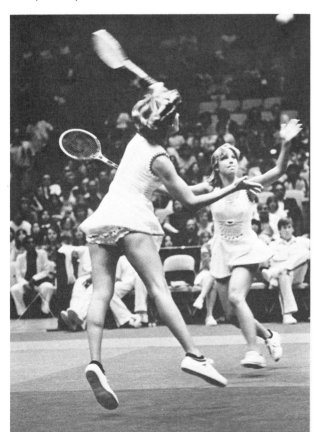

women's doubles combo could hardly believe that they were on the wrong end of a 6–0 set.

Men's singles was up next and the crowd settled back to watch Tom Okker get back at Sandy Mayer who had won their first championship encounter, 6–3. It didn't work out that way though. Mayer clobbered Okker 6–1, and the Sets' lead was suddenly 12–1. The Gaters bounced back and won the next three sets but it wasn't enough to wipe out New York's monstrous lead, and they lost 29–21.

Immediately following the second match in Oakland, Billie Jean, Betty Stove, and Virginia Wade hopped a plane for Philadelphia where they would represent their respective countries in the Federation Cup, the women's equivalent of the Davis Cup. A few nights later, Billie Jean defeated

Shaw and Evert were no match for Stove and Durr, the league's top women's doubles team.

Australia's Evonne Goolagong in the Federation
Cup finals and then joined forces with Rosie Casals
to beat Goolagong and Kerry Melville Reid for the
title. The United States' Fed Cup victory put Billie
Jean in the unique position of being able to win
two major team championships in a single week.
All the Sets had to do was get past the Gaters one
more time. It was no contest. New York swept all
five sets against the mysteriously inept Gaters in
match number 3 and took the WTT championship
31-13. Sandy Mayer continued to befuddle Okker
with another 6-1 drubbing. In his three
championship series wins over The Flying
Dutchman, Mayer yielded exactly five games. His
sterling playoffs performance earned him Male
Most Valuable Player honors, while Billie Jean King
was named the Female Most Valuable Player.

"This championship was my last big goal in
tennis," said the overjoyed Billie Jean, "and it feels
great to get it. I don't think a lot of people took me
seriously when I kept saying how much I wanted to
be part of a WTT championship team, but I worked
my buns off for it and so did everybody else on the
team. This is a team victory. We stayed together all
year and we worked hard to make this happen.
That's what team tennis is all about."

Victory at last for Billie Jean King.

*The New York Sets display the 1976 WTT
Championship banner after their victory over the
Golden Gators.*

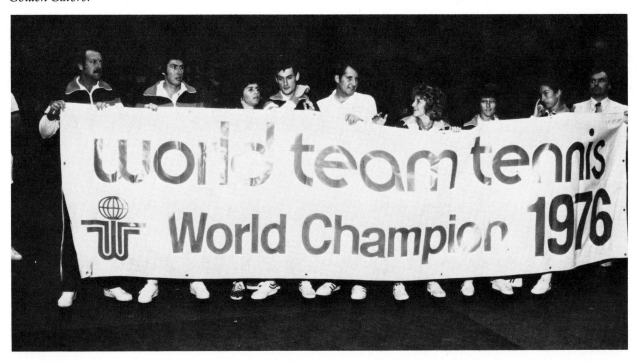

The New York Sets became the third WTT champions, and the second team to do so at the expense of the Golden Gaters. In 1974, the Denver Racquets won the prestigious Teflon Cup, symbolic of WTT supremacy, and in 1975 it was the Pittsburgh Triangles who took home the equally prestigious championship trophy, the Bancroft Cup. The trophy in 1976 was nameless, but it went to the Sets all the same. So did a large percentage of a small percentage of the total gate receipts. It wasn't much, however, because only about 14,000 people attended the three championship games.

The lackluster playoff attendance was surprising since the overall figures were up considerably. The final count, exclusive of the playoffs, All-Star game, and pre-season exhibitions, was an impressive 843,144. That averaged out to 3,850 for each of the league's 219 regular season matches, a 26 per cent gain over the previous year.

"The figures are overwhelming," said Larry King. "We felt we were going to grow, but I never expected to move so fast. The league's growth this year exceeded our most optimistic forecasts."

In its brief history, WTT had attracted well over two million fans, a milestone that many had thought unreachable, especially on those nights two years earlier when only handfuls of people were showing up for WTT matches. Phoenix led the league with an average attendance of 6,752 at home and 6,384 on the road. Pittsburgh and Los Angeles each averaged more than 4,000 for all of their matches, and only Boston and Indiana came in at less than 3,000.

Chris Evert completed her first WTT season by sweeping the individual honors for women. She was named Female Rookie-of-the-Year and the 1976 Female Most Valuable Player in recognition of her performance in women's singles and her contribution to the Racquet's first place finish in the Western Division. Evert won thirty-three sets and lost six while posting a games-won percentage of .700. Chris obviously enjoyed her initial contact with WTT. Shortly after the season, she renewed her 1-year contract with the Racquets, and later told *The New York Times,* "After another 2 or 3 years I plan to cut back on tournaments and concentrate on WTT."

Evonne Goolagong, 32–6 in sets, finished second in the women's singles Superstar stats with a .640 games-won percentage. Martina Navratilova of Cleveland, Virginia Wade of New York, and Rosie Casals of Los Angeles rounded out the top five. Billie Jean was absent from the women's singles superstar list because she failed to play enough games to qualify, but she did pick up several media votes for the Most Valuable Player award.

Sandy Mayer took top honors in the men's singles category. His performance also earned him the Male MVP award to go with his Playoffs Male MVP trophy. He won 19 sets and lost only 8 while compiling a games-won percentage of .575, some thirty points ahead of runnerup Rod Laver of the San Diego Friars. The Strings' Bob Lutz was third, and Tom Okker and Marty Riessen were fourth and fifth. Ilie Nastase recovered from his early season inconsistencies to finish sixth. He won 20 and dropped 15 sets and ended the season with a .504 games-won percentage.

Sandy Mayer beat Tom Okker three times in the championship series.

The Golden Gaters duo of Durr and Stove took the women's doubles title but they were followed closely by Goolagong and JoAnn Russell of Pittsburgh. The Loves' Mona Guerrant and Ann Kiyomura finished third.

The Gaters also came out on top in men's doubles. Frew McMillan and Tom Okker repeated their feat of the previous year, finishing the season just ahead of the Strings' Bob Lutz and Vijay Amritraj. Mark Cox and Bernie Mitton of the Triangles were third.

In mixed doubles, Ann Kiyomura and Ray Ruffels of Indiana ended up .005 points ahead of King and Phil Dent of New York. Durr and McMillan of the Gaters were third.

Individual honors in 1976 also went to Rod Laver who eclipsed Marty Riessen's record of being the oldest Rookie-of-the-Year in professional sports history. Riessen was thirty-five when he got his in 1975. Laver was a ripe, old thirty-eight in 1976.

The final award, Coach of the Year, must have come as a complete surprise to its recipient, Fred Stolle of the Sets. The previous year, that honor went to Frew McMillan, player/coach of the runnerup Golden Gaters, while the victorious coach, Vic Edwards of Pittsburgh, was fired. Stolle nevertheless accepted the award graciously.

The third annual WTT season was the most successful one yet. Attendance had risen tremendously, the tennis was superb, and ol' Mother Freedom finally captured the championship title she had been striving for.

Fred Stolle, Coach of the Year.

6 | 1976—Epilogue

At WTT's post-season owners' meeting in September the mood was buoyant. None of the teams had made any money, of course, but the losses were declining and the traditional end-of-the-season pessimism was not in evidence at the Occotillo Lodge in Palm Springs.

Joe Zingale and Jimmy Walker, the two owners who had recently locked horns over Walker's decision to bench his team just prior to the final regular season match, weren't exactly acting like long-lost buddies, but then again they weren't trying to push each other into the pool either. Walker managed to patch things up somewhat by giving Cleveland one of the Racquets' 1977 home games.

They and the other owners had more important matters to consider, such as the marketing study and audience survey that had been prepared by a San Francisco firm, Pacific Select Corporation. Among other things, the detailed survey showed that:

WTT attendance is female-dominated. A woman is more likely to influence a man to attend a match than vice-versa.

Less than 10% of the WTT audience are non-tennis players and 80% of the spectators play at least once a week.

Because of the relatively small percentage of new players among the audience, the primary learning emphasis is on strategy, not shot production.

Most spectators come to WTT matches because of a singles match-up, but they leave preferring the doubles by a wide margin.

Only a small percentage of the audience believes the players consider the league to be as important personally as a tournament. The doubters do, however, feel that WTT players are committed to the league, emotionally as well as contractually.

A majority of the spectators found the color court too distracting. They felt that a traditional court (i.e. one with lines) would make it easier for them to determine if a ball was in or out.

The overwhelming majority of fans thought the streamlined scoring system was valuable. This seemed to indicate that the *team* concept was becoming accepted.

Because the average WTT audience consists of

people who actually play tennis, most believed that heckling, especially during service, went beyond their sense of fair play and good sportsmanship.

Among tennis players who had never attended a WTT match it was felt that the lack of restraints on the fans would diminish the quality of play and probably disrupt their personal enjoyment of the match.

When asked to identify their favorite WTT player, many of those surveyed said Jimmy Connors.

The audience survey gave the owners something to think about, but so had Larry King. Several months earlier, he had announced his plans to resign after the third season, and he officially did so at the league meeting.

King was going off to the Big Apple to run the New York Sets for a while. He would still be part-owner of the Golden Gaters, of course, but Dave Peterson was running that show quite well and Sol Berg, the Sets' owner, had asked for some help.

Everyone agreed that the ultimate success of the league depended on the ultimate success of the New York franchise, but not all of the owners agreed that Larry King was the ideal choice to engineer that success. Berg did though, and his vote carried a lot of strength.

Almost immediately, King announced that he was going to move a dozen of the Sets' 1977 home matches from Long Island's Nassau Coliseum to Madison Square Garden in an effort to beef up attendance. Besides moving some of the Sets' matches to the Garden, he had persuaded the West Side Tennis Club, the site of the U.S. Open, to allow the Sets to play two of their 1977 home matches in the club's stadium. A new name had also been chosen for the New York franchise to go along with their occasional changes of venue. No, it wasn't the New York "Debts." Appropriate as that name might be, it was passed over in favor of the "Apples."

Meanwhile, the owners were faced with finding a replacement for King. They considered several candidates, before finally settling on a man whose WTT affiliations went back to the 1974 season: Earl (Butch) Buchholz.

The new commissioner had spent the first year of WTT as a member of the Chicago Aces. The following year he became the player/coach for the Hawaii Leis. In 1976 he also served as the non-playing coach of the Team America squad of WTT All-Stars who played the Russians.

Buchholz obviously knew his way around the league and in fact, he held a rather unique WTT record. On August 5, 1975, the new league

commissioner had been aced nine times in a single set by the Cleveland Nets' cannonballer, Bob Giltinan. Understandably, Buchholz doesn't like to go around bragging about that particular feat, especially since his pre-WTT tennis credentials greatly overshadow his unfortunate performance against Giltinan.

In 1958, Buchholz became the first and only player to capture the Junior Grand Slam of tennis by winning the 18-and-under titles of Australia, France, Great Britain, and the United States. A member of the U.S. Davis Cup team from 1958–60, he turned pro in 1961 and won the U.S. Professional title the following year. He later became one of the "Handsome Eight" players for WCT.

Buchholz wasted precious little time in getting things moving. Barely six weeks after taking office, he moved the league office from Newport Beach, California, to St. Louis, Missouri, his home base on those rare occasions when he wasn't globetrotting.

Butch Buchholz, the new WTT commissioner, during his playing days with the Hawaii Leis.

League headquarters, however, wasn't the only move WTT endured in 1976. The Hawaii Leis planned a move also. Well before the 1976 season had ended, in fact, it appeared that the islands might lose their franchise in 1977. Therefore it came as no great surprise when Leis' owner Donald Kelleher made it official.

Back in July, Kelleher had dropped a hint of things to come when he shifted the Leis last six home dates to Seattle and Portland. "It doesn't necessarily mean we're moving though," he said at the time. "That won't be decided until after the current (1976) season. But right now I'm extremely disappointed in our home attendance and I'm not entirely convinced we should take another chance on Honolulu." Two months later, Kelleher made another statement. "We're moving," he said.

Since the six Seattle/Portland test matches were well received, the relocated Leis said they would split their home matches between the two cities. The old Leis became the new Sea-Port Cascades.

A lot of people, including Donald Kelleher himself, were not overjoyed about leaving Hawaii, but the Leis were tired of the constant competition with Hawaii's beautiful natural attractions, the sun, surf, and sand. Besides, the islands had been inundated by several professional tennis events and it was becoming apparent that the inhabitants were approaching a saturation point. There was also the transportation factor, which was no small matter.

Meanwhile, another WTT franchise was making an even more dramatic move. The Pittsburgh Triangles closed up shop completely. Frank Fuhrer, the Triangles' owner, decided that the insurance business was less of a headache than running a tennis team and he bailed out of WTT in December. Since Fuhrer had been dropping hints that he might pull up stakes after the 1976 season, WTT had another franchise waiting in the wings. the Pennsylvania Keystones.

Initially, Larry King was the sole owner of the Triangles' replacement, but he quickly peddled shares of the Keystones to other WTT owners: Jerry Buss, of the Strings, Robert Kraft of the Lobsters, and Sol Berg of the Apples. The Keystones planned to divide their home matches between Pittsburgh and Philadelphia, but those plans were abandoned when Joe Zingale grabbed the open Pittsburgh territory for eleven of his Cleveland Nets' home matches.

While these geographic maneuverings were taking place, WTT scheduled a draft session for mid-January 1977. Conducted by telephone, the draft once again demonstrated that although the league had lost a charter franchise, its sense of humor was intact. The Keystones grabbed the

rights to Donald Dell, the player/agent who along with Jack Kramer provided WTT with some of its stiffest opposition three years earlier. The newest WTT franchise also drafted Renee Richards, the controversial transsexual, whose attempts to enter the women's field at Forest Hills the previous fall grabbed sports page headlines.

But before either of those draft choices had a chance to sign with Pennsylvania, a funny thing happened. The franchise was taken over by the Soviet Union. On January 29, 1977, after several months of negotiation with Larry King, the Soviet Tennis Federation signed a contract agreeing to field a Soviet team in WTT's fourth season. The Soviets will play the full 44-game WTT schedule, though only four of those matches will be played in their "home" city of Philadelphia. Two matches will take place in Moscow, and the others will be farmed out to non-WTT locations.

Though the Russian players are officially considered amateurs, they are not strangers to the world of international tennis. Alex Metreveli and

World Tennis *cover, November, 1976.*

Olga Morozova, the USSR's top male and female players, have both reached the finals at Wimbledon during their careers. Metreveli did it in 1973, and Morozova in 1974. Natasha Chmyreva, one of the most promising young players in the world; Marina Kroshina, Temuraz Kakulia, and Vadim Borisov, round out the Soviet team.

The addition of the Russian team to the WTT lineup wasn't the only big news out of the league in January. The same day the Soviet deal was announced, Bjorn Borg signed a three-year, $1.5 million contract with the Cleveland Nets, thus ending Joe Zingale's three year odyssey after the popular Swedish player.

Besides the lofty sum Borg extracted for signing, his contract carried an additional provision. His fiancée, Mariana Simionescu of Romania, also became a member of the Nets.

With Bjorn Borg and the Russians aboard, WTT was naturally optimistic about the future. The outlook was further brightened by indications that the media was finally beginning to acknowledge the league's position as a legitimate member of the tennis community.

A modicum of proof appeared on the cover of the November 1976 issue of *World Tennis*. There, in living color, was a photograph of the New York Sets, posed in a human pyramid. Beneath the photograph lay a bright green legend: WTT CHAMPIONS. And nestled inside the magazine was the World Team Tennis article, surrounded by sixteen pages of Forest Hills coverage.

No longer is WTT just "that American inter-city league" as the British press had sarcastically labeled it in 1974. No way. WTT is for real! Finally.

The WTT Innovations

1 | The Format

Here's the way world class tennis used to be:

Opening day, Wimbledon 1969. It is late in the afternoon as Pancho Gonzales, 41, and Charlie Pasarell, 25, stroll out onto Centre Court's hallowed grass to play a first-round match. Gonzales, who has never won the Wimbledon title in his illustrious, but now fading career, plays Pasarell evenly in the first set. After 45 games, the score is 23–22 in the younger man's favor. Pasarell has reached set point eleven times, but each time the wily veteran thwarts him. It seems as if the set is on the road to infinity.

Finally, on Pasarell's twelfth set point, Gonzales ignores a deep lob. His experienced eye tells him it is long. He is wrong. The 46-game set is over. It has lasted two hours and consumed most of the players' energies.

Though nightfall is fast approaching, the tournament referee orders play to continue, and in a manner of speaking, it does. Gonzales is in violent disagreement with the decision to continue play, claiming that the encroaching gloom has made it impossible to follow the flight of the ball. He registers his disapproval by dropping the second set in a quarter of an hour, 6–1. Mercifully, play is adjourned until the following day.

A rested Gonzales, down two sets in the best-of-five match, takes the third set, 16–14, and the fourth by a more reasonable score of 6–4. Going into the fifth and deciding set of the two-day match, Gonzales and Pasarell have played 83 games, the equivalent of nine 6–3 sets. Twenty games later, it is all over. Gonzales has survived his opening round confrontation 22–24, 1–6, 16–14, 6–4, 11–9. The 112 games have taken five hours and ten minutes to play.

Though the Gonzales/Pasarell match was not typical by any means, even by tournament standards, it is a prime example of what WTT wanted to avoid at all costs—namely long, tedious matches. But WTT wasn't alone. Many forward-thinking tournament officials also recognized that seemingly endless matches that threatened to run as long as "My Fair Lady" were the greatest cure for insomnia since political campaign speeches.

At the first Wimbledon Championships in 1877, a set was awarded to the first player to win six games. Period. At five-all then, the eleventh game of a set became a tiebreaker. The following year, however, the "advantage set" was introduced. Now the winner became the first player to take six games by a two-game margin. Since there was no longer a limit on the number of games, the sets occasionally became open-ended tests of endurance—for the players and the spectators.

Obviously something had to be done to eliminate tennis's version of the three-day weekend and in 1970 something was. That year USLTA authorized Forest Hills to experiment with a tiebreaker. The test was a success and the following year Wimbledon also adopted a tiebreaker to decide sets that became deadlocked at eight games (in all but the final set of a match).

The introduction of various tiebreak systems—usually either the 9-point "sudden death," or the 12-point "lingering death" variety—into tournament play brought tennis closer to the Jet Age. As far as WTT was concerned, however, it wasn't quite enough. WTT wanted to take tennis out of stuffy clubs and make it attractive to the modern sports fan. They wanted to mold tennis into a fast-paced, exciting spectacle that would appeal to spectators who were looking for an evening of quality sports entertainment.

They wanted to trim some fat from the existing product and present a leaner meaner version; they wanted to build a new house on an old foundation. They wanted . . . well, they wanted to do a lot of things.

But what they didn't want to do was get rid of tournaments. No, the WTT gang were not wild-eyed anarchists. They were in favor of alternatives, not destruction. They knew that it wasn't necessary to tear down New York City in order to start a commune upstate.

"Tournament tennis," they said, "certainly has its place and we're not out to eliminate it. We merely want to bring tennis to the masses. The tournament format, with its excruciatingly long matches and ancient scoring system, obviously will continue to appeal to the dedicated tennis fans and we wouldn't have it any other way.

"WTT, on the other hand, will present an exciting, compact form of tennis to those folks who might enjoy watching the sport, but who don't have the interest, stamina, or opportunity to sit through lengthy matches. World Team Tennis will not, as some have suggested, destroy or harm tennis. On the contrary, it will benefit the sport by bringing more good tennis to more people than ever before."

The initial WTT format, as designed by the league's architects, Larry King & Associates, may be found in an early promotional brochure, circa June 1973. The brochure states that the forty-four game WTT season will run from May through July;

that scoring will be "no ad" with tiebreakers (sudden death) at five–all in any set; that there will not be changes of ends of the court, except after sets (in tournaments, such changes occur on odd games); that substitutions will be permitted after two sets; and that the total league payroll is conservatively estimated at $2 million for the first year, not including unspecified "financial awards for the WTT playoffs."

Of the above, only the proposed number of matches and the season starting time were in effect when league play opened in May 1974. The original format of competition described in the promotional brochure had also undergone a few alterations by opening day.

"A WTT match," said the brochure, "will consist of three events: men's singles, women's singles, and mixed doubles. Match scores will be either 3–0 or 2–1."

It was quite a departure from the tournament structure where the men usually played best-of-five matches and the women best-of-three. Also, in tournament play, be it elimination or round robin, the winner was not determined until several matches, played over several days, had been contested. WTT would have had a definite winner every time two teams met.

When the league made its debut, however, the prototype format had been doubled from three events to six—two each of men's and women's singles and doubles, and two mixed doubles—and the notion of awarding one point for each set victory had been scrapped. The winner would be determined by the team capturing the greatest number of games during the six-set match.

Barely two weeks into the first season it became obvious that the modified structure of competition contained a fatal flaw; it was dull. Deadly dull. And in WTT's book, dullness was a cardinal sin. Even worse, the matches, which had been designed to run approximately two and a half hours, were becoming increasingly time consuming. About the only bright spot in the gloomy picture was the crowd enthusiasm generated by the mixed doubles events.

"We've gotta do something," said Larry King, who had called an emergency league meeting to deal with the problem.

He proposed a number of radical revisions to enliven the show. Beginning immediately, the WTT format would consist of only five sets: men's and women's singles and doubles, and the grand finale, mixed doubles. The sudden emphasis on the doubles game (now fully 60 per cent of the WTT program) was at odds with the position that aspect of the game occupied in the more traditional world of competitive tennis. Only very recently, in fact, has doubles begun to emerge from its fun-and-games stature, attracting big money and big names. WTT just happened to recognize the trend early.

King's insistence on giving mixed doubles permanent status as the rubber match was rooted in his desire to take full advantage of WTT's unique position of being the only professional sports league featuring sexually integrated teams. If a match went down to the wire, he wanted the men and the women on the court contributing equally to the final outcome.

Some strong opposition to the placement of mixed doubles at the end of the match surfaced at the early season emergency meeting. It came from a totally unexpected source: the two female owners. Betty Jones, owner of the Houston EZ Riders and Cathie Anderson, co-owner of the Golden Gaters, objected strenuously. They insisted that men's doubles was far more exciting than mixed doubles and that the men should play the final set.

"I couldn't believe what I was hearing," says Larry King. "I mean, here we were trying to make the women players completely equal partners in the team effort, and the only two women owners were fighting it."

Despite the objections, however, the format revisions were put into effect and they did indeed make things livelier and less time comsuming. The new format was so successful, in fact, that it remained unchanged until the 1976 season when the home team's coach was given control of the order of play.

Previously, the only decision possible regarding playing order was whether to play men's or women's singles in the second set or the fourth. The new ruling undoubtedly opened up the coaches to that great American pastime: second-guessing the head guy's strategy. The coaches still had to alternate singles and doubles, but in 1976 they were given the option of going for a big lead by using their strength early, or finishing up with the big guns.

2 | The Scoring

The third season also saw a solution to an obvious, oft-criticized flaw in WTT's cumulative game-scoring scheme. For the first time in the league's brief history a team could no longer mathematically clinch a match by the end of the third set, thereby reducing the remaining two sets to mere exhibitions.

From all indications, the method of scoring tennis games by the clock system—that is, 15 (quarter hour), 30 (half hour), 40 (most likely it was originally 45 for three-quarters of an hour), game (the final quarter hour that completes the cycle)—dates back to the Middle ages.

Nobody really knows exactly how "love" came to mean no score, but the most popular explanation seems to center on the French word, l'oeuf which means egg. Almost certainly, the term "deuce" is an anglicized form of the French a deux.

The Rt. Hon. Lord Aberdare, writing in The Encyclopedia of Tennis, tells us that the use of the word "service" to describe the opening stroke of each point stemmed from the fact that in the early days of tennis the ball was set in motion by a servant.

"Henry VIII (1509–47) certainly employed a servant for this purpose," writes Lord Aberdare, "and in those days there was clearly no intention of winning a point by service; it was just a convenient way of starting a rally and best performed by a lackey."

The winner of a game, then as now, was the player to win four points (i.e. 15, 30, 40, game) except when the game went to deuce (40–40). When that happened, the outcome of the game hung in the balance until one of the players managed to win two consecutive points. The extra points weren't numbered; they were called "advantage server," or "advantage receiver," or "ad in," or "ad out," or "my ad," or "your ad," or "advantage Jones," or something similar. If a player had an advantage point but lost the next one, the game score reverted to "deuce."

At least that's how it went until WTT came along and eliminated the deuce, the foul tip of tennis. The league also eliminated the strange, but well-established, point designations. Love, which means no score, was replaced by zero. The 15, 30, 40, game progression was supplanted by the far more basic 1, 2, 3, 4. The first player to make four points wins the game, plain and simple.

Mr. James Van Alen of Newport, Rhode Island, became an instant fan of the WTT scoring system. Of course, he was somewhat prejudiced, considering it was basically his invention. Van Alen had been attacking the confusing method of scoring for years, claiming that his Van Alen Streamlined Scoring System, (VASSS), would speed up the game and make it a contest of skill rather than stamina.

In Van Alen's "No Ad" system, games are scored 1, 2, 3, 4, and the first player to win six games takes the set. In the event a set is tied at five–all, a nine-point tiebreaker is played and the set ends at 6–5.

With only a few minor alterations, that is the scoring system WTT decided to adopt. The primary difference was that the set score could go to six–all in WTT before the tiebreaker, another Van Alen invention, was called in.

The nine-point tiebreaker works like this: Player A serves two points then relinquishes the serve to Player B who does likewise. Player A gets the serve back for the fifth and sixth points. Player B finishes up by serving the last three points. A court change occurs after four points and the first player to win five points is awarded a game and the set 7–6.

(The winner of the 12-point "lingering death" tiebreaker is the first player to win seven points with at least a two-point cushion. Theoretically, therefore, a 12-point tiebreaker could last forever.)

As soon as WTT decided to abandon its original plans of awarding a single scoreboard point for each set won and score cumulative game victories instead, several problems surfaced. The first and most obvious was the fact that the score could be tied in total games after all the events were played.

"No problem," said Larry King. "That's what we have a Super-Tiebreaker for."

"Super-Tiebreaker" is just a glittery name for the standard "sudden death" tiebreaker. It is still nine-points, but an entire WTT match hinges on the outcome. The league decreed that the players on the court when a match was tied after regulation play would play the Super-Tiebreaker. As might be expected, the final point of a Super-Tiebreaker was more pressure packed than a can of coffee, especially since it could make or break a team's entire season.

In 1977, the Super-Tiebreaker was extended to 13 points because WTT officials felt the additional points would intensify the drama inherent in the great match decider.

But although the Super-Tiebreaker nicely settled the close matches, what about those that were runaways? Like this hypothetical WTT match, for instance:

Team A wins the first set, 6–0. They duplicate that score in set number two. The match score stands at 12–0. But in the third set, Team B makes a comeback. Down 5–0, they fight back to tie it at six–all before losing the tiebreaker. The match score goes to 19–6, with two full sets remaining. Figure it out. Even if Team B wins the next 12 games while shutting out Team A, the final score will be: Team A, 19, Team B, 18.

Naturally, WTT was severely criticized for having such a monumental defect in its progressive scoring system. For two years the league endured the criticism while they searched for a solution.

Then shortly after the 1975 season, they found one. It was WTT "Overtime."

At first glance, the official description of "Overtime" sounds hopelessly confusing.

"The team leading the match must win the last set to be the winner. If the trailing team wins the last set, the match goes into 'Overtime.' Overtime continues until the leading team wins one game or until the trailing team ties the overall score. When the overall score is tied, a Super-Tiebreaker is played to determine the winner of the match."

A few words of explanation may be necessary, so let's let Larry King supply them.

"Let's say, for example, that Golden Gate is playing the Pittsburgh Triangles. After four sets, Pittsburgh holds a 24–17 lead. Now, under the old format, the match would have been clinched by the Triangles at that point. Even if Golden Gate were to win the final set, say 6–3, all that would have accomplished would have been to make the final score 27–23 in favor of Pittsburgh. With the overtime rule, however, play would continue.

"If Pittsburgh were to win the next game, the match would end with the Triangles winning, 28–23. But if Golden Gate were to win the first game of the overtime, the score would be 27–24 and at least one more game would have to be played.

"If Pittsburgh won that one, the final score would be 28–24, but if Golden Gate were to win the second game of the overtime, the score would become 27–25 with at least one more game to be played.

"If Golden Gate were to reach 27–all by winning four overtime games in a row without allowing Pittsburgh to win one, then we would go to the Super-Tiebreaker, and the team winning five points would be declared the overall winner of the match, 28–27.

"Of course, the whole overtime procedure depends on the trailing team winning the final set. If the leading team wins the final set, it's all over."

If WTT overtime seems complicated, just remember that the problem it was designed to solve wasn't exactly simple. And wait until you see what WTT did with the linespersons, those dedicated souls who seldom seem to see things your way.

3 | The Officiating

Tennis linespersons.

Ion Tiriac, for three years the player/coach of the Boston Lobsters, once had this to say about them: "They are all between fifty and dead."

And Tiriac's fellow Rumanian, Ilie Nastase, a player not especially noted for his habit of

Boston's Ion Tiriac puts a Rumanian curse on a linesperson.

exchanging pleasantries with the folks calling the shots, had the following conversation with a net cord judge during a close match:

"It was a let," Nasty suggested helpfully after an apparent ace blew past him.

"Not true," replied the man at the net. "If it was a let, I'd have heard it."

"How *could* you hear it?" screeched Nastase. "You're eighty years old!"

Both players, of course, were over-dramatizing the situation, but their remarks served to reinforce the unfortunate, stereotypical image shared by linespersons everywhere.

Sure, tennis officiating has its fair share of pensioners, but that doesn't necessarily mean that everyone who works a match has one foot in the grave and the other firmly wrapped around a folding chair on a tennis court. No, the main thing wrong with tennis officiating has little to do with age. It does, however, have a lot to do with experience and competence, or the lack of same.

Linespersons have traditionally been people who for a variety of reasons—love of the game, a chance to be part of the action, or perhaps a simple desire to grab one of the best seats in the house—have been volunteers. Sitting on a folding chair for several hours, often under a broiling sun, staring at a well-defined portion of a tennis court is not the easiest job in the world. Especially when

the primary reward one can expect for doing so is verbal abuse, and lots of it. Surely anyone who volunteers for such a masochistic assignment should be commended. They should also be well-trained and, above all, competent, but many are neither. And that is the problem.

For years, the quality of tennis officiating has been criticized, often with good reason. The sport, after all, had become major league—it was attracting big money and its stars were making headlines both on and off the court—but the officiating was still bush league. Nearly everyone, the fans, the players, and even many linespersons and umpires, agreed that something had to be done to upgrade that vital aspect of the game.

It was easier said than done though. What other sport has twelve officials on the field of combat with a maximum of four athletes? And although a dozen bodies are needed to oversee a tennis match, a hundred more are required to run a tournament when many matches are played simultaneously. Obviously, the sheer numbers make a comprehensive officials' training program impractical.

Naturally, the WTT brass were as concerned as the rest of the tennis world about the quality of the courtside jurists, and after the 1975 season, they decided to do something about it. Predictably, they developed a system that was guaranteed to raise a few eyebrows. And, if the league was to believed, it was also guaranteed to improve the officiating.

For starters, WTT eliminated six linespersons and took the chairs away from the remaining five. Presto, instant mobility. No more sitting around fighting to stay alert for the WTT officials, no sir! They would be on the move. That is, all of them except the referee, the only member of the corps who would remain stationary. But even he would be on his feet at all times, perched on a soap box near the net. The officials working the floor, however, two at each end of the court, would have to hustle.

WTT also did away with the customary blue blazers, long a mainstay of an official's uniform. The moving crew would be outfitted in gray slacks, complemented by blue shirts with green and white checked collars and a number on the sleeve. The fast-moving feet of the officials would be clad in appropriate footwear: tennis shoes. Ingenious!

During a WTT match, the line judge on the receiver's side of the court would crouch down and eyeball the service line waiting for the ball to barrel into the service court. Meanwhile, another official would keep an eye on the center service line. On the other side of the net, one linesperson would watch for a footfault while the other kept the service court side line in focus.

66

One of WTT's sartorially splendid, upright referees.

received hundreds of applications from prospective linespersons, but the league was primarily interested in applicants who had officiating experience in team sports.

"We figured we could teach the rules of tennis to someone with an officiating background regardless of the sport," said Larry King. "They would be coming to us already familiar with player and crowd control, two techniques that are difficult to teach."

That is how WTT came to have an NBA referee, an NFL official, and a former National League baseball umpire on its officials' payroll. Another innovation. The vast majority of tournament linespersons work gratis, but WTT was paying $25 a night. Not much perhaps, but a decent amount for a few hours' work.

Virtually all of the 144 training school graduates possessed impressive athletic credentials, either as athletes or officials or, in many cases, both. Each one also possessed excellent eyesight since passing an eye test was a prerequisite for securing a training school diploma. The WTT system didn't completely eliminate bad calls, but the general consensus among the players and spectators seemed to indicate that it was an improvement.

Still, it would probably be unwise to hold one's breath waiting for Wimbledon to adopt the WTT officiating system, although that prestigious event did borrow a paragraph from the league's officiating rulebook: the one that says the umpire may overrule a linesperson if necessary. WTT referees have always had the authority to overrule

If the serve was good, the officials on the receiver's side would pause until it was returned and then make a mad dash to cover a new area of responsibility. The service line judge would call the baseline and his partner would likewise do with one of the sidelines. The referee, backed up by a scorer seated nearby, would announce the game and set scores.

The streamlined system was given the acid test during the Wiesman Cup series between Team America and Team Russia in March 1976. It passed with flying colors. In fact an informal poll conducted among the players immediately following the Cup match in Cleveland showed that as far as the players were concerned, not a single officiating error had been made in the five sets.

WTT linespersons had become involved participants in the proceedings, not just spectators with authority. Every shot-caller was a certified graduate of another World Team Tennis innovation: an official's training school. Conducted in several cities around the country, the training schools

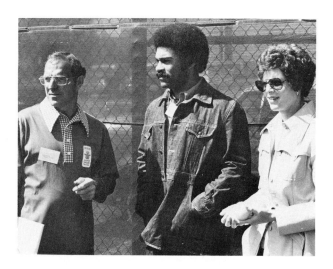

Dick Roberson, Director of Official Training, (left), with two star pupils, Carver Shannon, a Pacific Athletic Conference official, and Nancy Lewis, a veteran WTT linesperson.

an obviously incorrect call without having to badger the errant official to "yield his decision to the chair" as stipulated by the ILTF rules.

"The overrule is an essential part of a smoothly flowing match," says John Korff, WTT supervisor of officials. "There are occasions during every tennis match when a linesperson is unable to see the bounce of the ball and it is critical for the umpire to make the call without breaking into the match and embarrassing an official."

"Quite so," said the Wimbledon folks, and in 1976 that WTT procedure became a part of the oldest tennis championship in the world.

Most WTT linespersons—like Al Forman—have officiating experience in other team sports.

4 | The Court

It speaks for itself. Anybody who's ever seen it will tell you so. Hardly surprising though, is the fact that a few people think it speaks too loudly, that garish, multi-hued, lineless, hunk of carpet WTT calls a tennis court.

Well, the league's claim is true enough. The colorful rug is a real, honest-to-God, dyed-in-the-wool tennis court. The obligatory barrier, a net, slices it in half, and its dimensions mirror those outlined on the famed lawn of Wimbledon's Centre Court and etched into the gray-green Har-Tru floor of the weathered stadium at Forest Hills.

And like tennis courts everywhere, the WTT version plays host to victory and defeat in scrupulously equal measure. It seems sometimes too long, sometimes too short, and sometimes just right. It may befriend a player by catching a lob with its baseline one minute, then turn on that same player the next by refusing to accommodate a second serve on a crucial point.

Like tennis courts everywhere, it stoically endures hours of pounding by rubber-soled footwear and racquets guided by the hands of those who have been frustrated or angered to the extreme.

Unlike its less flamboyant brethren, however, the WTT tennis court has attracted a certain amount of comment concerning its appearance. Previously, tennis courts were seldom noticed. They were completely anonymous, functional backdrops at best. Oh, occasionally one of the damn things would make the ball travel in mysterious ways, but that was about it. There's always been a lot of talk about "fast" grass, "slow" clay, "slick" shags, and the like, but such chatter tended to focus on material composition, not physical appearance.

If the standard, lined court is a sedate tuxedo, the WTT court is definitely a Hawaiian shirt. The alternate service courts are blue and green, the doubles alleys are a blazing red, and the "no man's land" (the area between the service and baselines) is chocolate brown.

The "lines," therefore, are where the various colors butt up against each other. Besides adding a splash of color to the game, WTT officials claim that their creation makes it easier for the linespersons to follow the flight of the ball. No one can deny the accuracy of the former statement, but the latter may or may not be entirely true.

The brightly pigmented playing surface was originally tested by the league during a pre-season exhibition series in 1975 and it appeared on television at the All-Star match a few months later. There were no major negative reactions from the players, possibly because they knew the court could be a potentially strong selling point when WTT sat down to talk contract with the television networks.

Betty Stove's attitude is fairly typical. "I don't mind it at all," she says, "and it certainly hasn't affected my game one way or the other. But then again, I haven't seen the court from a distance."

An audience survey indicated that most WTT spectators found the court too distracting and they would like to see the league return to the traditional model. On the other hand, the WTT court has quite a few supporters. Larry King, for instance. He's the man who conceived it and is responsible for its status as WTT's permanent playground. King doesn't find it distracting, and for good reason. Larry King is color blind.

5 | The Fans

Shortly after World Team Tennis was formed, Larry King was asked if the league was really going to allow the fans to raise a ruckus during WTT matches.

"Not quite," he replied. "We're going to *encourage* the fans to raise a ruckus."

Why?

"Simply because it's unreasonable to expect someone to lay out hard-earned money to attend an athletic contest and then ask them to sit on their hands."

Anyone who attended any of WTT's 1974 early season scuffles will testify that very few spectators were guilty of sitting on their hands during the action. That's because most of them had their hands cupped around their mouths as ten-fingered amplifiers. Those early days were *loud.*

Some cities, of course, were worse than others. Pittsburgh, home of the cacophonous G-men, an organization of leather-larynxed fans, should have passed out earmuffs to the visiting teams. Cleveland didn't exactly seem to attract an over-abundance of the strong, silent type, and neither did Denver, Boston, Philadelphia, New York, etc.

A few players claimed they enjoyed the commotion, but most failed to see the humor in the fans' insistence on doing things like crashing a pair of cymbals together midway through the service toss. The players' lack of enthusiasm towards the noisy crowds was completely understandable. After years of performing in front of sedate galleries, they were suddenly forced to contend with hordes of screaming banshees.

It wasn't easy, but most of the players adjusted. And luckily, so did the fans. Gradually, the thrill of trying to get on the nerves of a big-time tennis player began to pale and they started to pay attention to other things, like the score. Still, it is a rare WTT match that fails to elicit at least a couple of outbursts.

Just ask Virginia Wade. During the second match of the 1976 Championship series between the New York Sets and the Golden Gaters, several Gaters' fans decided to give Virginia a hard time. The Sets had already iced the match for all intents and purposes, so the fans' behavior was undoubtedly motivated more by a sense of frustration than a hope of affecting the outcome. Regardless of the motivation, however, the noise finally got to Virginia. She faced the offenders and put her forefinger to her lips. It was, as she quickly discovered, a mistake. The next time Ms. Wade prepared to serve, approximately 5,000 people rattled the Oakland Coliseum walls by saying, "Ssssshhhhh!" in unison. It will probably be quite some time before Virginia asks another WTT crowd to hush up.

Allowing the crowd to act like sports fans instead of tennis fans though, did provide the players, including those who detested the policy, with at least one benefit. In most instances they found that their WTT experience greatly improved their concentration when they returned to the tournament circuit.

"WTT is like a conditioning school," is the way the Indiana Loves' Pat Bostrom put it. "After a few weeks of league play, you don't even notice normal distractions, like a crying baby."

"All I can say about the WTT fans," says the Cleveland Nets' Marty Riessen, "is God bless 'em."

Riessen's sentiments aside, the final verdict regarding the demeanor of the fans is not yet in. One thing's for sure though, the league isn't going to attempt to muzzle crowds. They would be foolish to try to do so and they know it. But they have stopped encouraging boisterous behavior, at least officially.

Recently, Larry King was asked if in retrospect, the lack of restraints on the fans was a good idea. "Definitely," he said. "The WTT fans don't need to have the league, or anyone else tell them how to behave. They'll decide that for themselves."

6 | Another Homily of Contemporary Tennis Lore

Sister Mary Mummy, the bionic nun, stood behind her massive desk and silently surveyed the cowering eighth graders arranged in symmetrical rows before her.

"Good morning, class," she said finally.

"Good morning, Sister," we chorused with the peculiar inflection favored by those anxious to please.

Since Sister Mary Mummy conducted her classes with a blend of crisp effeciency and iron-fisted discipline that Miss Ratched, the rigidly authoritarian Big Nurse of "One Flew Over The Cuckoo's Nest," could only envy, most of us desperately tried to remain as unobtrusive and anonymous as possible.

Only Dudley Mack, Our Lady of Pity's very own bull-goose looney, went out of his way to antagonize the good Sister. Dudley, who possessed the modesty of Bobby Riggs, the cunning of a Mafia hit man, the courage of a New York pedestrian, and the intelligence of a Pet Rock,

relentlessly conducted his personal brand of psychological warfare from his command post at the back of the room.

"Hey there, Sister," he yelled, waving a frisbee-sized hand wildly in the air.

Sister Mary Mummy ignored Dudley's theatrical plea for attention.

"Clear your desks," she said. "It's test time."

A ration cut on Devil's Island would have elicited a more enthusiastic response than the one that greeted her announcement, but Sister Mary Mummy was oblivious to our groans and our muttered threats of suicide. She merely began to distribute the test papers while whistling "Taps."

"Sister, Sister, Sister," hissed Dudley Mack. "Please, Sister."

"Yes, you may leave the room, Mr. Mack," said Sister Mary Mummy without looking up.

"No, Sister, it ain't that," said an out-of-breath Dudley Mack. "I just wanted to say something."

"Well, make it snappy."

Dudley grinned and winked at the class as we braced ourselves for another of his persistent, totally ineffective attempts to disrupt the educational process at Our Lady of Pity.

"You see, Sister," he said, "I managed to hustle . . . I mean, get my hands on a bunch of tickets for this Friday's World Team Tennis match and I was wonderin' if maybe you'd like to take the class on a tennis field trip?"

Sister Mary Mummy stopped passing out the tests.

"World Team *what?*"

"Tennis," chimed in Jimmy Sullivan, the class

informer and self-appointed chief of protocol. "World Team Tennis, alias WTT. It's quite an interesting concept, Sister."

"I'm sure it is," replied Sister Mary Mummy without enthusiasm, "but then so is suspended animation."

Though her love of sports was legendary, she still had not agreed to take us to the match even after listening to a half-hour class project known as begging.

"The San Diego Friars are playing," someone said finally. That did it.

"The San Diego Friars, huh? I guess we should check them out."

The class burst into a spontaneous round of applause and Dudley Mack bowed triumphantly. The test was forgotten as Sister Mary Mummy began to map out the logistics of the outing.

"I'll arrange for the use of the school bus," she said. "Of course, everyone will have to get written permission from their parents."

"Or guardians," said Jimmy Sullivan.

"Or guardians," sighed Sister Mary Mummy.

On Friday night, Sister Mary Mummy expertly wheeled Our Lady of Pity's ancient school bus, "The Yellow Peril," into the Coliseum parking lot and we joined the stream of spectators marching toward the domed arena.

"Why are they carrying those things?" asked Sister Mary Mummy, indicating a group of fans bearing cow bells and other assorted noise-making devices. "Don't they know that silence at a tennis match is almost as important as the net?"

"Not at WTT matches," answered Marty Shea. "The spectators are encouraged to make noise."

"Right," said Dudley Mack, proudly displaying a fistful of firecrackers and a battery-powered bullhorn. "This is a genuine S.W.A.T. model and I picked up the firecrackers . . ."

"I'll take those," interrupted Sister Mary Mummy.

"But, Sister . . ."

"Hand them over. The bullhorn too."

Dudley reluctantly complied and the confiscated items disappeared into the mysterious depths of Sister Mary Mummy's habit.

"I can't believe it," she muttered. "At Forest Hills in 1948, they asked the spectators to hold their breath during entire matches."

"Times change," said Marty Shea.

"And not always for the better," mumbled Sister Mary Mummy.

Upon entering the arena, our unruly procession attracted quite a bit of attention. With the Sister in the lead and a sulking Dudley Mack bringing up the rear, we roamed the aisles of the cavernous facility for nearly 20 minutes before locating our

70

seats. Just as we were settling in, Sister Mary Mummy gasped loudly.

"What in heaven's name is *that?*" she said, pointing to the color-coordinated tennis court.

"It's the playing surface, Sister."

"Who designed it? Salvador Dali?"

"I'm not sure."

"I can guarantee it wasn't Norman Rockwell," she said.

A few minutes later, the players came out to warm up and it took us a while to convince Sister Mary Mummy that their colorful uniforms did not violate a dress code.

"But they aren't wearing whites," she said.

"Of course not," said Marty Shea. "They're wearing their team colors."

"Did you hear that, Little Mo?" said Sister Mary Mummy, casting her eyes heavenward. "No whites! They're turning your sport into a circus."

When the women's doubles teams took the court for the evening's first match, Sister Mary Mummy applauded politely. "Which ones are the Pearly Gaters?" she asked.

"Uh, that's the Golden Gaters, Sister," said Marty Shea.

"Whatever," replied Sister Mary Mummy.

Down on the court, each team scored three quick points before commencing a long and exciting rally. After trading baseline shots for a few minutes, both teams were suddenly at the net. A rapid-fire exchange took place before the Gaters managed to place a lob deep into the Friars' backcourt. The crowd was on its feet as one of the Friars sprinted for the lob and miraculously belted a sizzling backhand past the surprised Gater duo. The ball touched down very close to the baseline.

"Out!" bellowed the linesman.

"That would have been in on a real court," muttered Sister Mary Mummy, wincing at the crowd's noisy celebration of the call.

"First game to the Golden Gaters, 4–3," said the public address system.

Immediately, Sister Mary Mummy was on her feet. "It's ad in," she yelled.

Marty Shea attempted to calm her down by explaining that WTT's streamlined scoring system eliminates deuces and ads.

"You mean the deuce has been aced?"

"I'm afraid so, Sister."

"Sequential digital scoring belongs in baseball," huffed Sister Mary Mummy. "It has no place in tennis."

"Speeds things up and makes the match more exciting," said Marty Shea.

"Maybe so," conceded the Sister. "But 2–0 is a lot less poetic than 30-love."

A few minutes later, the set was deadlocked at six games apiece and the umpire indicated that a tiebreaker would be played.

"Lay it on me," said Sister Mary Mummy. "What's a tiebreaker?" She listened to Marty Shea's explanation without comment.

Despite her highly negative initial reaction to the WTT format, Sister Mary Mummy had become a full-fledged Team Tennis convert long before the final match of the night was announced. She had completely abandoned her purist tennis stance sometime during the men's singles and, since then, her leathery voice could be heard shouting encouragement or bemoaning ill-fated flights of the ball on nearly every point.

The pattern of close play that had been established with the first match continued through the finale, men's doubles. The set went to 6–6 and the entire match was tied at 29 games apiece.

"Super tiebreaker!" screamed Sister Mary Mummy joyously. "Let's go, Friars!"

The Friars, serving first, double-faulted. Outraged, Sister Mary Mummy reached into the folks of her habit and withdrew Dudley's confiscated bullhorn.

"You should take out some no-fault insurance," she yelled at the thoroughly bewildered Friar.

Apparently unnerved by the nun with the bullhorn in Section EE, the same player was wide with an easy forehand on the next point.

"You probably have a hard time staying in the lines of your coloring book, too," screeched Sister Mary Mummy.

The Friars rallied briefly but finally lost the super-tiebreaker and the match. Sister Mary Mummy was, of course, disappointed but she recovered quickly.

"We'll get 'em next time," she yelled into the bullhorn. "I'll be back!"

Just then, the batteries gave out.

The Teams

1 | Survival of the Fittest

A new sports league is a lot like a television network's new Fall schedule. Some members of the lineup will probably make it, some won't, and some will have to be moved around a bit before they find acceptance.

WTT, of course, was no exception. Of the sixteen franchises that were handed out in May 1973, two were relocated within a matter of weeks. The Phoenix entry was shifted to Baltimore and the San Diego Swingers moved to Hawaii and became the Leis. The other fourteen WTT franchises stayed put for awhile, although a couple of them underwent ownership changes prior to the start of the 1974 season. Jerry Saperstein sold his New York team to Sol Berg, and Nick Mileti, with three other pro teams (the baseball Indians, the basketball Cavaliers, and the hockey Crusaders) in his back pocket, convinced his second-cousin, Joe Zingale, to take over the Cleveland Nets.

At the end of the 1974 season all sixteen· teams were still intact, but several were bordering on collapse. Minnesota was the first to go, but others quickly followed. Toronto/Buffalo, Florida, Chicago, Boston, and Baltimore also took the big fall within a few months after the conclusion of WTT's inaugural outing.

Three franchises sought a new lease on life in other locales. Denver went to Phoenix, Detroit to Indiana, and Philadelphia to Boston. On the eve of the second season's opening day, Houston became the seventh franchise to fold. Fortunately, a new team—San Diego—had been created as a hedge against the possibility of a team disappearing suddenly. The final toll: seven dropouts, three changes of location, and one new arrival.

The ten teams that comprised the 1975 WTT lineup finished that season intact and every one of them showed up for Year Three. The sudden stability was short-lived however. Shortly after the 1976 season, the Hawaii franchise moved to the mainland and became the Sea-Port Cascades. The champion Sets became the defending champion Apples; and the Pittsburgh Triangles became a fond memory, replaced first by the Pennsylvania Keystones and then by the Soviet Union team.

What follows is a brief look at the 1976 WTT teams, who they were, what they've done, where they've been, and, in a few cases, where they're going.

2 | The WTT Roll Call

1974

EASTERN DIVISION:

Atlantic Section
Philadelphia Freedoms
Boston Lobsters
Baltimore Banners
New York Sets

Central Section
Detroit Loves
Pittsburgh Triangles
Cleveland Nets
Toronto/Buffalo Royals

WESTERN DIVISION:

Gulf Plains Section
Minnesota Buckskins
Houston EZ Riders
Florida Flamingoes
Chicago Aces

Pacific Section
Denver Racquets
Golden Gaters
Los Angeles Strings
Hawaii Leis

1975 and 1976

EASTERN DIVISION:

New York Sets
Pittsburgh Triangles
Indiana Loves (formerly Detroit Loves)
Cleveland Nets
Boston Lobsters (formerly Philadelphia Freedoms)

WESTERN DIVISION:

Golden Gaters
Phoenix Racquets (formerly Denver Racquets)
Los Angeles Strings
Hawaii Leis
San Diego Friars (new franchise in 1975)

1977

EASTERN DIVISION:

New York Apples (name changed from Sets)
Boston Lobsters
Indiana Loves

Cleveland Nets
The Soviets (new franchise in 1977)

WESTERN DIVISION:

Golden Gaters
Phoenix Racquets
Los Angeles Strings
San Diego Friars
Sea-Port Cascades (formerly
Hawaii Leis)

3 | New York Sets/Apples

1974

Shortly before the first WTT season was scheduled to begin, Jerry Saperstein, the owner of the New York franchise, went looking for potential investors. Saperstein's lawyers approached Sol Berg, a soft-spoken commodities man, about putting some of his money into the team tennis scheme. Berg, whose only involvement with tennis at the time was as a recreational player, was understandably hesitant at first. But after thinking over Saperstein's proposal he decided he couldn't pass up the challenge. Sol Berg bought himself a tennis team.

Unfortunately, he didn't get much for his money. From the very beginning the Sets didn't win tennis matches and they didn't draw a crowd. The situation in New York was grave because the owners believed that the ultimate success of the league depended on the ultimate success of the Big Apple franchise. Since New York is the media capital of the U.S., the league needed a successful local operation to generate press coverage and possibly catch the attention of the folks charged with doling out the multi-million dollar advertising budgets that abound in Manhattan. A Sets disaster was bound to affect the rest of the league.

And that's exactly what the Sets were in 1974, a disaster. Even though Berg began to rebuild the team halfway through the season with the addition of Sandy Mayer and Virginia Wade, the New York team finished dead last in the Eastern Division's Atlantic Section.

1975

When the 1975 season began it quickly became obvious that Berg had managed to put together an instant contender. The Sets, strengthened by the

Billie Jean King and Virginia Wade

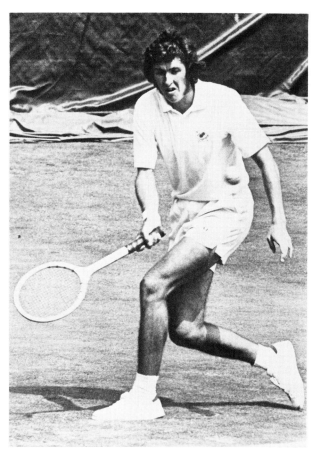

Phil Dent

Fred Stolle

off-season acquisition of Billie Jean King and Fred Stolle from the Philadelphia Freedoms, rolled off 16 wins in their first 16 matches. That was one win more than they had during the entire first year. They were unable to maintain the torrid pace, however, and the Pittsburgh Triangles overtook them in the standings late in the season. In a splendid coincidence, the two teams were scheduled to play each other on the final day of the regular season with only a single game separating them. The Sets needed the win to tie the Triangles for first place in the East. They didn't get it. They also didn't get the chance to seek revenge against Pittsburgh in the playoffs. That honor went to the Boston Lobsters who knocked off the Sets in a single-set playoff match to determine who would get to play the Triangles for the Eastern Division title.

The 1975 Sets season, which had begun with WTT's longest winning streak, ended with a bitter defeat. Berg and his players spent the next few months in a state of shock. The 1975 season ended in financial disappointment also. For the second year in a row, the Sets didn't draw well at the gate.

1976

In 1976, the Sets brought the World Team Tennis Championship to New York, but the story in the stands was as bleak as ever. Attendance had increased a bit over the previous year, though not nearly as dramatically as that experienced by other franchises.

Sol Berg had ridden the WTT roller coaster for three years. Although he was extremely pleased with the championship, he was also worried. The endless rows of Nassau Coliseum seats were getting to him so he decided to do something about it.

He hired Larry King as president of the Sets. Berg firmly believed that King was the only person who could reverse the financial fortunes of the Sets. He even threatened to pull out of the league if his fellow owners tried to block King's appointment. There was some grumbling, but Berg won out. New York was crucial to the league. Especially after the 1976 season. How would it look, after all, if the defending champs folded?

Besides launching a contest to rename the team, King booked a dozen matches into Madison Square Garden, and a pair of matches into Forest Hills' stadium. The remaining home matches on the Apples' schedule will be contested at the Nassau Coliseum. The locale changes, which are at least as expensive as they are risky, stand a good chance of either making or breaking the Apples.

Rosters:

1974
Sandy Mayer—USA
Charlie Owens—USA
Nikki Pilic—Yugoslavia
Manuel Santana—Spain
Gene Scott—USA
Fiorella Bonicelli—Peru
Carol Graebner—USA
Ceci Martinez—USA
Pam Teeguarden—USA
Virginia Wade—USA
Sharon Walsh—USA

1975
Fred Stolle—Australia
Sandy Mayer—USA
Charlie Owens—USA
Billie Jean King—USA
Virginia Wade—Great Britain
Mona Guerrant—USA
Betsy Nagelsen—USA

1976
Fred Stolle—Australia
Sandy Mayer—USA
Phil Dent—Australia
Billie Jean King—USA
Virginia Wade—Great Britain
Lindsey Beaven—USA
Linda Siegelman—USA

Season Standings:

Year	W	L	Pct.	Final Standing
1974	15	29	.341	4th Place, Atlantic Section, Eastern Division
1975	34	10	.773	2nd Place, Eastern Division
*1976	33	10	.767	1st Place, Eastern Division/WTT Champions

*The Sets only played 43 matches because hurricane Belle forced the cancellation of their August 9, 1976, match with Boston. The match was not made up.

Playoff Record:

Year	W	L	Pct.
1975	0	1	.000
1976	5	1	.833

Attendance:

Year	Total	Average
1974	63,121	2,869
1975	65,894	—
1976	78,408	3,564

Team Colors:

Green and red

Home Arenas:

Madison Square Garden (Capacity—19,500)
Nassau Veterans Coliseum (Capacity—8,600)

Draft History:

	1973	1974	1975	1976
1	Roy Emerson	—	Phil Dent	Billie Jean King
2	Pam Teeguarden	—	Julie Anthony	Virginia Wade
3	Sandy Mayer	Ilie Nastase	Ilie Nastase	Lindsey Beaven
4	Cliff Richey	Stan Smith	Victor Pecci	Sandy Mayer
5	Arthur Ashe	Racquel Giscafre	Andianno Panatta	Phil Dent
6	Barbara Downs	Helga Masthoff	Tom Gorman	Fred Stolle
7	Kazuko Sawamatsu	Sally Greer	Roger Taylor	Fred Stolle
8	Haroon Rahim	Jas Singh	Renato Tomanova	Vitas Gerulaitis
9	Gene Scott	Brenda Kirk	Regina Marisikova	Kathy Harter
10	Manuel Santana	—	Maria Bueno	Kim Warwick
11	Ingrid Bentzer	Haroon Rahim	Bob Carmichael	Laura Dupont
12	Cynthia Doerner	Marjorie Geneles Smith	Chris Lewis	Dick Bohrnstedt
13	Betty Ann Hansen	Donna Ganz	Victor Amaya	Steve Krulevitz
14	Beatriz Araujo	Nathalie Fuchs	Lynn Epstein	Mary Carillo
15	—	Ruta Gerulaitis	—	Bernie Mitton
16	Marjorie Genaler	Eugene Scott	—	Linda Siegelman
17	Nicky Kale	—	—	
18	Herb Fitz Gibbon	Mary Carillo	—	
19	—	—		
20	Wanaro N'Godrella			

1974½ Draft: 1. Kerry Melville; 2. Colin Dibley; 3. Ray Ruffels; 4. Patty Hogan; 5. John Lloyd; 6. Pancho Gonzales; 7. Graham Stillwell.

Sandy Mayer

Director of Player Personnel, was the logical choice for the coaching job. He had assisted Rosewall during the previous season, and he even called some of the shots during the playoffs so Rosewall could concentrate on his own game.

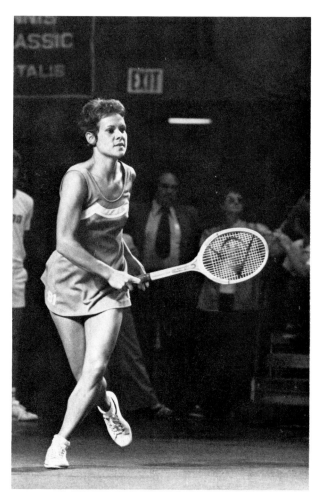

Evonne Goolagong

4 | Pittsburgh Triangles

1974

Pittsburgh was the first WTT franchise awarded in May 1973 and its principal owner was one of the men who had conceived the National Tennis League, Chuck Reichblum. Before the first WTT season had ended, however, Frank Fuhrer had acquired a controlling interest in the Triangles. A short time later he was elected president of the league. Fuhrer's reign as WTT's top administrative officer lasted only two months, and when it ended he focused his energy on bringing the league championship to Pittsburgh.

In 1974, the Triangles, anchored by player/coach Ken Rosewall and Evonne Goolagong, finished in a tie with the Detroit Loves for first place in the Central Section of the Eastern Division. The Triangles blasted Detroit out of the playoffs, but faltered slightly and were eliminated by the Philadelphia Freedoms.

After the first season, Rosewall decided to retire from WTT competition and Fuhrer began searching for a new coach. He didn't have to look far. Vic Edwards, Goolagong's mentor and the Triangles'

1975

One of the first things Edwards did was convince Fuhrer that the Triangles could use some help in the men's doubles category. With Rosewall gone, Vital Gerulaitis was pretty much the whole show as far as the men were concerned. Fuhrer immediately signed Mark Cox and the Triangles' primary weakness disappeared.

The importance of the Cox deal manifested itself when the league reconvened after the 1975

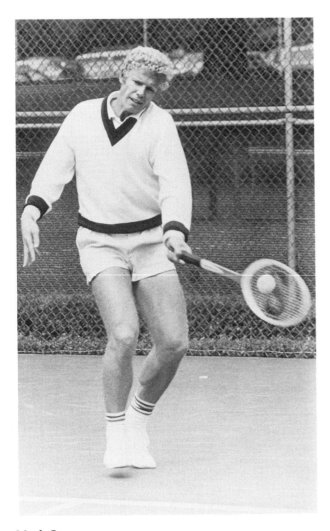

Mark Cox

Wimbledon break. The Triangles went on a rampage and won twenty of their final twenty–two matches, including a big one over the New York Sets on the last day of the regular season, giving Pittsburgh undisputed first place in the Eastern Division. More importantly, the Triangles continued their winning streak against Boston in the Eastern Division playoffs, and against the Golden Gaters in the championship series.

Frank Fuhrer had indeed brought the championship to Pittsburgh and he celebrated by firing Vic Edwards. It was something Fuhrer had wanted to do for quite a while. He and Edwards seldom saw eye to eye, but Edwards was able to hang on because of his extremely close relationship with Evonne Goolagong, who was named 1975's Female MVP shortly after the

season. Fuhrer didn't want to antagonize Goolagong by dumping Edwards.

As it turned out though, Evonne apparently had her own misgivings about Edwards. When she married Roger Cawley, a British businessman, in June 1975, Vic Edwards was conspicuously absent from the wedding guest list, and don't think for a minute that Fuhrer overlooked that.

In any event, Edward's departure meant that for the second year in a row Fuhrer had to shop for a new coach. And for the second year in a row, he didn't have to look beyond the Triangles' roster to find his man.

1976

Mark Cox, a player who had made tennis history of sorts when he became the first amateur to defeat a pro, Pancho Gonzales, in the first open tournament at Bournemouth in 1968, became the Triangles' new coach.

Cox's job was hardly a bed of roses. The first half of the 1976 season was a total disaster for the Triangles. Evonne missed several matches because of an injury and the team plummeted to last place. Then Evonne's doubles partner, Peggy Michel, was let go despite having a no-cut contract. And Vitas Gerulaitis aroused Fuhrer's considerable ire with a few public remarks about the owner's alleged threats to fine the team for losing.

As a result, Fuhrer was making a few public statements of his own. "If his (Gerulaitis's) deportment doesn't change radically, he won't be back," Fuhrer said.

Even Evonne, perhaps the gentlest soul in the sport, found herself on Fuhrer's bad side. She and new hubby Roger had confronted Fuhrer over what they considered to be unreasonable demands on her off-court time for promotional appearances. Barely three weeks into the season, Fuhrer and the Cawleys were not on speaking terms. And Fuhrer was hinting about getting rid of his prize player after the season.

"I don't want anyone playing here who doesn't want to play for me," he said. "I don't care who it is."

He also hinted that he might just throw in the towel and unload his franchise after the season.

The Triangles began the second half of the third WTT season in a less-than-harmonious atmosphere, and without Mark Cox, who had been relieved of his coaching duties. His replacement was General Manager and Publicity Director, Dan McGibbeny. But Fuhrer was still exerting considerable influence on how the team should be run.

Bernie Mitton

Sue Stap

JoAnn Russell

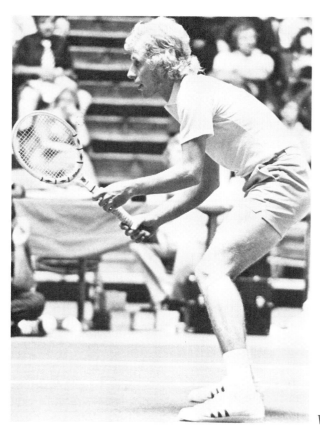

Vitas Gerulaitis

Sue Stap, a former Triangle, rejoined the team to play women's doubles with JoAnn Russell; Evonne was playing singles and mixed doubles; and Vitas Gerulaitis was handling men's singles and teaming with Mark Cox in doubles. And, just as they'd done the year before, the Pittsburgh contingent began to win matches on a regular basis. New York had first place all sewn up by mid-July, barring a total collapse or an act of God, but the Triangles ran right past the sagging Cleveland Nets to clinch second place and a playoff berth.

Despite their thoroughly dismal first half, the Triangles salvaged the season with a strong finish, thus becoming the first WTT team to be in a position to retain the league championship for two years in a row. Their chances looked even better when they beat the Sets in the first match of the best-of-three Eastern Division playoffs. The New Yorkers, however, came back to take the next two matches and the defense of the defending champions was over.

A few weeks after the season, Evonne Goolagong announced that she was expecting a baby on or about WTT's opening day in 1977. In an unrelated move, Fuhrer quietly looked for a way to unload his franchise. Apparently unable to find a buyer, he closed up shop on December 1, 1976. The three-year run of the Pittsburgh Triangles was abruptly over.

Rosters:

1974
Ken Rosewall—Australia
Gerald Barttick—Great Britain
Vitas Gerulaitis—USA
Evonne Goolagong—Australia
Peggy Michel—USA
Isabel Fernandez—Colombia
Laura DuPont—USA

1975
Mark Cox—Great Britain
Vitas Gerulaitis—USA
Kim Warwick—Australia
Evonne Goolagong—Australia
Peggy Michel—USA
Nancy Gunter—USA
Rayni Fox—USA

1976
Mark Cox—Great Britain
Vitas Gerulaitis—USA
Bernie Mitton—South Africa
Evonne Goolagong—Australia
Peggy Michel—USA
Sue Stap—USA
JoAnn Russell—USA

Season Standings:

Year	W	L	Pct.	Final Standing
1974	30	14	.682	1st Place, Central Section, Eastern Division
1975	38	8	.818	1st Place, Eastern Division
1976	24	20	.545	2nd Place, Eastern Division

Playoff Record:

Year	W	L	Pct.
1974	3	1	.750
1975	4	1	.800
1976	1	2	.333

Attendance:

Year	Total	Average
1974	66,270	3,012
1975	82,270	—
1976	102,608	4,664

Team Colors:

Green and yellow

Home Arena:

Pittsburgh Civic Arena (Capacity—16,400)

Draft History:

	1973	1974	1975
1	Ken Rosewall	Kathy May	Guillermo Vilas
2	Evonne Goolagong	John Whitlinger Rayni Fox	Dennis Ralston
3	Harold Solomon	Balasz Taroczy	Marie Neumannova
4	Vitas Gerulaitis	Jeanne Evert	Lea Antonopolis
5	Laura DuPont	Ferdi Taygan	Brian Gottfried
6	Mona Schallau	Pat Pretorius	Walter Redondo
7	Jeff Borowiak	Colin Dowdeswell	Walter Redondo
8	Kathy Blake	Pat Coleman	Barbara Downs
9	Patrick DuPre	Angelo Botch	Trey Waltke
10	Jane Stratton	Mark Farrell	Bruce Manson
11	Tom Edlefsen	Patty Shoolman	Katja Ebbinghaus
12	Gerald Battrick	Fred DeJesus	Byron Bertram
13	Linda Lewis	—	Peaches Bartkowicz
14	Jill Cooper		Berta McCallum
15	Brian Teacher		
16	Isabel Fernandez	—	
17	Anand Amritraj	—	—
18	Paolo Bertolucci	—	
19	Marcy O'Keefe	—	—
20	Bob Chappell	—	—

1974½ Draft: Guillermo Vilas; 2. Wendy Overton; 3. Janet Young; 4. Eddie Dibbs; 5. Juan Gisbert; 6. Wendy Parish.

5 | Boston Lobsters

1974

The 1974 Lobsters coasted to a second-place finish in the Atlantic Section of the Eastern Division, some 20 games behind the powerful Philadelphia Freedoms. Despite their position as runner-up, however, the Lobsters failed to qualify for a playoff berth. The third place finishers in the Central Section, the Cleveland Nets, were given the opportunity to meet the Freedoms in post-season play. The Nets won this honor by posting a won/loss record that was slightly better than Boston's 19–25 showing.

Besides being the only sectional runner-up that failed to make it to the WTT playoffs, the 1974 Lobsters suffered a greater indignity by folding a few months after the first season ended. By January 1975 it appeared that Boston's tenure as a WTT host city was over almost before it had begun.

1975

Then, in March, WTT announced that the Philadelphia Freedoms, sans Billie Jean and Fred Stolle, had been sold to a Boston group. At first the new team was prevented from assuming the name "Lobsters" so the new owners decided to call their property the "Lobs." Before long, however, the legal obstacles were removed, and the Boston Lobsters were back on the league roster.

Although confusion with the original Lobster team is inevitable, league officials are quick to point out that the 1975 Lobsters were really the

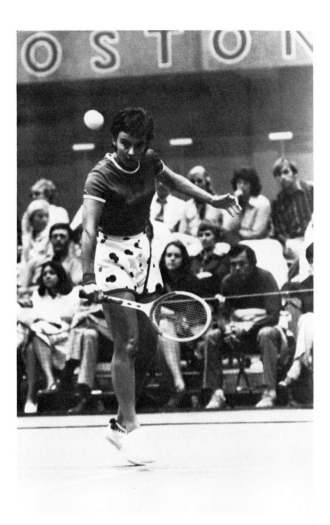

Kerry Melville Reid

Ion Tiriac

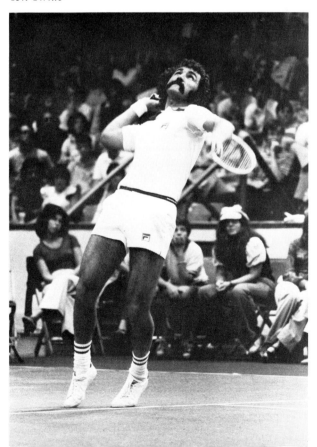

Philadelphia Freedoms. Be that as it may, the new Lobsters' roster did not have a single Freedom player. It did have three members of the original Lobsters though: Ion Tiriac, Kerry Melville and Raz Reid.

The latter two individuals decided to get married on the eve of the 1975 season. As far as can be determined, they became the first and only professional sports teammates to do so. If nothing else, the marriage gave quite a few people the opportunity to point out that WTT hadn't completely taken "love" out of tennis.

The three original Lobsters were joined by Bob Hewitt, Wendy Turnbull and Val Ziegenfuss. In 1975, the Boston team did qualify for the Eastern Division playoffs.

Only a thousand people were in the stands at the Nassau Coliseum to watch the New York Sets go through the formality of bumping Boston out of the

Pam Teeguarden

Greer Stevens

John Alexander

Mike Estep

playoffs on August 17, 1975. At least that's what the crowd thought it was going to see that night. Instead, they watched in stunned disbelief as the lowly Lobsters eliminated the Sets, the team that had beaten them seven times during the regular season. Billie Jean had some harsh words for the Lobsters following the bitter defeat. "The Boston Lobsters will not beat us once in 1976," she said.

Even though his team was subsequently stomped by the Triangles in the next round of the playoffs, player/coach Ion Tiriac voiced an opinion contrary to Billie Jean's. "We'll win the WTT championship next year," he said.

1976

Tiriac's projection turned out to be wide of the mark. The Lobsters not only failed to win the league championship, they found themselves in the Eastern Division cellar when the season ended, one-half game behind the Indiana Loves. Billie Jean's vow, on the other hand, was surprisingly accurate. The Sets beat the Lobsters five out of five in 1976 and it might have been six out of six had hurricane Belle not forced the cancellation of the final regular-season match between the two teams.

Part of the reason for the Lobsters' poor showing may be traced to the fact that both of their singles players, Kerry Melville Reid and John Alexander, played far below their capabilities for much of the season. Greer Stevens, the Female-Rookie-of-the-Year in 1975, and Mike Estep played well in mixed doubles, and Stevens also anchored the women's doubles with either Pam Teeguarden or Reid. Coach Tiriac, however, was reluctant to play Stevens in singles because WTT rules stipulate that a player may only participate in two sets per match. Moving her would have necessarily weakened either women's or mixed doubles.

Tiriac won't have to face that particular problem in the future though, at least not with the Boston Lobsters. Following the 1976 season the owners of that team announced that his three-year association as coach of the various Lobster teams had terminated. Roy Emerson, previously the player/coach of the 1974 Golden Gaters, was named as Tiriac's replacement.

The following "promotional" recipe is provided courtesy of Marcia Young, Publicity Director of the Boston Lobsters. It is her claim that the end result is not only edible, but delicious.

THE BOSTON LOBSTER

Two 1¼ lb. live lobsters
enough salt water and white wine to cover lobsters   (one part wine to 5 parts water)

Bring salt water to boil. Add wine and lobsters. Simmer 8–10 minutes. Drain, cool, cut down middle and split back open. Take off tail membrane. Take out tail meat and cube and place back in tail. Take meat out of claws. Clean chest cavity. Line chest cavity with claw meat. Brush meat with melted butter and place on cookie sheet.

STUFFING

½ lb. unsalted butter
1 sprig each, fresh thyme, parsley, and tarragon
½ lb. sliced mushrooms
6 minced shallots
1¼ lb. crabmeat
¼ cup slivered almonds
½ cup sliced black olives
¼ cup cognac
1 cup sour cream

Melt butter and stir in shallots and almonds. Fry until shallots turn clear. Add crabmeat and fry. Add herbs, olives, mushrooms. Add cognac. Blend in sour cream.
Stuff chest cavity and tail. Brush with melted butter and ¼ cup bread crumbs. Brown in 425° oven.
Garnish with lemon wedges and parsley.
Serves two.

Rosters:

1975
Ion Tiriac (player/coach)—Rumania
Bob Hewitt—South Africa
Raz Reid—USA
Kerry Melville Reid—Australia
Valerie Ziegenfuss—USA
Wendy Turnbull—USA
Greer Stevens—South Africa
1976
Ion Tiriac (player/coach)—Rumania
John Alexander—Australia
Mike Estep—USA
Kerry Melville Reid—USA
Greer Stevens—South Africa
Pam Teeguarden—USA

Season Standings:

Year	W	L	Pct.	Final Standing
1975	20	24	.455	3rd Place, Eastern Division
1976	18	25	.419	4th Place, Eastern Division

Playoffs Record:

Year	W	L	Pct.
1975	1	2	.333

The 1976 Lobsters. Left to right: *Pam Teeguarden, player/coach Ion Tiriac, Kerry Melville Reid, Greer Stevens, Mike Estep, and John Alexander.*

Attendance:

Year	Total	Average
1975	30,789	—
1976	59,180	2,690

Team Colors:

Red and white

Home Arena:

Walter Brown Arena (Capacity—4,000)
Hartford Civic Center (Capacity—10,500)

Television:

Channel 38, Boston's sports station—10 matches in 1977

Draft History

1973 [*]	1974 [*]	1975	1976
1 Billie Jean King	Betsy Nagelson	Natasha Chymreva	John Alexander
2 Fred Stolle	Roscoe Tanner	Mike Estep	Mike Estep
3 Brian Fairlie	Bob Giltinan	Roscoe Tanner	Bob Hewitt
4 Cliff Drysdale	Leslie Charles	Pam Teeguarden	Kerry Reid
5 Laura Rossouw	Tina Zwaan	Janet Newberry	Greer Stevens
6 Tory Ann Fretz	Patricia Cornejo	Harold Solomon	Pam Teeguarden
7 Laurie Fleming	Bobby Riggs	Eddie Dibbs	Roy Emerson
8 Christopher Mottram	Barbara Hallquist	Leslie Charles	Kathy May
9 Dianne Fromholtz	Vicky Berner	Paulina Peischov	Victor Pecci
10 John Paish	Elton John	Paolo Bertolucci	Barbara Hallquist
11 —	Karl Meiler	Brian Fairlie	Onny Parun
12 Zan Guerry	Terry Addison	Patrice Dominguez	Mariana Simionescu
13 Wendy Appleby	Jan O'Neil	Bailey Brown	Jim Delaney
14 Jun Kuki	Arthur Carrington	Juan Gisbert	Paolo Bertolucci
15 Chris Mattison	—	Charlie Owens	Chris Gonzales
16 John Bartlett	—	Ken Rosewall	
17 Maria Nasueli	—	Jurgen Fassbender	
18 —	—	—	
19 Hans-Jurgen Pohmann	—	—	
20 Hans-Joachin Plotz	—		

1974½ Draft: 1. Mike Estep; 2. Butch Buchholz; 3. Kathy Latham; 4. Ken Fletcher; 5. Andriana Panatta; 6. Jerry Van Linge; 7. Byron Bertram.

[*]—All drafts were by Philadelphia. Franchise was sold to Boston prior to second season of competition. This franchise should not be confused with the one that operated in Boston during the 1975 season.

6 | The Indiana Loves

1975

When Bill Bereman bought the Loves and moved them to Indianapolis from Detroit, Allan Stone was the only team member to relocate. Phil Dent, Butch Seewagen, Lendward Simpson, Mary Ann Beattie, Pat Faulkner, and Kerry Harris all went their separate ways. Some joined other franchises and others retired from WTT. Rosie Casals didn't make the trip to Speedway City either. She didn't fit into Bereman's philosophy of team tennis. She was considered a star in some circles, and stars Bereman neither needed or wanted.

Bereman strongly believed that the team was all important. No high-priced superstars were going to bring a championship to Indianapolis all by themselves. They would only bring a lot of grief and high salary demands. And Bereman had a point. Wilt Chamberlain had never played on an NBA Championship team and O.J. Simpson has spent seven years in the NFL without once suiting up for the Super Bowl.

Bereman was in the market for good, solid tennis talent and he found some. Wendy Overton, Carrie Meyer, Pat Bostrom, Roy Barth, and Ray Ruffels joined the Loves' roster in 1975 and the team didn't fare badly. They won eighteen matches and lost twenty-six which put them only one match behind the third place Boston Lobsters in the Eastern Division.

1976

In 1976, a slightly modified Loves team entertained their visitors in the 17,500-seat Indianapolis Convention Center. Wendy Overton had become a Cleveland Net and Roy Barth was also gone. They were replaced by Syd Ball, Ann Kiyomura, and Mona Guerrant. Kiyomura was obtained from the Golden Gaters, and Guerrant arrived from the New York Sets. Syd Ball was making his league debut.

And for the second year in a row, the Indiana Loves finished only one game out of third place in the Eastern Division. They also finished only one-half a game ahead of the last place Lobsters.

The Loves lost ground in one important category, however. In 1975 they ranked seventh in home attendance; in 1976 they were last. Then in September 1976, Larry Noble, a Los Angeles real estate man and a native of Indiana, became the principal owner of the Loves. Bill Bereman retains a share of the ownership and will stay on as

Pat Bostrom

Carrie Meyer

84

Ann Kiyomura

Syd Ball

Ray Ruffels

president and general manager of the franchise. But Noble's presence on the scene signalled a departure from Bereman's no-star philosophy.

Several weeks prior to the start of the 1977 WTT season, the Loves signed Vitas Gerulaitis, the former Triangles' star, and Sue Barker, the 20-year-old Britisher, who was runner-up to Chris Evert at the 1977 Virginia Slims championships.

Rosters:

1975
Allan Stone (player/coach)—Australia
Roy Barth—Australia
Ray Ruffels—Australia
Wendy Overton—USA
Carrie Meyer—USA
Pat Bostrom—USA
1976
Allan Stone (player/coach)—Australia
Ray Ruffels—Australia
Syd Ball—Australia
Mona Guerrant—USA
Ann Kiyomura—USA
Pat Bostrom—USA
Carrie Meyer—USA

Allan Stone

Mona Guerrant

Season Standings:

Year	W	L	Pct.	Final Standing
1975	18	26	.409	4th Place, Eastern Division
1976	19	25	.432	4th Place, Eastern Division

Attendance:

Year	Total	Average
1975	33,782	—
1976	48,642	2,211

Team Colors: Maroon, green, and gold

Home Arenas: Indiana Convention Center (Capacity—6,800)
Main Arena (Capacity—15,000)

Draft History:

1973*	1974	1975	1976
1 Rosie Casals	Jun Kamiwazumi	Olga Morozova	Syd Ball
2 Brian Gottfried	Roy Barth	Beth Norton	Pat Bostrom
3 Kerry Harris	Paul Gerken	Barbara Jordan	Ann Kiyomura
4 Phillip Dent	Sue Mappin	Julie Heldman	Olga Morozova
5 Virgina Wade	Vic Amaya	Lele Forood	Beth Norton
Allan Stone	Brenda Leiss	Barbara Hallqist	Ray Ruffels
7 Mary Eisel Beattie	Lindsey Blachford	Kerry Harris	Mona Guerrant
8 Corinne Molesworth	Maricaye Christenson	Marina Kroshina	Allan Stone
9 Jaime Fillal	Linda Lewis	Candy Reynolds	Ruta Gerulaitis
10 Nancy Ornstein	Bob Maud	Ferdi Taygan	Sue Mappin
11 Manuel Orantes	—	Jenifer Balent	Barbara Jordan
12 Patricia Faulkner	Paulina Peisachov	Roy Barth	Mima Jausovec
13 Freddy DeJesus	Maria Nasvelli	Iris Reidel	Lele Forood
14 Butch Seewagen	Stan Malless	Dick Denny	Leslie Charles
15 Jaime Pinto-Bravo	—	Syd Ball	Bill Benner
16 Zeliko Franulovic	—	—	
17 James Osborne	—	—	
18 Bob Maud	—	—	
19 Spencer Segura	—	—	
20 Sue Pritula	—	—	

1974½ Draft: 1. Raz Reid; 2. Ion Tiriac; 3. Tom Gorman; 4. Gail Chanfreau; 5. Ingrid Bentzer; 6. Belus Parajoux; 7. Veronica Burton.
°—1973 draft was by Detroit. Franchise was moved to Indiana after its first year of competition.

Marty Riessen, player/coach

The Nets' bench. Left to right: *Haroom Rahim, Rayni Fox, Bob Giltinan, Martina Navratilova, and Wendy Overton.*

7. | Cleveland Nets

1974

Nets' owner, Joe Zingale, a bald, bearded, bespectacled ex-disc jockey with a penchant for denims, somehow managed to come out of the first WTT season with his considerable optimism intact. It was an achievement of epic proportions considering what he'd been through.

For starters, he had spent a lot of time and energy in an unsuccessful attempt to sign his number one draft pick, Björn Borg. Every time Zingale made the Swedish teenager an offer, it was topped by Swedish government. Zingale also failed to sign his number twelve draft pick, 16-year-old Martina Navratilova, then an unknown.

He was luckier with Nancy Gunter, Peaches Bartkowicz, Ray Moore, Cliff Richey and the Graebners, Clark and Carole. Well, maybe not all *that* lucky. Shortly before the season opened, player/coach Clark Graebner approached Zingale with an unusual request.

"Trade my wife," said Clark, "please!" (Mr. Graebner's plea seemed to indicate that all was not well with the marriage. Sure enough, the Graebners were divorced shortly thereafter.)

Zingale obliged, sending Carole to Pittsburgh who in turn shipped her off to New York. Not long after Mrs. Graebner left Cleveland, another one of Zingale's players jumped ship. Peaches Bartkowicz left one day and never came back.

Then there was Nancy Gunter, Cliff Richey's sister. She was in the habit of changing into her street clothes after playing her singles matches and returning to the bench to join her teammates in riding the opposing team, usually in language more colorful than repeatable.

One night following a round of such bench-jockeying, Nancy was mugged in the parking lot of the Nets' less than plush stomping grounds, Cleveland's Public Hall. She lost some money, but not nearly as much as Joe Zingale.

He, of course, had dropped a bundle running a team that finished in 4th Place in the Eastern Division's Central Section.

1975

By the second season things were definitely looking up for the Nets. They moved out of the drafty, 5,000-seat Public Hall and into a beautiful sports palace, The Coliseum.

Marty Riessen was the new player/coach and former Wimbledon champ, Ann Hayden Jones

Bob Giltinan

Haroom Rahim

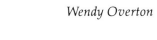
Wendy Overton

Martina Navratilova

became the Nets number one women's singles player. Clark Graebner was back, but Cliff Richey and Nancy Gunter were gone, as was Ray Moore. Bob Giltinan, Sue Stap, and Laura DuPont rounded out the roster. During the season, Val Ziegenfuss was obtained from the Boston Lobsters.

The team's playing environment, unfortunately, was the Nets' principle improvement in 1975. They wound up the second season in the Eastern Division cellar, twenty games out of first place.

1976

Zingale was still unable to sign Björn Borg but he did land another young player of note, Martina Navratilova. She had signed shortly after defecting from Czechoslovakia in September.

With Marty Riessen, 1975's Rookie-of-the-Year, and the league's top men's singles player, back for another year, the Nets would be very tough in singles. In an effort to improve their women's doubles efforts, Zingale got Wendy Overton from Indiana. Haroon Rahim replaced Clark Graebner and Rayni Fox came over from Pittsburgh for Sue Stap.

The 1976 edition of the Cleveland Nets finished the first half of the season in second place. They continued to play well after the Wimbledon break, but the Pittsburgh Triangles played a little better. Cleveland's run for a playoff spot came to an abrupt halt in the last week of the regular season when they lost four of their final five matches. They finally settled for third place in the Eastern Division with a 20-24 record.

After the season, Zingale took time out to plot a way to boost the Nets' home attendance. Most of the owners believed that twenty-two home matches might be a few too many and several teams had decided to spread their home stands around a bit. In 1976, in fact, each WTT franchise had taken between two and six home matches to non-WTT cities within their respective areas, a trend that would continue in 1977.

The newly-monikered New York Apples would be playing their home matches in three different facilities; the Sea-Port Cascades would alternate matches between Seattle and Portland, appropriately enough; and the Boston Lobsters would once again play a few home games in Hartford. "Why not move the Nets around?" thought Zingale. "But where?"

The Pittsburgh Triangles provided him with the answer. After the Triangles folded, Joe Zingale announced that his Cleveland Nets would play

Rayni Fox

eleven 1977 matches in the Steel City. And they would be doing so with a player named Bjorn Borg on the roster. He had finally come to terms with his tireless pursuer. Now the only question remaining is what's Joe Zingale going to do with his winters from now on?

Rosters:

1974
Clark Graebner (player/coach)—USA
Peaches Bartkowicz—USA
Nancy Gunter—USA
Cliff Richey—USA
Ray Moore—South Africa
Laura DuPont—USA
Pat Thomas—USA
Winnie Woolridge—Scotland
1975
Marty Riessen (player/coach)—USA
Bob Giltinan—Australia
Clark Graebner—USA
Ann Hayden Jones—Great Britain
Sue Stap—USA
Margo Tiff—USA

Valerie Ziegenfuss—USA
1976
Marty Riessen (player/coach)—USA
Martina Navratilova—Czechoslovakia
Rayni Fox—USA
Wendy Overton—USA
Haroon Rahim—Pakistan
Bob Giltinan—Australia

Season Standings:

Year	W	L	Pct.	Final Standing
1974	21	23	.477	4th Place, Central Section, Eastern Division
1975	16	28	.364	5th Place, Eastern Division
1976	20	24	.455	3rd Place, Eastern Division

Attendance:

Year	Total	Average
1974	48,887	2,222
1975	55,924	—
1976	73,108	3,323

Team Colors:

Red, white, and blue

Home Arenas:

The Coliseum (Capacity—20,000)
Pittsburgh Civic Arena (Capacity—16,400)

Bjorn Borg

Draft History:

1973	1974	1975	1976
1 Bjorn Borg	—	Arthur Ashe	Marty Riessen
2 Nancy Richey Gunter	Marty Riessen	Bjorn Borg	Martina Navratilova
	Arthur Ashe		Wendy Overton
3 Ray Moore	Bjorn Borg	Jimmy Connors	Haroon Rahim
4 Carole Graebner	Martina Navratilova	Wojtek Fibak	Hans Gildemeister
Clark Graebner			Bjorn Borg
5 Peaches Bartkowicz	Linky Boshoff	Val Ziegenfuss	Jimmy Connors
6 Pancho Gonzales	Harold Solomon	Ray Moore	Wojtek Fibak
7 Bill Lloyd	Mima Jausovec	Karen Krantzke	Owen Davidson
8 Onny Parun	Laura Rossouw	Judy Dalton	Karen Krantzcke
9 Katja Ebbinghaus	Clark Graebner	Alex Metrevelli	Helen Gourlay
10 Mal Anderson	Ove Bengston	Wendy Turnbull	Janice Metcalf
11 —	Marcie Louie	Jan Kodes	Mark Edmundson
12 Martina Navratilova	Laurie Tenney	Ruta Gerulaitis	David Lloyd
13 Thomas Koch	John Feaver	Joyce Hume	Carrie Meyer
14 Richard Gonzales, Jr.	Jaime Pinto-Bravo	Hans Pohmann	
15 Tom Kreiss	Barry Phillips-Moore	Tina Zwaan	
16 Byron Bertram	—	—	
17 Patty Ann Reese	—	—	
18 Richard Russell	—	—	
19 Ingo Budding	—	—	
20 David Blaushield	—	—	

8 | Golden Gaters

1974

Of the sixteen WTT franchises that operated in 1974 the Golden Gaters was the only one lacking a specific geographic moniker. They weren't the San Francisco Golden Gaters, or the Daly City Golden Gaters, or even the Oakland Golden Gaters despite the fact that Oakland was their home base. They were just the Golden Gaters, but that designation left little or no doubt as to which area they represented.

Co-owners Larry King and Cathy Anderson put together a well-balanced squad. Player/coach Roy Emerson finished fifth in the men's singles statistics, and he and Frew McMillan combined for an eighth place finish in the men's doubles. Lesley Hunt performed well in women's singles and anchored the women's doubles efforts with a young South African, Ilana Kloss.

The Gaters wound up their first season with a

Betty Stove

Tom Okker

23-21 record, good enough for second place in the Pacific Section of the Western Division and a playoff berth. Unfortunately, their post-season opponent was the Denver Racquets, the team that had finished seven games ahead of the Gaters in the regular season standings. The Gaters had won three of the four regular season meetings between the two teams, but the Racquets, who were destined to go all the way, took two straight wins in the playoffs.

1975

Larry King retained his share of the team, but Cathy Anderson sold hers to Dave Peterson, who had made his fortune by establishing a chain of restaurants. Roy Emerson left and was replaced by Frew McMillan as player/coach. Peterson and King also acquired The Dutch Connection; Betty Stove and Tom Okker from Baltimore and Toronto/Buffalo respectively. They picked up Ann Kiyomura from Hawaii and traded Lesley Hunt to San Diego. Ilana Kloss, Whitney Reed and Dick Bohrnstedt were holdovers from the 1974 team.

Okker and McMillan quickly established themselves as a dominant force in men's doubles, and Kloss and Kiyomura, did likewise in women's doubles. Okker, in fact, was named the league's Male MVP at the conclusion of the 1975 season and McMillan became WTT's Coach-of-the-Year for taking his team most of the way to the Championships. They would have gone all the way, but the Pittsburgh Triangles neatly foiled those plans by winning the second and third matches in the championship series.

1976

Ilana Kloss joined the tournament circuit and Ann Kiyomura went to the Indiana Loves, but the Gaters retained their women's doubles strength with the acquisition of Francoise Durr from the Phoenix Racquets. Two-year Gaters' vets Dick Bohrnstedt and Whitney Reed left the fold, and Jeff Boworiak climbed aboard. McMillan and Okker stayed on for the third season.

The Gaters would once again present a strong, well-balanced team and they were considered prime contenders for the 1976 championships. A month into the season, however, they were in third place in the Western Division, behind the Phoenix Racquets and the L.A. Strings. A few weeks later, they overtook the Strings and were gaining on Chris Evert and her Racquet teammates. The Gaters never caught up, but finished only one game behind Phoenix in the regular season.

The 1976 Golden Gators. **Left to right:** *Player/coach Frew McMillan, John Lucas (the NBA's number one draft pick in 1976 and currently a member of the Houston Rockets), Racquel Giscafre, Francoise Durr, Betty Stove, and Tom Okker.*

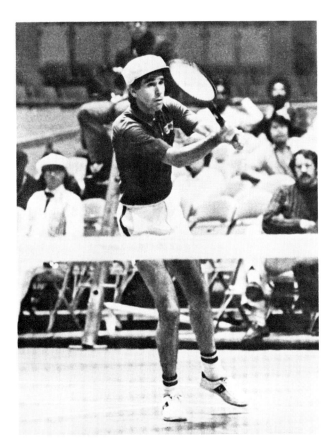

Frew McMillan

The team lost Jeff Borowiak in mid-season, but made headlines by signing John Lucas in his place. Lucas was a 6'4'' basketball and tennis All-American. Earlier, he had been the first player selected in the NBA draft, by the Houston Rockets. This was his second contract with a professional sports team.

Lucas, who was called "the second best black tennis player in the country," by his agent, Donald Dell, spent more time on the bench for the Gaters than on the court. However, he refused to get discouraged and concentrated on learning from his more experienced teammates.

"Lucas," said Gaters' general manager, Jerry Diamond, "is ready to go one-on-one with Arthur Ashe any time . . . on the basketball court. One day I hope he'll be ready to take him on in tennis."

From his vantage point on the bench, Lucas watched his team crush the Racquets in the Western Division playoffs and then promptly roll over and play dead against the New York Sets in the championship series.

For the third time in three years, the Gaters had made the playoffs, but for the second year in a row they ended up as the WTT bridesmaid.

Rosters:

1974
Roy Emerson (player/coach)—Australia
Dick Bohrnstedt—USA
Frew McMillan—South Africa
Whitney Reed—USA
Lesley Hunt—Australia
Ilana Kloss—South Africa
Denise Triolo—USA
Barbara Downs—USA

1975
Frew McMillan (player/coach)—South Africa
Tom Okker—The Netherlands
Dick Bohrnstedt—USA
Whitney Reed—USA
Ann Kiyomura—USA
Ilana Kloss—South Africa
Betty Stove—The Netherlands
Kate Latham—USA

1976
Frew McMillan (player/coach)—South Africa
Tom Okker—The Netherlands
Jeff Borowiak—USA
John Lucas—USA
Francoise Durr—France
Betty Stove—The Netherlands
Racquel Giscafre—Argentina

Season Standings:

Year	W	L	Pct.	Final Standing
1974	23	21	.523	2nd Place; Pacific Section, Western Division
1975	29	15	.659	1st Place; Western Division
1976	28	16	.636	2nd Place, Western Division

Playoff Record:

Year	W	L	Pct.
1974	0	2	.000
1975	3	2	.600
1976	2	3	.400

Attendance:

	Total	Average
1974	54,080	2,458
1975	47,345	—
1976	87,208	3,964

Team Colors:

Maroon and gold

Home Arena:

Oakland Coliseum (Capacity—12,000)

Television:

KTVU—Channel 2—six away matches in 1977

Draft History:

	1973	1974	1975	1976
1	Margaret Court	—	Raul Ramirez	Francoise Durr
2	Frew McMillan	Margaret Court	Jeff Borowiak	John Lucas
3	Dennis Ralston	Bob Lutz	Racquel Giscafre	Frew McMillan
4	Tom Gorman	Ashok Amritraj	Gene Mayer	Tom Okker
		Raul Ramirez		Adrianno Panatta
5	Ann Kiyomura	Lea Antonopolis	Cliff Richey	Marita Redondo
6	Jurgen Fassbender	Dick Crealy	Kathy May	Betty Stove
7	Jim McManus	Rick Fisher	Sharon Walsh	Evonne Goolagong
8	Ilana Kloss	Corinee Molesworth	Colin Dowdswell	Fred McNair
9	Susan Mehmedbasich	Barbara Jordan	Isabel Fernandez	Brigitte Cuypers
10	Pancho Segura	Bruce Manson	Whitney Reed	Cliff Letcher
11	Denise Tiolo	Joaquin Loyo-Moyo	James Delaney	Paul Kronk
12	Ove Bengston	John Cooper	—	Peggy Michel
13	Katie Lathram	Marie Neumannova	—	Pam Austin
14	Whitney Reed	Whitney Reed	—	Susan Hagey
15	Rick Fisher	—	—	
16	John Whitlinger	—	—	
17	Jim Delaney	Jim Delaney	—	
18	Nick Saviano	—	—	
19	Chip Fisher	Chris Mattison	—	
20	Cathi Anderson	Marina Kroshina	—	

1974½ Draft: 1. Betty Stove; 2. Tom Okker; 3. Steve Krulevitz; 4. Sue Mahmedbasich; 5. Barry McKay; 6. Ceci Martinez; 7. Janet Haas.

Chris Evert

Stephanie Tolleson

9 | Phoenix Racquets

1975

The 1975 Phoenix Racquets, transplanted from Denver, arrived in Arizona with their championship roster basically intact. Player/coach Tony Roche, the Austins, brother Jeff and sister Pam, Francoise Durr, Andrew Pattison, and Kristien Kemmer Shaw each owned a piece of the Teflon Cup, the 1974 WTT Championship trophy. Brian Fairlie, a former Philadelphia Freedom, rounded out the Racquets roster.

The Racquets rounded out the 1975 season by establishing a 22-22 record. It wasn't spectacular, but it was enough to get them into the playoffs. They annihilated the third place Los Angeles Strings in their one-match playoff to see who would earn the right to go against the Western Division champions, the Golden Gaters, but the Gaters quickly eliminated Phoenix from further contention.

1976

The big news in 1976 was Chris Evert. She and the Racquets won just about everything except the New York lottery and the Western Division playoffs. Evert swept WTT's top individual honors when she was named Female Rookie-of-the-Year and the Female MVP. In singles, she had an amazing .700 games-won percentage with a 226-97 record which was sixty percentage points ahead of Evonne Goolagong. In doubles, with Kris Shaw, she tied for fifth at .547. Evert also did well in tournament play that year. Besides winning Wimbledon during the mid-season recess, she won the U.S. Open in September.

But Evert and the rest of the Racquets, Roche, Pattison, Butch Walts, Shaw, and the league's only amateur, Stephanie Tolleson, the 1975 Women's Intercollegiate Singles Champion, were denied a shot at the WTT title by the Gaters. Phoenix and Golden Gate battled for supremacy in the Western Division all year long and the Racquets finished on top in the regular season. The Gaters, however, took the playoffs in two straight victories.

Although the Racquets failed to win the WTT Championship, they won an undisputed first place in the attendance race. At home in the 12,000-seat Veteran's Memorial Coliseum, the team drew close to 150,000 fans, an 85 per cent increase over the previous year when they drew 80,000. The Racquets also led the league in season ticket sales by selling close to 3,000 tickets. Owner Jimmy Walker, obviously disappointed by his troops' failure

Andrew Pattison

Kristien Shaw

Butch Walts

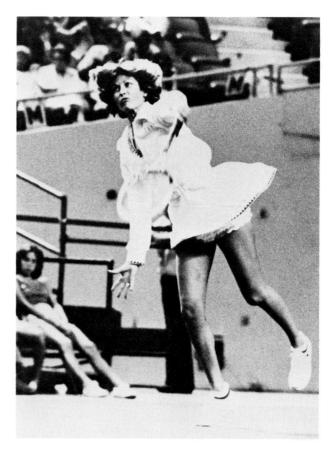

to win the league title, was at least able to console himself with the knowledge that they were attracting a large audience.

Rosters:

1975
Tony Roche (player/coach)—Australia
Jeff Austin—USA
Brian Fairlie—New Zealand
Andrew Pattison—Rhodesia
Roger Taylor—Great Britain
Pam Austin—USA
Kristien Shaw—USA
Francoise Durr—France
Stephanie Tolleson—USA

1976
Tony Roche (player/coach)—Australia
Andrew Pattison—Rhodesia
Butch Walts—USA
Chris Evert—USA
Kristien Shaw—USA
Stephanie Tolleson—USA

Season Standings:

Year	W	L	Pct.	Final Standing
1975	22	22	.500	2nd Place, Western Division
1976	30	14	.682	1st Place, Western Division

Playoff Record:

Year	W	L	Pct.
1975	1	2	.333
1976	0	2	.000

Attendance:

	Total	Average
1975	80,140	—
1976	148,544	6,752

Team Colors:

Blue and gold

Home Arena:

Veteran's Memorial Coliseum (Capacity—12,000)

Tony Roche

Draft History

1973*	1974*	1975	1976
1 Tony Roche	Judy Dalton	Rod Laver	Chris Evert
2 Francoise Durr	Susan Hagey	Stan Smith	Kristien Shaw
3 Eric Van Dillen	Pancho Walthal	Colin Dibley	Tony Roche
4 Kristien Kemmer	Eric Van Dillen	Jeanne Evert	Andrew Pattison
5 Andrew Pattison	Brian Teacher	Butch Walts	Butch Walts
6 Colin Dibley	Tom Edelson	Howard Schoenfield	Stephanie Tolleson
7 Alex Olmedo	Chico Hagey	Sherwood Stewart	Bill Scanlon
8 Stephanie Johnson	John Lucas	Brian Teacher	JoAnn Russell
9 Pam Austin	Tom Leonard	Paul Gerken	Hank Pfister
10 Jeff Austin	Stephanie Johnson	Mark Joffey	Ken Rosewall
11 Ian Crookenden	Dick Dell	Chris Penn	Brian Chaney
12 Steve Avoyer	Pam Austin	Bruce Nichols	Jan Kodes
13 Pam Farmer	Cliff Buchholtz	Bruce Kleege	Jeremy Cohen
14 Billy Higgins	Richard Gore	Jon Erik Palm	Nikki Pilic
15 Carol Bailey	Mike Springlemeyer	—	Valerie Ziegenfuss
16 Chico Hagey	—		
17 Reyno Seegers	—		
18 Walter Redondo	—		
19 Cindy Ursich	—		
20 Lew Hoad	—		

1974½ Draft: 1. Janet Newberry; 2. Valerie Ziegenfuss; 3. Bob Carmichael; 4. Christy Pigeon; 5. Ismail elShafei; 6. Cynthia Doerner; 7. William Brown.

*—1973 and 1974 drafts were by Denver. Franchise was moved to Phoenix after its first year of competition and after the second draft. The redistribution draft was made by Phoenix.

10 | Hawaii Leis/Sea-Port Cascades

1974

It could have been almost anything. The endless white beaches, or maybe the clear, blue Pacific. The only thing for certain was that something seemed to be distracting the Hawaii Leis during the 1974 season. Even the Leis' unique fan club, the 200-member strong Oahu Refuse Collectors' booster club, was generally unsuccessful when it came to inspiring the Leis to victory. The booster club sure looked nice though, decked out in T-shirts bearing the Leis' logo superimposed over a garbage truck.

Despite overwhelming displays of affection from their fans, the Leis, led by player/coach Dennis Ralston, managed only 14 wins in the 1974 season. They finished in last place in the Pacific Section of the Western Division.

1975

The beaches, palm trees, sand, and surf still abounded in 1975, and so did the lack of Hawaii Lei victories. Ralston went over to the San Diego Friars and Butch Buchholz took over coaching duties, but without much success. John Newcombe, who saw his Houston EZ Riders bite the dust just before the second season began, wound up in a Leis' uniform but he was plagued by aches and pains much of the year. Margaret Court also played for Hawaii in 1975 but was unable to reverse the team's fortunes. The Leis finished fourth in the Western Division just ahead of San Diego.

1976

With both Newcombe and Court in self-imposed retirement, the Leis were in the market for replacements in 1976. They chose Ilie Nastase.

"It makes sense," said the WTT detractors. "After all, the league is a circus so why not bring in the clown?"

Though Nastase didn't cause a barrage of international incidents he didn't exactly distinguish himself on the court either. When he showed up that is, which wasn't all that often. By mid-season, the Leis and their high-priced, part-time employee had won only twice in their first eighteen matches. Due to his many absences Nastase was confronted by Larry King at Wimbledon and was convinced to

return to the Leis for the second half. Margaret Court also agreed to rejoin the team after the Wimbledon break. The team's performance improved somewhat, but not enough to avert a last place finish in the Western Division.

Donald Kelleher, the Leis' owner, then confirmed the speculations that he was planning to pack up his team and move to the Pacific Northwest. After three years he finally decided that the climate in Hawaii was more conducive to suntans than a lucrative team tennis franchise. Beginning in 1977, the Hawaii Leis will be known as the Sea-Port Cascades, alternating their home matches between Seattle, Washington and Portland, Oregon.

The franchise also lost a player/coach. In September 1976, Butch Buchholz was named as WTT's new commissioner.

Rosters:

1974
Dennis Ralston (player/coach)—USA
Butch Buchholz—USA
Ross Case—Australia
Barry McKay—USA
Mike Machette—USA
Charles Panui—USA
Charlie Pasarell—USA
Ann Kiyomura—USA
Kristy Pigeon—USA
Judy Vincent—USA
Val Ziegenfuss—USA
Brigitte Cuypers—France

1975
Butch Buchholz (player/coach)—USA
Owen Davidson—Australia
Tom Edelfsen—USA
John Newcombe—Australia
Barry McKay—USA
Charles Panui—USA
Mary Ann Beattie—USA
Joyce Champaigne—USA
Margaret Court—Australia
Heather Dalgren—USA
Helen Gourlay—Australia
Kathy Kuykendall—USA
Bridgitte Cuypers—France

1976
Butch Buchholz (player/coach)—USA
Owen Davidson—Australia
Ilie Nastase—Rumania
Margaret Court—Australia
Helen Gourlay—Australia
Nancy Gunter—USA
Sue Stap—USA
Marcie Louie—USA

Season Standings:

Year	W	L	Pct.	Final Standing
1974	14	29	.326	4th Place, Pacific Section, Western Division
1975	14	30	.318	4th Place, Western Division
1976	12	32	.272	5th Place, Western Division

Attendance:

	Total	Average
1974	32,191	1,463
1975	56,470	—
1976	67,452	3,066

Team Colors:

Hawaii Leis—Green and white
Sea-Port Cascades—Green and white (uniforms)
Blue and green (logo)

Home Arenas:

Hawaii Leis—Blaisdell Memorial Center (Capacity—7,829)
Sea-Port Cascades—Seattle Center Coliseum (Capacity—13,500)
Portland Memorial Coliseum (Capacity—11,655)

The 1976 Hawaii Leis. **Left to right:** *player/coach Butch Buchholz, Helen Gourlay, Margaret Court, Nancy Richey, Owen Davidson, and Ilie Nastase.*

Draft History

	1973*	1974	1975	1976*
1	Rod Laver	Kazuko Sawamatsu	Eric Van Dillen	Ilie Nastase
2	Karen Susman	Onny Parun	Billy Martin	Stan Smith
3	Wendy Overton	Charles Pasarell	Onny Parun	John Lloyd
4	Ilie Nastase	Nancy Ornstein	Zenda Leiss	Tom Gorman
5	Jan Kodes	Jun Kuki	Manuel Orantes	Margaret Court
6	Alexander Metreveli	Toshiro Sakai	Fred McNair	Nancy Richey
7	Marie Bueno	Ching Ling Chang	Karen Susman	Manuel Orantes
8	Roy Barth	Heather Dahlgren	Nancy Ornstein	Lea Antonopolis
9	Ann Jones	James Osborne	Patty Hogan	Marise Kruger
10	Glynis Coles	—	John Lucas	Sherwood Stewart
11	Susie Minford	Butch Walts	Mary Eisel Beattie	Janet Young
12	Joyce Schwikert	Barbara Downs	Carl Meiler	Steve Docherty
13	Jill Schwikert	Bill Cosby	Sue Mahmedbasich	Larry Gottfried
14	Mari Coronado	Stan Pasarrell	Laura Dupont	Peter Pearson
15	Yevgeniya Biryukova	Peter Burwash	Spencer Segura	Eric Van Dillen
16	Dick Bohrnstedt	—	—	
17	Bill Bond	—	—	
18	John Andrews	—	—	
19	Steve Krulevitz 3	—	—	
20	J. Shalem	—	—	

1974½ Draft: 1. Chris Evert; 2. Brian Gottfried; 3. Joyce Hume; 4. Jurgen Fassbender; 5. Naha Sato; 6. Jeri Hrebic; 7. Fred McNair.

*—1973 draft was by San Diego. Franchise was moved to Hawaii prior to its first year of competition. The team that drafted in 1973 should not be confused with the one currently operating in San Diego which is a new franchise.
*1976 draft for Sea-Port Cascades

Terry Holladay

Bettyann Stuart

11 | San Diego Friars

1975

The San Diego Friars were created as an insurance team following the 1974 WTT season. League officials were afraid that the Philadelphia Freedoms were going to fold and they wanted to have a franchise that could be plugged into the forty-four vacancies in the schedule that would be left in the wake of the Freedoms' departure. The anticipated disappearance never materialized, but the Freedoms did move north to Boston. As things turned out, the Houston EZ Riders surprised everyone by going under just before the start of the 1975 season and San Diego took their place.

San Diego had been the original home of the WTT franchise that became the Hawaii Leis, but the citizens of that fair city never had a chance to root for the home team. Now with another franchise, they would finally get a chance to see what WTT was all about. Not very many did, however. A paltry

Rod Laver

Cliff Drysdale

22,000 spectators showed up at the San Diego Sports Arena to watch the Friars during 1975. A few times, in fact, the players outnumbered the audience three to one. And that's not counting the linespersons, ballboys, and ballgirls.

The Friars didn't lack tennis players, however. Fifteen of them, six women and nine men, donned the team colors during the season. Most of them didn't accumulate much playing time, however. Bill Schoen, for instance, played exactly one set of mixed doubles, winning 6-4, before deciding to quit the team. Jeff Cowan, Tom Leonard, Shushi Menon, Ken Stuart, Marita Redondo, and Francis Troll each played less than forty games during the 1975 season. Vijay Amritraj and Lesley Hunt carried most of the singles burden and Amritraj was the only San Diego Friar named to the WTT All-Star squad.

Unfortunately, the team's record was as bad as its attendance. They finished in last place in the Western Division standings.

1976

The Friars began their second season in much the same circumstances that the league had been in when it began its second season. There was no where to go but up.

A certain red-haired tennis player who had won more than a million dollars with his broad left wrist, and who had twice (1962 and 1969) won the Grand Slam, was bound to help the Friars.

"I'm not ready to be put in a box yet," said Rod Laver as he signed a lucrative contract with San Diego.

Terry Holladay, a big-hitting left-hander, also became a Friar, giving the team a strong women's singles weapon. Holladay eventually finished tenth in the women's singles season stats, but she certainly began her Friars' career in fine fashion when she beat Evonne Goolagong in San Diego's opening match. Laver wasn't quite so lucky. He lost to Vitas Gerulaitis in his first WTT match.

Under the guidance of player/coach Cliff Drysdale the team's overall performance was highly encouraging during the first half of the 1976 season. They were 9-15 going into the recess, good enough for fourth place in the tough Western Division. After the break, however, the Friars went on a downhill slide and they won only four more matches while losing sixteen. Still, they ended up one game out of the cellar.

Though the team's on-court record didn't quite meet the pre-season expectations, the previous year's attendance figure was more than tripled in 1976. The people in San Diego had discovered WTT.

Chico Hagey

Rosters:

1975
Dennis Ralston (player/coach)—USA
Vijay Amritraj—India
Lesley Hunt—Australia
Ashok Amritraj—India
Brigitte Cuypers—France
Janet Young—Australia
Mike Machette—USA
John Andrews—USA
Jeff Cowan—USA
Tom Leonard—USA
Bill Schoen—USA
Ken Stuart—USA
Helen Gourlay—Australia
Marita Redondo—USA
Francis Troll—USA

1976
Cliff Drysdale (player/coach)—South Africa
Ross Case—Australia
Rod Laver—Australia
Terry Holladay—USA
Janet Young—Australia
Bettyann Stuart—USA

Season Standings:

Year	W	L	Pct.	Final Standing
1975	12	32	.308	Fifth Place, Western Division
1976	13	31	.273	4th Place, Western Division

Attendance:

Year	Total	Average
1975	22,274	—
1976	74,624	3,392

Team Colors:

Gold and light brown

Home Arena:

San Diego Sports Arena (Capacity 9,500)

Draft History:

1975	1976
Linky Boshoff	Rod Laver
Nancy Richey-Gunter	Terry Holladay
Janice Metcalf	Cliff Drysdale
Charlie Passarell	Dick Stockton
Kazuko Sawamatsu	Linky Boshoff
Glynes Coles	Sue Barker
Jaime Fillol	Peter Fleming
Jane Stratton	Wendy Turnbull
Peter Fleming	Cynthia Doerner
Balazs Taroczy	Chico Hagey
Sue Mappin	Rayni Fox
Pancho Segura	Brian Teacher
	Raul Ramirez
	Walter Redondo
	Karen Susman

Lesley Hunt

Ross Case

12 | Los Angeles Strings

1974

Jerry Buss, a physical chemist, who made his fortune in real estate, movies, and, other assorted ventures, acquired part ownership in the Los Angeles Strings in 1973. With such a varied and unusual background, Dr. Buss's involvement in WTT seems only natural. The crazy league and the mad scientist were made for each other.

In true Southern California fashion, the Strings made their debut in the L.A. Sports Arena in 1974 with a brief in-person monologue by Johnny Carson (also a Strings' owner) and a few songs courtesy of the USC marching band. They also emerged with a victory over the visiting Florida Flamingoes, one of sixteen wins they were to enjoy during the inaugural season. Buss and the other owners lost a lot of money that first season. Their team lost twenty-eight matches and finished third in the four-team Pacific Section of the Western Division.

Dennis Ralston

Bob Lutz

1975

Only two original Strings returned for the second season, Geoff Masters and Kathy Harter. Rosie Casals arrived from the Detroit Loves, Bettyann Stuart from the Florida Flamingoes, Ross Case from the Leis, Bob Lutz from the tournaments, and Mike Machette from the Hawaii Leis following a brief stopover with the Friars.

In 1975 the Strings most memorable moments occurred when they halted the New York Sets' 16-match winning streak and when they qualified for the post-season playoffs. The team posted a 20-24 record enroute to its third-place finish behind the Racquets and Golden Gaters but their playoff appearance was shortlived. Phoenix defeated the Strings with ease, 20-8.

1976

Once again only two members of the previous year's roster were in Strings' uniforms when the season began: Rosie Casals and Bob Lutz. Vijay Amritraj was obtained from the Friars, and his brother, Ashok, also joined the team. Dianne Fromholtz, a Margaret Court protégé, and Ann Haydon Jones were signed and Dennis Ralston was named as the Strings' player/coach.

The biggest fish, however, had gotten away. Buss had mounted every effort to land Jimmy Connors but Connors wasn't ready for WTT. Buss doesn't

Rosie Casals

Vijay Amritraj

Dianne Fromholtz

The 1975 Los Angeles Strings. Standing (left to right): Bill Norris, Bob Lutz, Ross Case, Rosie Casals, Geoff Masters, and Delroy Reid. Seated: Bettyann Stuart and Kathy Harter.

give up easily though, and in September 1976 he dangled another hook before Connors, one that was baited with almost a quarter of a million dollars. Connors again demurred, but Ilie Nastase didn't. The mercurial Rumanian late of the Hawaii Leis, attached himself to the Strings in March 1977.

In 1976 the Strings finished in third place in the Western Division for the third straight year. The team's won/lost record had improved in each of their three years in the league, but in 1976 their attendance record had skyrocketed. A move from the L.A. Sports Arena to the plusher Forum undoubtedly helped because the Strings became one of only three WTT franchises to draw over 100,000 spectators.

Rosters:

1974
John Alexander—Australia
Jean Baptiste Chanfreau—France
Pat Cramer—South Africa
Geoff Masters—Australia
Jerry Van Linge—USA
Kathy Harter—USA
Marita Redondo—USA
Karen Susman—USA
1975
Ross Case—Australia
Bob Lutz—USA
Mike Machette—USA
Rosie Casals—USA
Geoff Masters—Australia
Bettyann Stuart—USA

1976
Bob Lutz—USA
Vijay Amritraj—India
Ashok Amritraj—India
Dennis Ralston—USA
Charles Pasarell—Puerto Rico
Rosie Casals—USA
Ann Haydon Jones—Great Britain
Dianne Fromholtz—Australia

Season Standings:

Year	W	L	Pct.	Final Standing
1974	16	28	.364	3rd Place, Pacific Section, Western Division
1975	19	24	.455	3rd Place, Western Division
1976	22	22	.500	3rd Place, Western Division

Playoff Record:

Year	W	L	Pct.
1975	0	1	.000

Attendance:

	Total	Average
1974	38,707	1,759
1975	28,970	—
1976	103,370	4,699

Team Colors:

Orange and yellow

Home Arena:

The Forum (Capacity—11,250)

Draft History:

	1973	1974	1975	1976
1	John Alexander	Jeff Borowick	Dianne Fromholtz	Vijay Amritraj
2	Valerie Ziegenfuss	Dianne Fromholtz	Marcie Louie	Rosemary Casals
3	Julie Anthony	Rod Laver	Mima Jausovec	Dianne Fromholtz
4	Ross Case	Walter Redondo	Pam Stockton	Sue Stap
5	Vijay Amritraj	Mal Anderson	John Alexander	John Newcombe
6	Kathy Kuykendall	Pat Cramer	Cindy Doerner	Charles Pasarell
7	Geoff Masters	Roy Emerson	Sue Barker	Roscoe Tanner
8	Kathy May	John Andrews	Terry Holladay	Betsy Nagelsen
9	Leif Johansson	Madeline Pegel	Bob Lutz	Jaime Fillol
10	Jane Albert Willens	Christina Sandberg	Hank Pfister	John Andrews
11	Robert Kreiss	Trey Waltke	Janet Young	Ray Moore
12	Sherwood Stewart	Tracy Austin	Diane Morrison	Colin Dibley
13	Jun Kamiwazumi	Dean Martin, Jr.	Ulli Pinner	Mary Struthers
14	Penny Moor	Johnny Carson	Kathy Harter	Billy Martin
15	Terry Ryan	—	Mary Struthers	
16	Bruce Manson	—	John Holladay	
17	Trey Waltke	—	David Ryan	
18	Butch Walts	—	Tracy Austin	
19	Robin Tenney	—	Stewart Keller	
20	Jerry Van Linge	—	Sheila MacKenerni	

1974½: 1. Lesley Hunt; 2. Betty Grubb; 3. Janice Metcalf; 4. Anand Amritraj; 5. Ivan Molina; 6. Paul Kronk; 7. Bob Hewitt.

13 | Draft Selections by Ex-franchises

Baltimore

Franchise Did Not Operate After 1974 Season
1973: Round 1. Jimmy Connors; 2. Betty Stove; 3. Janet Newberry; 4. Bob Carmichael; 5. Berry Phillips-Moore; 6. Janice Metcalf; 7. Joyce Williams; 8. Dick Crealy; 9. Pass; 10. Joachim Loyo-Mayo; 11. Kristy Pigeon; 12. John Cooper; 13. Ron Holmberg; 14. Torben Ulrich; 15. Mike Machette; 16. Ken Fletcher; 17. Gail Elliott; 18. Audrey Morse; 19. Pass; 20. Lenny Schloss.

1974: Round 1. Jan Kodes; 2. Pass; 3. Joyce Metcalf; 4. William Brown; 5. Cathy Latham; 6. Jurgen Fassbender; 7. Susan Mehmedbasich; 8. Elly Appel; 9. Pass; 10. Christina Sandberg; 11. Steve Krulevich; 12. Pass; 13. Ceci Martinez; 14. Nancy Sato; 15. Helen Anliot; 16. through 20. None.

Boston*

Franchise Did Not Operate after 1974 Season
1973: Round 1. Kerry Melville; 2. Nikki Pilic; 3. Roger Taylor; 4. Sharon Walsh; 5. Paul Gerken; 6. Jeanne Evert; 7. Mike Estep; 8. Ismail El Shafei; 9. Patricia Bostrom; 10. Ion Tiriac; 11. Charles Pasarell; 12. Peggy Michael; 13. Ian Fletcher; 14. Victor Amaya; 15. Esme Emanuel; 16. Gene Mayer; 17. Ferdi Taygan; 18. Ashok Amritraj; 19. Steve Faulk; 20. Fran Taylow.

1974: Round 1. Colin Dibley; 2. Gail Chanfreau and Patty Hogan; 3. Carrie Flemming; 4. Anand Amritraj; 5. Sherwood Stewart; 6. Sue Barker; 7. John Lloyd; 8. Virginia Ruzici; 9. Linda Mottram; 10. Paul Kronk; 11. Marianna Simionescu; 12. Steve Warboys; 13. through 20. None.

1974½: Round 1. Mike Estep; 2. Butch Buchholtz; 3. Kathy Latham; 4. Ken Fletcher; 5. Andriano Panatta; 6. Jerry Van Linge; 7. Byron Bertram

*—Not to be confused with franchise currently operating in Boston.

Chicago

Franchise Did Not Operate After 1974 Season
1973: Round 1: Marty Riessen; 2. Julie Heldman; 3. Bob Lutz; 4. Judy Dalton; 5. Ray Ruffels; 6. Janet Young; 7. Billy Martin; 8. Marie Neumannova; 9. Bobby Riggs; 10. Andres Gimeno; 11. Gail Chanfreau; 12. Tam O'Shaughnessy; 13. Graham Stillwell; 14. Pat Cramer; 15. Lita Liem Sugiarto; 16. Sue Vinton; 17. Frantisek Pala; 18. Jean Baptiste Chanfreau; 19. Bernard Mitton; 20. Mimi Henreid.

1974: Round 1: Julie Heldman; 2. Pass; 3. Billy Martin; 4. Manuel Orantes; 5. Eddie Dibbs; 6. Andriano Panatta; 7. Jeri Hrebic; 8. Pat Faulkner; 9. Hans-Jurgen Pohmann; 10. Kristy Pigeon; 11. Christine O'Neil; 12. Cynthia Doerner; 13. Pass; 14. F.D. Robbins, 15. Byron Bertram; 16. through 20. None.

Florida

Franchise Did Not Operate After 1974 Season
1973: Round 1. Chris Evert; 2. Roscoe Tanner; 3. Frank Froehling; 4. Marcie Louie; 5. Adriano Panatta; 6. Patrice Dominguez; 7. Patti Hogan; 8. Mark Cox; 9. Olga Morozova; 10. Neale Fraser; 11. Wendy Paish; 12. Madeline Pegel; 13. Norman Holmes; 14. Toshiro Sakai; 15. Pam Richmond; 16. Joey Williams; 17. Juan Gisbert; 18. Sally Greer; 19. F.D. Robbins; 20. Fiorella Bonicelli.

1974: Round 1. Chris Evert and Tom Gorman; 2. Brian Gottfried; 3. Jaime Fillol; 4. Valerie Ziegenfuss; 5. Veronica Burton; 6. Fred McNair; 7. Belus Prajoux; 8. Ivan Molina; 9. Ingrid Bentzer; 10. Milan Holecek; 11. Wendy Paish; 12. Graham Stillwell; 13. Jerry Van Linge; 14. through 20. None.

Houston

Franchise Did Not Operate After 1974 Season
1973: Round 1. John Newcombe; 2. Dick Stockton; 3. Karen Krantcke; 4. Leslie Bowrey; 5. Helen Gourlay; 6. Bill Bowrey; 7. Cecilia Martinez; 8. Bob McKinley; 9. Ray Keldie; 10. Daryl Gralka; 11. Terry Addison; 12. Marilyn Tesch; 13. Peter Doerner; 14. Becky Vest; 15. Linda Ruppert; 16. Pancho Walthall; 17. Mary McLean; 18. Chris Bovett; 19. Jo Ann Russell; 20. Sam Giammalva.

1974: Round 1. Glynis Coles; 2. Neil Fraser; 3. Olga Morazova; 4. Syd Ball; 5. Robin Tenney; 6. JoAnn Russell; 7. Bob McKinley; 8. Stephanie Tollson; 9. Sandy Stap; 10. Jim Parker; 11. Jim McManus; 12. Zan Guerry; 13. Denise Triolo.

1974½: Round 1. Billy Martin; 2. Julie Heldman; 3. Sue Barker; 4. Kim Warwick; 5. Carrie Flemming; 6. Maria Bueno; 7. Donna Stockton.

Minnesota

Franchise Did Not Operate After 1974 Season
1973: Round 1. Linda Tuero; 2. Owen Davidson; 3. Stan Smith; 4. Patricia Pretorius; 5. Bob Hewitt; 6. Brenda Kirk; 7. Patrick Proisy; 8. Corrado Barazzutti; 9. Nathalie Fuchs; 10. Sue Stap; 11. Jim Ebbitt; 12. Eddie Dibbs; 13. Steve Wilkinson; 14. Tom Leonard; 15. Lany Kaligis; 16. Shari Barman; 17. Pass; 18. Maricaye Christenson; 19. Frank Sedgman; 20. Larry Loeb.

Toronto-Buffalo

Franchise Did Not Operate After 1974 Season
1973: Round 1. Tom Okker; 2. Marita Redondo; 3. Pierre Barthes; 4. Lesley Hunt; 5. Karl Meiler; 6. Raul Ramirez; 7. Helga Masthoff; 8. Laurie Tenney; 9. Guillermo Vilas; 10. Mike Belkin; 11. Carrie Fleming; 12. Christina Sandberg; 13. Janice Tindle; 14. Marina Kroshina; 15. Pass; 16. David Lloyd; 17. Rolf Norberg; 18. John Lloyd; 19. Antonio Zugarelli; 20. George Gross.

1974: Round 1. Pass; 2. Katja Ebbinghaus; 3. Ismail El Shafei; 4. Thomas Koch; 5. Guillermo Vilas; 6. Juan Gisbert; 7. Linda Tuero; 8. Ken Rosewall; 9. Alex Metreveli; 10. Manuel Santana; 11. Pass; 12. Pancho Gonzales; 13. Andres Gimeno; 14. Pierre Barthes; 15. Pat Proisy; 16. Shiela McInerney; 17. Barry McKay; 18. Tim Ryan; 19. and 20. None.

14 | Rosters of Ex-franchises

Baltimore Banners

Byron Bertram, Don Candy, Bob Carmichael, Jimmy Connors, Ian Crookenden, J. Makuerjea, Joyce Hume, Audrey Morse, Betty Stove, Kathy Kuykendall (Phila.)

Chicago Aces

Butch Buchholz, Ray Ruffels, Graham Stilwell, Kim Warwick, Barbara Downs, Sue Eastman, Marcie Louie, Sue Stap, Janet Young

Minnesota Buckskins

Owen Davidson, Bob Hewitt, Bill Lloyd, Judy Holladay, Ann Hayden Jones, Mona Shallau, Wendy Turnbull

Florida Flamingoes

Mike Belkin, Mark Cox, Cliff Drysdale, Frank Froehling, Ester Bueno, Lynn Epstein, Donna Fales, Laurie Fleming, Donna Ganz, Bettyann Stuart

Toronto/Buffalo Royals

Mike Estep, Ian Fletcher, Tom Okker, Jane O'Neill, Wendy Overton, Laura Rossouw

Houston EZ Riders

Bill Bowrey, Peter Doerner, Bob McKinley, John Newcombe, Dick Stockton, Lesley Bowrey, Cynthia Doerner, Helen Gourley, Karen Krantzcke

Boston Lobsters

Doug Crawford, Raz Reid, Roger Taylor, Ion Tiriac, Stephan Warboys, Pat Bostrom, Kerry Melville, Janet Newberry, Francis Taylor, Andrea Volkos

Philadelphia Freedoms (Boston 1975)

Brian Fairlie, Buster Mottram, Fred Stolle, Julie Anthony, Tory Fretz, Billie Jean King, Kathy Kuykendall

Denver Racquets (Phoenix)

Jeff Austin, Andrew Pattison, Tony Roche, Pam Austin, Francoise Durr, Stephanie Johnson, Kristien Kemmer Shaw

Detroit Loves (Indiana)

Phil Dent, Butch Seewagen, Lendward Simpson, Allan Stone, Mary Ann Beattie, Rosie Casals, Pat Faulkner, Kerry Harris

Tennis Tips

In 1976, WTT and the makers of Minute Maid put together a unique booklet of tennis tips featuring members of the 1975 WTT All-Star team demonstrating various technical aspects of the game. The booklet also included a comprehensive section on tennis basics (etiquette, court surfaces, conditioning, equipment, etc.) several suggested practice drills for singles and doubles, and a section on World Team Tennis.

Portions of the WTT Tennis Tips instructional guide appear here in book form for the first time.

We wish to thank The Coca-Cola Company Foods Division and Robert W. Boyle, Manager, Promotion Material and Packaging Coordination, for allowing us to reprint the following material. May it help your game.

1 | Courts and Surfaces

The day of the grass court is all but gone. Today's more popular surfaces are mainly made of an asphalt, cement, hard clay or clay-like material. Indoor courts, which are becoming more popular, feature a variety of surfaces ranging from fast-playing (like cement or asphalt based materials) to the slower playing type like synthetic carpet.

Each type of surface will have its own playing characteristic. It's best to just practice hitting the ball first on a surface that's new to you. Study how the ball bounces on this particular surface. Note the height of the ball bounce, the speed with which it will bounce, the effect that a spin or twist may have. Then adjust your ready position and stroking motions to match the relative characteristics of that surface. You'll discover that faster surfaces demand quicker stroke preparation. Slower surfaces allow greater time to prepare for your stroke. Learning to adjust to a different playing surface should become an important part of your thinking about our strokes.

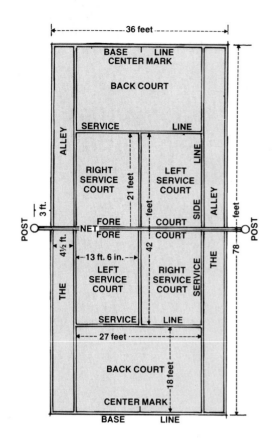

"CARRY THE BALL" FORWARD

2 | Ball Contact

Margaret Court

As you move your racquet forward to hit the ball several things should be happening:

1—your body weight should be shifting forward naturally toward that point where the ball should be making contact with your racquet strings;

2—you're concentrating on watching that ball all the way;

3—once that ball bounces into your court, you should be thinking about making contact with the ball as it either begins to rise or is at the peak of it's bounce;

4—concentrate on hitting the ball at a point that's in front of you and just about even with your left foot—try not to let the ball crowd you;

5—as the ball hits the center of your racquet strings think about how it "feels" on the strings and imagine that you are, momentarily at least, carrying that ball forward with your strings. In reality, during any well hit forehand stroke, the ball is actually carried forward by the racquet strings for a distance of about six to ten inches.

3 | Spins and Slices

To achieve greater topspin on your basic backhand stroke think about bringing your racquet strings up and over the ball as you carry it forward during point of contact To add slice, tilt the angle of your racquet face slightly backwards. Now, with your racquet in this position you'll be coming across and under the ball as you carry it forward on your racquet strings. This action causes a reverse motion on the spin of the ball resulting in a low, halting ball bounce for your opponent.

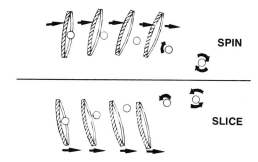

4 | Foot Action (Forehand)

Margaret Court

Footwork is the key to controlling the balance of your body weight and its motion. If your footwork is good it will add greater mobility and more of a fluid motion to your strokes and overall game. You simply can not hit a solid forehand when your feet are flat on the court and your legs are straight like sticks. Since your feet allow your body to do these necessary actions, you shouldn't overlook the importance of good footwork as an integral part of your forehand stroke.

5 | Body Weight and Following Through (Forehand)

Margaret Court

Now, assuming that you've prepared properly to hit your forehand, you'll soon find that the shifting of your body weight forward and into the ball becomes rather automatic . . . and a natural action within the total physical rhythm of your stroke. Be sensitive to the fact that the varying height of a ball bounce will dictate a need for you to either raise or lower your body while you're moving forward. Bend your knees or extend your legs to their fullest if need be.

6 | Forehand Practice Drills

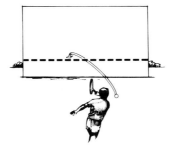

Stepping into The Ball
Stand behind the base line. Start each stroke by dropping the ball at a point on the court that causes you to step forward as you practice your forehand stroke. Try hitting 20 to 30 balls in a row like this without making an error. Aim for the baseline on the opposite side of the court.

Against A Wall or Backboard
Try hitting 20 to 30 forehands against the wall. Concentrate on getting your racquet straight back and complete your stroke with a full follow through up and out. Stand about 25 to 30 feet from the wall. If necessary indicate the net height as follows:

CORRECT NET HEIGHT

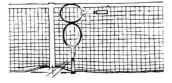

Preparing for a Forehand
Stand at about a 40° angle to the net. Hold a ball in your non-racquet hand. Bounce the ball in front and to the outside of your left foot. Swing your racquet arm forward (without the racquet in your hand) just as your would from a normal forehand ready position. Be sure you shift your weight naturally forward during your swing, then catch the ball with your racquet hand after it's bounced. Practice this drill carefully 10 to 20 times. (see illustration)

7 | The Backhand

Tony Roche

   Many beginning players tend to be afraid of the backhand stroke. There's no essential reason for this attitude. When you follow a few fundamentals, the backhand stroke should be the most natural of all your groundstrokes. You'll discover that the elements of a good backhand are virtually the same as the forehand . . . correct GRIP, GETTING READY, BALL CONTACT, BODY WEIGHT and FOLLOW THROUGH. A well executed backhand involves getting to the ball early, stepping into it and following all the way through smoothly and out toward your ultimate target area. As you bring your racquet back, one important key to your making a good stroke will be to move your shoulders and waist parallel with the side of the court. As you move to the ball, your front foot should be crossing toward the ball thereby providing you with a solid base for your stroke. As with your forehand, be sure you're bending your knees to help move your body weight gracefully into the shot.

GETTING READY

BALL CONTACT

FOLLOW THROUGH

8 | Body Weight and Following Through (Backhand)   Tony Roche

By the time the ball starts to make contact with your racquet, the physical rhythm of your stroking action should cause your body weight to be moving forward into the ball. Remember, when you're stroking smoothly the shift in your body weight will occur automatically and naturally. Bend your knees slightly to help this shift in your body weight. Try to get the feel of the ball on your strings as you carry it forward while completing your follow through action. By now, your arm and body motion should be working together. It's important to concentrate on keeping your shoulder low, your head down as you watch the ball closely. You complete your follow through by moving your extended racquet arm (still comfortably straight with a locked, firm wrist) up and out toward your target. Work at keeping your head down even as you complete your follow through. At the completion of your stroke you should have brought your arm fully through its swing, and up. This total motion in your backhand stroke will tend to add a little natural topspin to the ball.

9 | The Toss

John Newcombe

Simply stated, the objective of a good ball toss is to throw a tennis ball to that location where your racquet will meet the ball without forcing you to compensate by changing your body position or your serving motion. It's better to re-toss your ball if you happen to make a bad toss than to alter your body position or serving motion.

The release of your ball should actually occur after your arm has become fully extended during the toss. As you start your toss, hold the ball lightly with your finger tips.

Try thinking of the court surface as sort of a ''mirror'' when you begin your toss. Prior to starting your toss, bounce the ball at a point on the court that is opposite to where you want it to go in the air. You'll find that this action will help you to concentrate better as to where you want your toss to go.

Think about tossing or ''lifting'' the ball to a height equal to the fullest extension of your arm and racquet during your service motion. Your ball tossing arm should always be relaxed but generally straight at your elbow. Also think about lifting your head to watch the ball continuously. You should be ready to make contact with the ball when it's at the peak of your toss . . . not while it's going up or coming down. Being able to make a consistent ball toss is vital to a good serve.

10 | Varying Your Serve

John Newcombe

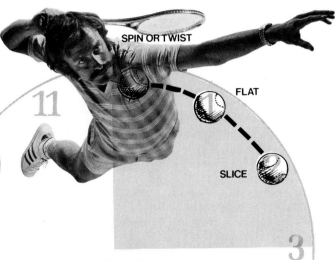

Many players, when they prepare to serve, will imagine that they are standing at the center of a circle that resembles a clock.

To help achieve variations on their service they will toss the ball to different points on this imaginary clock. Here's how you can use this technique to improve your service variations.

The Slice Service

Toss ball up, out and toward the 2 o'clock position: Note how the face of your racquet must then come around the ball as it makes contact thus creating a side spin. Depending on where you're aiming, this motion is used whenever you want to make the ball run away from or in toward the opposing player.

The Flat Service

Toss ball up, out, and toward the one o'clock position. In this case, note how the face of your racquet makes the fullest, head-on impact with the ball thus providing you with more power. This type of service is used most often for the first serve.

The Spin or Twist Service

Toss ball up toward the 12 o'clock position. However, in this case you should toss the ball more directly over your head. If you want to achieve even more twist, toss the ball up and to a location that is slightly behind your head. This will force you to arch your back more and as a result will make your racquet strings brush up and over the ball at the point of contact during your serving motion. This serve is used most often for a second serve.

11 | The Grip

Billie Jean King

If you're a beginner stay with the EASTERN or "shake hands" grip. As your ability and confidence grows, you'll find the same grip used for your service and backhand will probably suit most of your volleying needs. Since you really don't have much time to either think about or actually change grips during the volley, experiment a bit to discover which grip gives you greater confidence and shot consistency. The Continental Grip is suggested for advanced players since it's about halfway between the forehand and backhand grip.

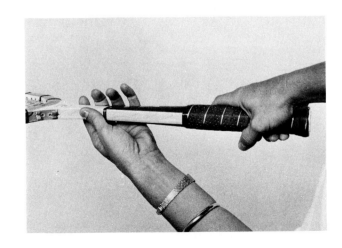

12 | The Volley

Billie Jean King

A good volley is really quite easy to learn and it's one of the best offensive strokes you can use in tennis. When you combine it with an accurate, consistently good service, you can win a point quickly and decisively. On windy days or if you're playing on uneven or rough court surfaces it will reduce your chances of making an error. However, to master the volley you must adjust your stroke to meet the need for more exact timing. Generally speaking, volleys are hit in the forecourt to either your forehand or backhand side. Since you are now closer to the net you have obviously shortened the distance and the time it takes for the ball to reach you after it leaves your opponent's racquet. The volley is far more demanding on your natural reflexes and coordination than virtually any other stroke. Whether you are hitting a forehand or backhand volley, the cardinal rule is to keep and hit that ball in front of you. You should let your racquet strings do most of your work for you. Your basic stroke should have little or no backswing. Rather, you should be moving toward the ball utilizing a punching motion rather than the full follow through that's needed on a good ground stroke. Punch out and toward the baseline of your target area.

Position in Preparation for a Volley

Execute your volleys in the forecourt and approximately 4 to 6 feet from the net. This will tend to reduce your margin for error and increase the amount of angle available for a forehand or backhand volley. In an exchange of volleys, try to close in on the net after each shot.

Move quickly to the point at which you want to hit your volley. From your ready position on a forehand volley, for example, you should be stepping into the shot. Foot action is important. Your feet should be a little more than a shoulder width apart. Keep your weight forward on the balls of your feet. Your shoulders should be generally parallel but at a slight angle to the net. Be really ready mentally. Remember not to bring your racket further back than your back shoulder. Lock your wrist. Keep your elbows well in front of your body. Watch that ball all the way to your racquet. Remember, on your backhand volley this action should be just the reverse or like a mirror image of what you are doing on your forehand volley. If you let that ball get even with or past your body you won't be able to execute an effective volley.

Point of Ball Contact

As you punch through at the ball, imagine you're pushing the ball with the open face of your hand. Push out and toward your target. Imagine you're carrying the ball toward your target with your racquet strings. Never take a full swing at the ball when you volley. The odds are stacked against you hitting a winner if you try to volley with a swing. Instead concentrate on watching that ball hit the face of your racquet. This isn't easy to do but it's the best way to make sure you'll be in position to hit variations on your volley.

Adjusting to Different Types of Volleys

The high backhand volley, the low wide volley or even the half-volley will require enormous concentration on your getting into position to execute the shot effectively.

At best, the high backhand volley is a difficult shot for any good player. A key element to proper execution is a firmly locked wrist. This enables your forearm to execute the stroke for you as you move your body weight into the ball. Remember to hit through at the ball, not down on it.

Use your knees and legs to raise and lower your body even with the path of flight to the oncoming ball. The lower the level of the oncoming shot, the lower you should bring your body. When you bend those knees you are also helping to keep your racquet head parallel with the ground at the moment the ball makes contact with your racquet.

The half-volley requires that you hit the ball the instant after it bounces. This is a defensive stroke used whenever your opponent returns a well hit ball at your feet as you approach the net. Most likely you'll use a half-volley in mid-court. The essential difference in this volley is that you are forced to let the ball hit the court just before you start your stroke. To execute a half-volley successfully you must get down with the ball as much as possible. Hit it in front of you using an upward motion to your racquet. Part of your stroking motion should be generated from your springing up as you hit the shot and continue in toward the net. Only a lot of practice with this shot will give you a sense of the timing, a feel to the motion and ability to judge the proper angle needed for your racquet face as you make the half-volley. Watch the ball all the way to your racquet. This is a difficult shot. To play winning tennis, it's best to avoid using it unless it's absolutely necessary.

13 | The Overhead Smash

Billie Jean King

Think of the overhead as a variation on the service motion. However, getting into position quickly for the overhead smash is critical to proper execution. The basic differences in physical action between the service motion and the overhead smash are that in the smash you should be:

(1)—keeping your weight on the balls of your feet (remember, in serving you begin with a comfortably firm stance).

(2)—taking a shorter backswing. However, you should still continue to let your racquet "scratch your back" as you prepare to hit the ball.

(3)—getting into position to hit a high lob, for example, may require a small jumping action to help keep the ball more in front of you as you begin your overhead.

Keep your head up and your eye on the ball during every overhead smash. To help you watch the ball use your free hand and point your index finger toward the ball. This also will assist you in maintaining your body balance.

As in serving, you should strive for a continuous, fluid motion and a smooth, easy stroke.

This insures greater accuracy in hitting the ball to the point at which you're aiming. If possible, try stepping forward while you're stroking your overhead. You'll automatically add power to your stroke. Strive first for accuracy then concentrate on adding power.

As a rule, on windy days let the ball bounce before you attempt an overhead smash during play. Letting the ball bounce gives you more time to get into position to hit it accurately. As another guideline, you'll find it's also better to let the ball bounce whenever it's hit to you shallow or in mid-court. On sunny days, letting the ball bounce allows you to get into a better position and avoid the glaring distraction of the sun.

The Statistics

1 | WTT Attendance

Individual Franchises and League Totals

Team	1974	1975	1976
Baltimore	40,472	—	—
Boston	56,404	—	—
Boston	—	30,789	59,180
Chicago	30,840	—	—
Cleveland	48,887	55,924	73,108
Denver	44,286	—	—
Detroit	48,978	—	—
Florida	44,227	—	—
Golden Gaters	54,080	47,345	87,208
Hawaii	32,191	56,470	67,452
Houston	38,366	—	—
Indiana	—	33,782	48,642
Los Angeles	38,807	28,970	103,370
Minnesota	62,165	—	—
New York	63,121	65,894	78,408
Philadelphia	92,364	—	—
Phoenix	—	80,140	148,544
Pittsburgh	66,270	82,270	102,608
San Diego	—	22,274	74,624
Toronto-Buffalo	72,508	—	—

Year	Playing Dates	Attendance	Average
1974	352	833,966	2,369
1975	165	503,858	3,053
1976	219	843,144	3,850
Total	736	2,180,968	3,091

Playoffs Attendance:

Year	Playoff Matches	Attendance	Average
*1974	10	31,481	3,148
1975	6	9,081	1,513
1976	5	21,093	4,219

*Two 1974 playoff matches are not included here because someone neglected to count the number of spectators. They were Minnesota vs Houston and Philadelphia vs Cleveland. Both were played on August 20, 1974.

Championship Series Attendance:

Year	Championship Matches	Total	Average
1974	2	9,539	4,769
1975	3	11,224	3,741
1976	3	13,925	4,641

All-Star Attendance:

Year	Attendance	Place
1975	7,112	Los Angeles
1976	12,581	Oakland

2 | Team Statistics

Final Season Standings:

1974

Eastern Division

Atlantic Section	W	L	Pct.	GB
Philadelphia	39	5	.886	—
Boston	19	25	.432	20
Baltimore	16	28	.364	23
New York	15	29	.341	24
Central Section				
Detroit	30	14	.682	—
Pittsburgh	30	14	.682	—
Cleveland	21	23	.477	8
Toronto-Buffalo	13	31	.295	17

Western Division

Gulf Plains Section	W	L	Pct.	GB
Minnesota	27	17	.614	—
Houston	24	19	.558	2½
Florida	19	25	.432	8
Chicago	15	29	.341	12
Pacific Section				
Denver	30	14	.682	—
Golden Gaters	23	21	.523	7
Los Angeles	16	28	.364	14
Hawaii	14	29	.326	15½

1975

Eastern Division

	W	L	Pct.	GB
Pittsburgh	36	8	.818	—
New York	34	10	.773	2
Boston	20	24	.455	17
Indiana	18	26	.409	18
Cleveland	16	28	.364	20

Western Division

	W	L	Pct.	GB
Golden Gaters	29	15	.659	—
Phoenix	22	22	.500	7
Los Angeles	20	24	.455	9
Hawaii	14	30	.318	15
San Diego	12	34	.272	17

1976

Eastern Division

	W	L	PCT	GB
New York	33	10	.767	—
Pittsburgh	24	20	.545	9½
Cleveland	20	24	.455	13½
Indiana	19	25	.432	14½
Boston	18	25	.419	15

Western Division

	W	L	PCT	GB
Phoenix	30	14	.682	—
Golden Gaters	28	16	.636	2
Los Angeles	22	22	.500	8
San Diego	13	31	.295	17
Hawaii	12	32	.273	18

Playoff Standings and Results:

1974

	W	L	Pct.	GW	GL
Denver	5	1	.833	170	130
Pittsburgh	3	1	.750	108	79
Philadelphia	3	3	.500	146	144
Minnesota	2	2	.500	92	101
Houston	1	1	.500	47	48
Cleveland	0	2	.000	44	49
Detroit	0	2	.000	27	63
Golden Gaters	0	2	.000	41	61

August 19, 1974
Denver 29, Golden Gaters 17 — Att. 2404 — at Denver
Houston 28, Minnesota 19 — Att. 1504 — at Houston
Pittsburgh 31, Detroit 10 — Att. 1622 — at Detroit
Phildelphia 26, Cleveland 22 — Att. 2148 — at Cleveland
August 20, 1974
Pittsburgh 32, Detroit 17 — Att. 3685 — at Pittsburgh
Minnesota 29, Houston 19 — Att. — — at Houston
Philadelphia 23, Cleveland 22 — Att. — — at Cleveland
Denver 32, Golden Gaters 24 — Att. 1971 — at Oakland
August 22, 1974
Phildelphia 31, Pittsburgh 21 — Att. 5362 — at Pittsburgh
Denver 29, Minnesota 18 — Att. 3126 — at Denver
August 23, 1974
Minnesota 26, Denver 25 — Att. 2547 — at Minnesota
Pittsburgh 24, Philadelphia 21 — Att. 7112 — at Philadelphia

1975

	W	L	Pct.	GW	GL
Pittsburgh	4	1	.800	122	95
Golden Gaters	3	2	.600	116	118
Boston	1	2	.333	55	72
Phoenix	1	2	.333	64	59
Los Angeles	0	1	.000	8	20
New York	0	1	.000	24	25

August 17, 1975
Phoenix 20, Los Angeles 8   Att. 1214   at Phoenix
Boston 25, New York 24   Att. 1025   at New York
August 18, 1975
Pittsburgh 25, Boston 16   Att. 912   at Boston
Golden Gaters 25, Phoenix 24   Att. 1308   at Phoenix
August 19, 1975
Pittsburgh 23, Boston 14   Att. 2803   at Pittsburgh
Golden Gaters 26, Phoenix 20   Att. 1819   at Golden Gaters

1976

	W	L	Pct.	GW	GL
New York	5	1	.833	173	130
Golden Gaters	2	3	.400	113	125
Pittsburgh	1	2	.333	73	82
Phoenix	0	2	.333	34	56

August 16, 1976
Golden Gaters 32, Phoenix 16,   Att. 5848   at Phoenix
August 17, 1976
Golden Gaters 24, Phoenix 18   Att. 6025   at Oakland
Pittsburgh 26, New York 25   Att. 3385   at Pittsburgh
August 18, 1976
New York 29, Pittsburgh 21   Att. 3227   at New York
August 19, 1976
New York 28, Pittsburgh 26   Att. 2608   at New York

Championship Series Results:

1974

August 25 at Denver	Phila.	Dvr.
WS— Francoise Durr (D) def. Billie Jean King (P), 6–4	4	6
MS— Andy Pattison (D) def. Brian Fairlie (P), 6–2	6	12
WD—Durr-Kristien Kemmer (D) def. Julie Anthony-King (P), 6–3	9	18
MD—Pattison-Tony Roche (D) def. Fairlie-Fred Stolle (P), 7–6	15	25
MX— Anthony-Stolle (P) def. Kemmer-Roche (D), 6–2	21	27

August 26 at Philadelphia	Dvr.	Phila.
WS—Billie Jean King (P) def. Francoise Durr (D), 6–4	4	6
MS— Andy Pattison (D) def. Buster Mottram (Brian Fairlie) (P), 6–0	10	6
WD—King-Julie Anthony (P) def. Durr-Kristien Kemmer (D), 7–6	16	13
MD—Brian Fairlie-Fred Stolle (P) def. Tony Roche-Pattison (D), 7–6	22	20
MX— Kemmer-Roche (D) ef. Anthony-Stolle (P), 6–4	28	24

1975

August 21 at Golden Gaters	Pgh.	GG
WD Evonne Goolagong (P) def. Ann Kiyomura/Ilana Kloss (GG), 6–4	6	4
MS— Tom Okker (GG) def. Mark Cox (P), 7–5	11	11
MD—Mark Cox-Vitas Gerulaitis (P) def. Frew McMillan-Okker (GG), 7–6 (tiebreaker 5–4)	18	17
WS—Goolagong (P) def. Betty Stove (GG), 6–3	24	20
MX—Stove-McMillan (GG) def. Peggy Michel-Kim Warwick (P), 6–1	25	26

August 24 at Pittsburgh	GG	Pgh.
WD—Evonne Goolagong-Peggy Michel (P) def. Ilana Kloss-Betty Stove (GG), 7–6 (tiebreaker 5–2)	6	7
WS—Goolagong (P) def. Stove (GG), 7–6 (tiebreaker 5–3)	12	14
MD—Mark Cox-Vitas Gerulaitis (P) def. Frew McMillan-Tom Okker (GG), 6–3	15	20
MS— Okker (GG) def. Gerulaitis (P), 6–4	21	24
MX— Michel-Cox (P) tied Kloss-McMillan (GG), 4–4*	25	28

August 25 at Pittsburgh	GG	Pgh.
WD—Ilana Kloss-Betty Stove (GG) def. Evonne Goolagong-Peggy Michel (P), 6–2	6	2
WS—Goolagong (P) def. Stove (GG), 6–2	8	8
MD—Mark Cox-Vitas Gerulaitis (P) def. Frew McMillan-Tom Okker (GG), 7–5	13	15
MS— Gerulaitis (P) def. Okker (GG), 6–1*	14	21

*—Match play suspended when team victory assured.

1976

August 21 at Oakland	NY	GG
MX— King/Dent (N) def. Durr/McMillan (G) 6–2	6	2
WS— Wade (N) def. Stove (G) 7–6 (5–3 TB)	13	8
MD—Dent/Mayer (N) def. McMillan/Okker (G) 6–4	19	12
MS— Mayer (N) def. Okker (G) 6–3	25	15
WD—Durr/Stove (G) def. King/Wade (N) 7–5	30	22
Overtime—King/Wade (N) def. Durr/Stove (G) 1–1	31	23

August 23 at Oakland	NY	GG
WD—Wade/King (N) def. Durr/Stove (G) 6–0	6	0
MS— Mayer (N) def. Okker (G) 6–1	12	1
MX— King/Dent (N) def. Stove/McMillan (G) 7–6 (5–2 TB)	19	7
WS— Durr (G) def. Wade (N) 7–5	24	14
MD—McMillan/Okker (G) def. Dent/Mayer (N) 6–4	28	20
Overtime: Dent/Mayer (N) def. McMillan/Okker (G) 1–1	29	21

August 27 at New York	NY	GG
MX— King/Dent (N) def. Stove/McMillan (G) 7–6 (5–3 TB)	7	6
MS— Mayer (N) def. Okker (G) 6–1	13	7
WD—Wade/King (N) def.Stove/Durr (G) 6–2	19	9
WS— Wade (N) def. Durr (G) 6–1	25	10
MD—Mayer/Dent (N) def. Okker/McMillan (G) 6–3	31	13

All-Star Games:

1975

In the first ever WTT All-Star game, the East powered past the West, 28–21, at the Los Angeles Sports Arena on July 21, 1975. A national television audience viewed the spectacle along with an arena crowd of 7,112.

	East	West
WD—Evonne Goolagong-Cawley (Pittsburgh)-Virginia Wade (New York) (EAST) def. Francoise Durr (Phoenix)-Betty Stove (Golden Gaters) (WEST), 6–3.	6	3
MS— Marty Riessen (Cleveland) (EAST) def. Tom Okker (Golden Gaters) (WEST), 6–4	12	7

MD— Mark Cox (Pittsburgh)-Bob Hewitt (Boston) (EAST) def. Vijay Amritraj (San Diego)-Frew McMillan (Golden Gaters) (WEST), 6–4   18   11
WS— Francoise Durr (Phoenix) (WEST) def. Billie Jean King (New York) (EAST), 6–4.   22   17
MX— Allan Stone (Indiana)-Billie Jean King (New York) (EAST) def. Geoff Masters (Los Angeles)-Rosie Casals (Los Angeles) (WEST), 6–4.   28   21

Rosters

East: Coach—Fred Stolle, New York
Boston—Bob Hewitt and Kerry Melville-Reid; Cleveland—Marty Riessen; Indiana—Allan Stone; New York—Billie Jean King and Virginia Wade; Pittsburgh—Evonne Goolagong-Cawley and Mark Cox. Ann Haydon Jones of Cleveland replaced Kerry Melville-Reid who was unable to play due to illness.
West: Coach—Tony Roche, Phoenix.
Golden Gaters—Tom Okker and Betty Stove; Hawaii—Margaret Court and John Newcombe; Los Angeles—Rosie Casals and Geoff Masters; Phoenix—Francoise Durr; San Diego—Vijay Amritraj. Helen Gourlay of Hawaii replaced Margaret Court who was unable to play due to illness; the Golden Gaters' Frew McMillan replaced John Newcombe who was unable to play due to injuries.

Female Most Valuable Player—Francoise Durr, Phoenix
Male Most Valuable Player—Marty Riessen, Golden Gaters

1976

In the second WTT All-Star match, the West avenged their defeat of the previous year by downing the East, 28–27, at the Oakland Coliseum on July 10, 1976. For the second year in a row, NBC televised the All-Star match. Along with the television audience, 12,581 saw the contest in person.

	East	West
MD— Rod Laver (San Diego)-Tom Okker (Golden Gaters) (WEST) def. John Alexander (Boston)-Phil Dent (New York) (EAST), 6–2.	2	6
WS— Evonne Goolagong (Pittsburgh) (EAST) def. Chris Evert (Phoenix) (WEST), 6–3.	8	9
MX— Billie Jean King (New York)-Sandy Mayer (New York) (EAST) def. Tony Roche (Phoenix)-Francoise Durr (Golden Gaters) (WEST), 6–2.	14	11
MS— Vitas Gerulaitis (Pittsburgh) (EAST) def. Bob Lutz (Los Angeles) (WEST), 7–6.	21	17
WD— Betty Stove (Golden Dianne Fromholtz (Los Angeles) (WEST) def. Virginia Wade (New York)-Martina Navratilova (Cleveland) (EAST), 7–6.	27	24
OVERTIME— Betty Stove (Golden Gaters)-Chris Evert (Phoenix) (WEST) def. Billie Jean King (New York)-Evonne Goolagong (Pittsburgh) (EAST), 4–0.	27	28

Rosters

East: Coach—Fred Stolle, New York
Boston—John Alexander; Cleveland—Martina Navratilova; New York—Billie Jean King, Sandy Mayer, Phil Dent, Virginia Wade; Pittsburgh—Evonne Goolagong, Vitas Gerulaitis.
West: Coach—Frew McMillan, Golden Gaters
Golden Gaters—Betty Stove, Tom Okker, Francoise Durr; Los Angeles—Dianne Fromholtz, Bob Lutz; Phoenix—Tony Roche, Chris Evert; San Diego, Rod Laver.

Female Most Valuable Player—Dianne Fromholtz, Los Angeles
Male Most Valuable Player—Tom Okker, Golden Gaters

3 | Individual Statistics

Awards

Because of WTT, tennis players suddenly have the opportunity to become Most Valuable Players and Rookies-of-the-Year. Such awards have been a part of professional sports—baseball, football, basketball, and hockey—for years but are new to the tennis world.

WTT individual honors are bestowed upon the players at the conclusion of the season, which makes more sense than bestowing them before the season. It is not surprising, therefore, to learn that WTT's individual awards are known as "Post-season Honors."

The individual WTT franchises play a large role in determining which players will receive a specific post-season honor because they are charged with polling the media in their respective areas to ascertain nominees for each award category. A media ballot is then held in each area and the ballots are forwarded to the league office, which in turn tabulates them and announces the winners.

Here is a rollcall of WTT's individual award winners for the first three years:

1974

Coach of the Year	Tony Roche, Denver Racquets
Most Valuable Player	Billie Jean King, Philadelphia Freedoms

1975

Coach of the Year	Frew McMillan, Golden Gaters
Female MVP	Evonne Goolagong, Pittsburgh Triangles
Male MVP	Tom Okker, Golden Gaters
Male Rookie of the Year	Marty Riessen, Cleveland Nets
Female Rookie of the Year	Greer Stevens, Boston Lobsters
All-Star Game Male MVP	Marty Riessen, Cleveland Nets
All-Star Game Female MVP	Francois Durr, Phoenix Racquets
Playoff MVP	Vitas Gerulaitis, Pittsburgh Triangles

1976

Coach of the Year	Fred Stolle, New York Sets
Female MVP	Chris Evert, Phoenix Racquets
Male MVP	Sandy Mayer, New York Sets
Male Rookie of the Year	Rod Laver, San Diego Friars
Female Rookie of the Year	Chris Evert, Phoenix Racquets
All-Star Game Male MVP	Tom Okker, Golden Gaters
All-Star Game Female MVP	Dianne Fromholtz Los Angeles Strings
Playoff MVP (Male)	Sandy Mayer, New York Sets
Playoff MVP (Female)	Billie Jean King, New York Sets

WTT Super Stars

WTT Super Star status is achieved by those players who come out on top in each of the league's five statistical categories. In 1974 and 1975, the respective Super Stars must have played in at least half of the sets available in a category and ranked in the top ten percentage-wise. In 1976, a qualifier must have played at least 132 games in a category to be eligible to become a Super Star.

1974

		Sets Played	Games won Pct.
Women's Singles	Billie Jean King, Philadelphia	56	.637
Men's Singles	John Newcombe, Houston	32	.593
Women's Doubles	Billie Jean King/Julie Anthony, Philadelphia	35	.645
Men's Doubles	John Newcombe/Dick Stockton, Houston	32	.583
Mixed Doubles	Kerry Harris/Allan Stone, Indiana	27	.578

1975

Women's Singles	Billie Jean King, New York	29	.641
Men's Singles	Marty Riessen, Cleveland	33	.570
Women's Doubles	Billie Jean King/Mona Guerrant, New York	26	.624
Men's Doubles	Frew McMillan/Tom Okker, Golden Gaters	41	.570
Mixed Doubles	No qualifiers		

1976

Women's Singles	Chris Evert, Phoenix	39	.700
Men's Singles	Sandy Mayer, New York	27	.575
Women's Doubles	Francoise Durr/Betty Stove, Golden Gaters	42	.575
Men's Doubles	Frew McMillan/Tom Okker, Golden Gaters	37	.582
Mixed Doubles	Ann Kiyomura/Ray Ruffels, Indiana	14	.599

Rankings:

1974

Women's Singles (Minimum 15 sets played)

	Sets	Pct.
*1. Billie Jean King, Philadelphia	56	.637
2. Rosie Casals, Detroit	50	.610
3. Evonne Goolagong, Pittsburgh	45	.589
4. Nancy Gunter, Cleveland	41	.585
5. Virginia Wade, New York	20	.548
6. Ann Jones, Minnesota	44	.548
7. Francoise Durr, Denver	48	.546
8. Kerry Melville, Boston	45	.519
9. Betty Ann Grubb, Florida	41	.512
10. Lesley Hunt, Golden Gaters	43	.506
11. Helen Gourlay, Houston	15	.503
12. Sue Stap, Chicago	39	.491

13. Marita Redondo, Los Angeles	46	.491
15. Pam Teeguarden, New York	27	.481
15. Karen Krantzcke, Houston	26	.472
16. Wendy Overton, Toronto-Buffalo	37	.456
17. Bridgitte Cuypers, Hawaii	22	.437
18. Val Ziegenfuss, Hawaii	24	.408
19. Kathy Kuykendall, Baltimore	20	.349
20. Joyce Hume, Baltimore	15	.286

Men's Singles (Minimum 15 sets played)

	Sets	Pct.
1. Jimmy Connors, Baltimore	18	.627
*2. John Newcombe, Houston	32	.593
3. Tom Okker, Toronto-Buffalo	42	.592
4. Dick Stockton, Houston	18	.572
5. Roy Emerson, Golden Gaters	17	.559
6. Ken Rosewall, Pittsburgh	51	.537
7. John Alexander, Los Angeles	22	.534
8. Andrew Pattison, Denver	45	.522
9. Cliff Drysdale, Florida	34	.511
10. Cliff Richey, Cleveland	42	.510
11. Buster Mottram, Philadelphia	32	.504
12. Phil Dent, Detroit	46	.497
13. Raz Reid, Boston	18	.493
14. Bob Carmichael, Baltimore	25	.492
15. Earl Buchholz, Chicago	22	.490
16. Nikki Pilic, New York	28	.489

*WTT Super Stars

Men's Doubles (Minimum 10 sets played)

	Sets	Pct.
*1. Newcombe—Stockton, Houston	32	.583
2. Davidson—Hewitt, Minnesota	33	.552
3. Pattison—Roche, Denver	39	.546
4. Alexander—Masters, Los Angeles	18	.544
5. Case—Machette, Hawaii	11	.540
6. Estep—Okker, Toronto-Buffalo	27	.531
7. Carmichael—Connors, Baltimore	10	.528
8. Emerson—McMillan, Golden Gaters	12	.525
9. Gerulaitis—Rosewall, Pittsburgh	15	.522
10. Dent—Stone, Detroit	34	.522
11. Cox—Drysdale, Florida	23	.522
12. Fairlie—Stolle, Philadelphia	35	.513
13. Graebner—Moore, Cleveland	42	.505
14. Battrick—Rosewall, Pittsburgh	24	.492
15. Bohrnstedt—McMillan, Golden Gaters	28	.491
16. Stillwell—Warwick, Chicago	18	.491
17. Buchholz—Warwick, Chicago	14	.486
18. Case—Ralston, Hawaii	15	.476
19. Pilic—Santana, New York	13	.465
20. Reid—Taylor, Boston	20	.465
21. Carmichael—Mukerjea, Baltimore	15	.460
22. Owens—Pilic, New York	10	.456
23. Chanfreau—Cramer	12	.398

Women's Doubles (Minimum 10 sets played)

	Sets	Pct.
*1. Anthony—King, Philadelphia	35	.645
2. Goolagong—Michel, Pittsburgh	37	.625
3. Durr—Kemmer, Denver	39	.565
4. Hume—Stove, Baltimore	39	.564
5. Beattie—Casals, Detroit	11	.561
6. Wade—Walsh, New York	12	.543
7. Casals—Harris, Detroit	29	.541
8. Bartkowicz—Gunter, Cleveland	20	.538
9. Bowrey—Krantzcke, Houston	15	.532
10. Bostrom—Melville, Boston	12	.532
11. Schallau—Turnbull, Minnesota	38	.532
12. Hunt—Kloss, Golden Gaters	36	.517
13. Harter—Susman, Los Angeles	38	.498
14. Bostrom—Newberry, Boston	23	.475
15. Stap—Young, Chicago	36	.460
16. Gourlay—Krantzcke, Houston	22	.449
17. Kiyomura—Ziegenfuss, Hawaii	26	.448
18. Fleming—Grubb, Florida	31	.446
19. Wade—Teeguarden, New York	10	.402
20. Overton—Rossouw, Toronto-Buffalo	28	.393

*WTT Super Stars

Mixed Doubles (Minimum 10 sets played)

	Sets	Pct.
1. Bartkowicz—Graebner, Cleveland	10	.632
*2. Harris—Stone, Detroit	27	.578
3. Fleming—Cox, Florida	24	.565
4. Anthony—Stolle, Philadelphia	48	.559
5. Stove—Carmichael, Baltimore	18	.556
6. Kemmer—Roche, Denver	29	.552
7. Kiyomura—Ralston, Hawaii	12	.546
8. Schallau—Lloyd, Minnesota	10	.537
9. Teeguarden—Owens, New York	10	.536
10. Kloss—McMillan, Golden Gaters	25	.529
11. Overton—Estep, Toronto-Buffalo	17	.524
12. Bowrey—Stockton, Houston	13	.523
14. Susman—Masters, Los Angeles	36	.517
15. Jones—Lloyd, Minnesota	26	.513
16. Michel—Battrick, Pittsburgh	20	.505
17. O'Neill—Estep, Toronto-Buffalo	20	.502
18. Young—Warwick, Chicago	13	.495
19. Bostrom—Tiriac, Boston	13	.487
20. Dupont—Moore, Cleveland	10	.470
21. Beattie—Stone, Detroit	13	.464
22. Fernandez—Gerulaitis, Pittsburgh	16	.460
23. Dupont—Graebner, Cleveland	15	.459
24. Young—Stilwell, Chicago	15	.434

1975

Women's Singles

	SP	SW	SL	GW	GL	PCT
*1. Billie Jean King, New York	29	23	6	161	90	.641
2. Evonne Goolagong, Pittsburgh	40	33	7	227	132	.632
3. Rosemary Casals, Los Angeles	40	27	13	209	145	.590
4. Nancy Gunter, Pittsburgh	2	2	0	13	10	.565
5. Virginia Wade, New York	15	10	5	77	69	.527
6. Francoise Durr, Phoenix	42	21	21	201	181	.526
7. Betty Stove, Golden Gaters	40	22	18	195	177	.524
8. Greer Stevens, Boston	10	5	5	51	48	.515
9. Kerry Melville Reid, Boston	33	20	13	162	154	.513
10. Margaret Court, Hawaii	27	15	12	131	126	.510
11. Sue Stap, Cleveland	15	6	9	60	66	.476
12. Peggy Michel, Pittsburgh	2	1	1	8	9	.471
13. Kristien Kemmer-Shaw, Philadelphia	1	0	1	6	7	.462
14. Ann Jones, Cleveland	26	9	17	118	143	.452
15. Lesley Hunt, San Diego	26	9	17	116	147	.442
16. Carrie Meyer, Indiana	28	8	20	118	157	.430
17. Valerie Ziegenfuss, Boston	2	1	1	9	12	.429
18. Kathy Kuykendall, Hawaii	18	4	14	75	103	.421
19. Wendy Turnbull, Boston	1	0	1	4	6	.400
20. Wendy Overton, Indiana	15	5	10	52	•78	.400
21. Helen Gourlay, Hawaii	2	0	2	7	12	.368
22. Brigette Cuypers, San Diego	17	3	14	55	105	.344
23. Valerie Ziegenfuss, Cleveland	1	0	1	4	9	.308
24. Bettyann Stuart, Los Angeles	4	0	4	10	25	.285
25. Ilana Kloss, Golden Gaters	3	0	3	7	18	.280
26. Laura DuPont, Cleveland	2	0	2	3	10	.231
27. Marita Redondo, San Diego	2	0	2	3	12	.200
28. Ann Kiyomura, Golden Gaters	1	0	1	1	4	.200
29. Pat Bostrom, Indiana	1	0	1	1	6	.143
30. Stephanie Tolleson, Phoenix	1	0	1	1	6	.143

*WTT Super Star

Men's Singles

	SP	SW	SL	GW	GL	PCT
*1. Marty Riessen, Cleveland	33	25	8	187	141	.570
2. Mark Cox, Pittsburgh	20	15	5	115	89	.564
3. John Newcombe, Hawaii	11	8	3	59	47	.557
4. Tom Okker, Golden Gaters	42	24	18	230	202	.532
5. Vijay Amritraj, San Diego	33	19	14	180	158	.532
6. Tony Roche, Philadelphia	7	4	3	40	37	.519
7. John Andrews, San Diego	5	4	1	28	26	.519
8. Ray Ruffels, Indiana	20	10	10	99	93	.516
9. Andrew Pattison, Phoenix	12	6	6	61	58	.513
10. Allan Stone, Indiana	21	10	11	102	97	.512
11. Sandy Mayer, New York	41	22	19	211	202	.511
12. Dick Bohrnstedt, Golden Gaters	2	1	1	9	9	.500
13. Vitas Gerulaitis, Pittsburgh	23	12	11	115	117	.496
14. Bob Lutz, Los Angeles	27	15	12	131	134	.494
15. Dennis Ralston, San Diego	6	2	4	31	32	.492
16. Bob Hewitt, Boston	19	9	10	88	99	.471
17. Butch Buchholz, Hawaii	33	11	22	149	168	.470
18. Brian Fairlie, Phoenix	21	8	13	96	110	.466
19. Geoff Masters, Los Angeles	8	2	6	39	48	.448
20. Raz Reid, Boston	21	8	13	88	112	.440
21. Bob Giltinan, Cleveland	11	4	7	41	53	.436
22. Shushi Menon, San Diego	1	0	1	5	7	.417
23. Ion Tiriac, Boston	6	1	5	22	31	.415
24. Tom Edelfsen, Hawaii	2	1	1	9	13	.409
25. Ross Case, Los Angeles	9	0	9	37	57	.394
26. Jeff Austin, Phoenix	4	1	3	14	22	.389
27. Roy Barth, Indiana	3	0	3	9	15	.375
28. Fred Stolle, New York	1	0	1	3	6	.333
29. Kim Warwick, Pittsburgh	1	0	1	3	6	.333
30. Mike Machette, San Diego	1	0	1	2	6	.250
31. Charlie Owens, New York	2	0	2	3	12	.200

*WTT Super Star

Men's Doubles

	SP	SW	SL	GW	GL	PCT
1. Leonard/Andrews, San Diego	1	1	0	6	2	.750
2. Okker/Bohrnstedt, Golden Gaters	1	1	0	6	4	.600
*3. McMillan/Okker, Golden Gaters	41	31	10	223	168	.570
4. Tiriac/Hewitt, Boston	37	24	13	199	159	.556
5. Ruffels/Stone, Indiana	39	22	17	204	166	.552
6. Roche/Fairlie, Phoenix	21	14	7	113	94	.546
7. Davidson/Newcombe, Hawaii	8	4	4	44	37	.543
8. Gerulaitis/Cox, Pittsburgh	20	13	7	108	94	.535
9. Mayer/Owens, New York	2	1	1	10	9	.526
10. Pattison/Roche, Phoenix	3	2	1	20	19	.513
11. Riessen/Graebner, Cleveland	26	13	13	134	128	.511
12. Case/Lutz, Los Angeles	5	3	2	26	25	.510
13. Masters/Case, Los Angeles	38	22	16	197	191	.508
14. McMillan/Bohrnstedt, Golden Gaters	2	1	1	9	9	.500
15. Fairlie/Austin, Phoenix	2	1	1	9	9	.500
16. Cox/Warwick, Pittsburgh	12	6	6	62	63	.496
17. Austin/Pattison, Phoenix	9	5	4	45	46	.495
18. Mayer/Stolle, New York	42	19	23	198	206	.489
19. Buchholz/Newcombe, Hawaii	12	5	7	59	64	.480
20. Reid/Hewitt, Boston	7	4	3	32	35	.478
21. V. Amritraj/A. Amritraj, San Diego	27	10	17	124	141	.468
22. Riessen/Giltinan, Cleveland	11	4	7	48	55	.466
23. Stone/Barth, Indiana	5	1	4	23	27	.460
24. Buchholz/Davidson, Hawaii	12	4	8	52	61	.460
25. Giltinan/Graebner, Cleveland	7	2	5	32	39	.451
26. Ralston/Andrews, San Diego	9	2	7	40	49	.449
27. Gerulaitis/Warwick, Pittsburgh	12	3	9	48	63	.432

		SP	SW	SL	GW	GL	PCT
28.	Buchholz/Edelfsen, Hawaii	14	4	10	58	80	.420
29.	Tiriac/Reid, Boston	2	0	2	9	13	.409
30.	Austin/Roche, Phoenix	8	1	7	34	51	.400
31.	V. Amritraj/Andrews, San Diego	1	0	1	4	6	.400
32.	Ralston/Machette, San Diego	1	0	1	3	6	.333
33.	Menon/Machette, San Diego	1	0	1	3	6	.333
34.	A. Amritraj/Ralston, San Diego	3	0	3	8	18	.308
35.	Ralston/Cowan, San Diego	2	0	2	4	12	.250
36.	Case/Machette, Los Angeles	1	0	1	2	6	.250
37.	Austin/Taylor, Phoenix	1	0	1	1	6	.143
38.	V. Amritraj/Ralston, San Diego	1	0	1	1	7	.125

*WTT Super Star

Women's Doubles

		SP	SW	SL	GW	GL	PCT
1.	Shaw/Tolleson, Philadelphia	2	2	0	13	6	.684
2.	Turnbull/Troll, Boston	1	1	0	6	3	.667
3.	Fox/Michel, Pittsburgh	2	2	0	12	7	.632
4.	King/Schallau, New York	26	21	5	146	88	.624
5.	Wade/Schallau, New York	6	5	1	37	24	.607
6.	Goolagong/Michel, Pittsburgh	37	30	7	204	136	.600
7.	King/Wade, New York	12	9	3	69	46	.600
8.	Casals/Stuart, Los Angeles	20	13	7	99	83	.543
9.	Durr/Shaw, Philadelphia	42	25	17	216	185	.540
10.	Kiyomura/Kloss, Golden Gaters	32	22	10	161	136	.539
11.	Court/Pigeon, Hawaii	3	2	1	14	12	.538
12.	Turnbull/Stevens, Boston	17	8	9	81	74	.523
13.	Court/Cuypers, Hawaii	4	2	2	21	20	.512
14.	Stuart/Harter, Los Angeles	18	7	11	88	90	.494
15.	Casals/Harter, Los Angeles	6	3	3	31	33	.484
16.	Bostrom/Meyer, Indiana	14	7	7	62	69	.473
17.	Stove/Kloss, Golden Gaters	4	1	3	17	19	.472
18.	Court/Gourlay, Hawaii	24	9	15	105	120	.467
19.	Cuypers/Redondo, San Diego	1	0	1	6	7	.462
20.	Stove/Kiyomura, Golden Gaters	8	4	4	35	41	.460
21.	Jones/Stap, Cleveland	22	9	13	91	107	.459
22.	Hunt/Young, San Diego	26	10	16	114	137	.454
23.	Jones/DuPont, Cleveland	14	4	10	65	79	.451
24.	Ziegenfuss/Reid, Boston	16	4	12	71	87	.449
25.	Young/Gourlay, San Diego	3	1	2	15	19	.441
26.	Bostrom/Overton, Indiana	16	6	10	61	78	.439
27.	Meyer/Overton, Indiana	14	4	10	61	78	.439
28.	Jones/Ziegenfuss, Cleveland	3	1	2	14	18	.438
29.	Ziegenfuss/Turnbull, Boston	5	2	3	20	26	.435
30.	Hunt/Cuypers, San Diego	8	2	6	32	46	.410
31.	Stap/Ziegenfuss, Cleveland	5	1	4	20	29	.408
32.	Fox/Goolagong, Pittsburgh	3	1	2	11	16	.407
33.	Court/Beattie, Hawaii	1	0	1	4	6	.400
34.	Stevens/Reid, Boston	4	0	4	17	27	.386
35.	Turnbull/Reid, Boston	3	1	2	10	16	.385
36.	Gourlay/Kuykendall, Hawaii	13	4	9	47	76	.382
37.	Young/Cuypers, San Diego	8	1	7	26	47	.356
38.	Fox/Gunter, Pittsburgh	2	0	2	6	13	.316
39.	Young/Troll, San Diego	0	0	0	0	1	.000
40.	Court/Kuykendall, Hawaii	1	0	1	0	6	.000

*WTT Super Star

Mixed Doubles

	SP	SW	SL	GW	GL	PCT.
1. Stevens/Drake, Boston	1	1	0	6	2	.750
2. Hunt/Machette, San Diego	1	1	0	6	2	.750
3. Cuypers/V. Amritraj, San Diego	1	1	0	6	3	.667
4. Reid/Drake, Boston	1	1	0	6	3	.667
5. Stap/Riessen, Cleveland	1	1	0	6	3	.667
6. Turnbull/Hewitt, Boston	5	3	2	25	13	.658
7. Harter/Case, Los Angeles	3	3	0	17	9	.654
8. King/Stolle, New York	8	7	1	46	27	.630
9. Reid/Tiriac, Boston	2	2	0	13	8	.619
10. Stevens/Tiriac, Boston	3	2	1	17	11	.607
11. Stevens/Hewitt, Boston	1	1	0	6	4	.600
12. Gourlay/Schoen, San Diego	1	1	0	6	4	.600
13. Stove/Bohrnstedt, Golden Gaters	3	2	1	16	11	.593
14. Kuykendall/Newcombe, Hawaii	2	2	0	13	9	.591
15. Redondo/Ralston, San Diego	1	1	0	7	5	.583
16. Gourlay/Newcombe, Hawaii	9	8	1	60	44	.577
17. Meyer/Stone, Indiana	3	2	1	19	14	.576
18. Wade/Stolle, New York	10	7	3	51	38	.573
19. Stuart/Case, Los Angeles	4	3	1	20	15	.571
20. Schallau/Stolle, New York	13	8	5	67	51	.568
21. Schallau/Owens, New York	9	7	2	51	39	.567
22. Stove/McMillan, Golden Gaters	13	9	4	77	59	.566
23. Michel/Cox, Pittsburgh	8	5	3	45	36	.556
24. Stap/Graebner, Cleveland	20	13	7	113	92	.551
25. Meyer/Ruffels Indiana	2	1	1	11	9	.550
26. Kloss/McMillan, Golden Gaters	4	2	2	17	14	.548
27. Michel/Gerulaitis, Pittsburgh	3	2	1	17	14	.548
28. Casals/Masters, Los Angeles	17	12	5	105	87	.545
29. Stuart/Lutz, Los Angeles	3	2	1	13	11	.542
30. Overton/Barth, Indiana	3	2	1	13	11	.542
31. Goolagong/Warwick, Pittsburgh	1	1	0	7	6	.538
32. Young/Leonard, San Diego	1	1	0	7	6	.538
33. Ziegenfuss/Hewitt, Boston	1	1	0	7	6	.538
34. Dalgren/Edelfsen, Hawaii	1	1	0	7	6	.538
35. Turnbull/Tiriac, Boston	7	5	2	41	36	.532
36. Fox/Cox, Pittsburgh	2	1	1	9	8	.529
37. Jones/Riessen, Cleveland	3	2	1	19	17	.528
38. Stap/Giltinan, Cleveland	2	1	1	11	10	.524
39. Cuypers/Andrews, San Diego	2	1	1	12	11	.522
40. Harter/Masters, Los Angeles	7	4	3	37	34	.521
41. Cuypers/Ralston, San Diego	6	3	3	27	25	.519
42. Bostrom/Ruffels, Indiana	5	3	2	28	26	.519
43. Fox/Warwick, Pittsburgh	11	7	4	60	56	.517

1976

Women's Singles

		SP	SW	SL	GW	GL	GWP
*1.	Chris Evert, Phoenix	39	33	6	226	97	.700
2.	Evonne Goolagong, Pittsburgh	38	32	6	215	121	.640
3.	Billie Jean King, New York	14	12	2	80	50	.615
4.	Martina Navratilova, Cleveland	44	26	18	227	198	.534
5.	Virginia Wade, New York	29	16	13	146	129	.531
6.	Rosie Casals, Los Angeles	15	8	7	67	66	.504
7.	Dianne Fromholtz, Los Angeles	29	14	15	131	136	.491
8.	Margaret Court, Hawaii	3	1	2	14	16	.467
9.	Nancy Richey Gunter, Hawaii	34	14	20	150	172	.466
10.	Francoise Durr, Golden Gaters	14	7	7	61	70	.466
11.	Mona Guerrant, Indiana	34	13	21	153	180	.459
12.	Kerry Reid, Boston	26	10	16	115	142	.447
13.	Marcie Louie, Hawaii	9	3	6	33	42	.440
14.	Ann Kiyomura, Indiana	1	0	1	7	9	.438
15.	Terry Holladay, San Diego	42	13	29	170	228	.427
16.	Betty Stove, Golden Gaters	30	11	19	118	161	.423
17.	Pam Teeguarden, Boston	6	1	5	23	32	.418
18.	Greer Stevens, Boston	11	3	8	38	57	.400
19.	Kristien Shaw, Phoenix	3	1	2	11	18	.379
20.	Stephanie Tolleson, Phoenix	2	0	2	6	12	.333
21.	Carrie Meyer, Indiana	9	1	8	20	47	.299
22.	Helen Gourlay, Hawaii	1	0	1	2	6	.250
23.	Sue Stap, Hawaii	4	0	4	5	20	.200
24.	Bettyann Stuart, San Diego	2	0	2	3	12	.200

*WTT Super Star

Men's Singles

		SP	SW	SL	GW	GL	GWP
1.	Cliff Richey, Los Angeles	1	1	0	6	3	.667
2.	Ross Case, San Diego	4	4	0	26	18	.591
*3.	Sandy Mayer, New York	27	19	8	154	114	.575
4.	Rod Laver, San Diego	35	23	12	188	158	.543
5.	Jeff Borowiak, Golden Gaters	4	2	2	19	16	.543
6.	Bob Lutz, Los Angeles	19	10	9	95	84	.531
7.	Tom Okker, Golden Gaters	38	23	15	210	186	.530
8.	Marty Riessen, Cleveland	28	15	13	145	134	.520
9.	Tony Roche, Phoenix	7	4	3	37	35	.514
10.	Cliff Drysdale, San Diego	5	2	3	28	27	.509
11.	Ilie Nastase, Hawaii	35	20	15	179	176	.504
12.	Vitas Gerulaitis, Pittsburgh	35	18	17	175	173	.503
13.	Allan Stone, Indiana	24	11	13	123	123	.500
14.	Bernie Mitton, Pittsburgh	9	4	5	47	47	.500
15.	Vijay Amritraj, Los Angeles	19	9	10	93	98	.487
16.	Andrew Pattison, Phoenix	35	15	20	171	187	.478
17.	Charles Pasarell, Los Angeles	4	1	3	20	22	.476
18.	John Alexander, Boston	43	18	25	203	224	.475
19.	Haroon Rahim, Cleveland	16	7	9	78	91	.462
20.	Ray Ruffels, Indiana	20	7	13	91	111	.450
21.	Dick Stockton, Hawaii	2	1	1	9	11	.450
22.	Phil Dent, New York	15	4	11	58	81	.417
23.	John Lucas, Golden Gaters	2	0	2	7	10	.412
24.	Butch Buchholz, Hawaii	5	1	4	18	29	.383
25.	Fred Stolle, New York	1	0	1	3	6	.333
26.	Butch Walts, Phoenix	2	0	2	5	12	.294
27.	Ken Rosewall, Hawaii	2	0	2	5	12	.294
28.	Ashok Amritraj, Los Angeles	1	0	1	1	6	.143

*WTT Super Star

Men's Doubles

		SP	SW	SL	GW	GL	GWP
1.	A. Amritraj/V. Amritraj, Los Angeles	1	1	0	6	1	.857
2.	Rosewall/Davidson, Hawaii	1	1	0	6	3	.667
3.	Pasarell/V. Amritraj, Los Angeles	2	2	0	12	7	.632
4.	Mayer/Stolle, New York	3	3	0	18	11	.621
*5.	McMillan/Okker, Golden Gaters	37	27	10	206	148	.582
6.	Lutz/V. Amritraj, Los Angeles	18	14	4	105	83	.559
7.	Cox/Mitton, Pittsburgh	21	14	7	123	98	.557
8.	Mayer/Dent, New York	39	23	16	219	181	.548
9.	Ball/Ruffels, Indiana	11	7	4	61	52	.540
10.	Riessen/Gildemeister, Cleveland	1	1	0	7	6	.538
11.	Alexander/Brown, Boston	3	2	1	11	10	.524
12.	Laver/Case, San Diego	33	17	16	171	158	.520
13.	Ralston/Lutz, Los Angeles	8	4	4	46	43	.517
14.	Roche/Pattison, Phoenix	27	17	10	140	131	.517
15.	Alexander/Tiriac, Boston	32	16	16	176	173	.504
16.	Walts/Pattison, Phoenix	11	5	6	52	52	.500
17.	Cheney/Pattison, Phoenix	1	1	0	7	7	.500
18.	Nastase/Davidson, Hawaii	20	8	12	113	118	.489
19.	Rahim/Gildemeister, Cleveland	3	1	2	18	19	.486
20.	Stone/Ruffels, Indiana	19	9	10	97	103	.485
21.	Riessen/Rahim, Cleveland	39	18	21	198	218	.476
22.	Alexander/Estep, Boston	6	3	3	28	32	.467
23.	Cox/Gerulaitis, Pittsburgh	10	3	7	49	57	.462
24.	Nastase/Buchholz, Hawaii	1	0	1	6	7	.462
25.	Cheney/Walts, Phoenix	1	0	1	6	7	.462
26.	Dent/Stolle, New York	1	0	1	6	7	.462
27.	Mitton/Gerulaitis, Pittsburgh	13	6	7	58	68	.460
28.	Borowiak/McMillan, Golden Gaters	5	2	3	17	20	.459
29.	Case/Drysdale, San Diego	5	2	3	23	28	.451
30.	Walts/Roche, Phoenix	3	1	2	15	19	.441
31.	Drysdale/Laver, San Diego	6	2	4	27	35	.435
32.	Pasarell/Lutz, Los Angeles	8	3	5	35	47	.427
33.	Stone/Ball, Indiana	14	3	11	61	86	.415
34.	Estep/Tiriac, Boston	2	0	2	8	12	.400
35.	Cheney/Roche, Phoenix	1	0	1	4	6	.400
36.	Lucas/Okker, Golden Gaters	1	0	1	4	6	.400
37.	Pasarell/Ralston, Los Angeles	5	1	4	20	31	.392
38.	Buchholz/Davidson, Hawaii	21	2	19	78	130	.375
39.	Borowiak/Okker, Golden Gaters	1	0	1	3	6	.333
40.	Stockton/Davidson, Hawaii	1	0	1	3	6	.333
41.	Giltinan/Riessen, Cleveland	1	0	1	2	4	.333
42.	A. Amritraj/Ralston, Los Angeles	1	0	1	2	6	.250
43.	Richey/Ralston, Los Angeles	1	0	1	1	6	.143

*WTT Super Star

Women's Doubles

		SP	SW	SL	GW	GL	GWP
1.	Kiyomura/Meyer, Indiana	1	1	0	6	3	.667
*2.	Durr/Stove, Golden Gaters	42	30	12	226	167	.575
3.	Goolagong/Russell, Pittsburgh	17	11	6	90	70	.563
4.	Kiyomura/Guerrant, Indiana	43	28	15	229	180	.560
5.	Wade/King, New York	40	27	13	220	178	.553
6.	Navratilova/Overton, Cleveland	42	27	15	222	184	.547
7.	Evert/Shaw, Phoenix	38	24	14	205	170	.547
8.	Michel/Goolagong, Pittsburgh	12	6	6	63	57	.525
9.	Stuart/Young, San Diego	8	4	4	40	37	.519
10.	Casals/Fromholtz, Los Angeles	9	5	4	46	45	.505

11.	Court/Gourlay, Hawaii	3	1	2	16	17	.485
12.	Casals/Jones, Los Angeles	29	13	16	129	140	.480
13.	Stove/Giscafre, Golden Gaters	2	1	1	10	11	.476
14.	Stevens/Teeguarden, Boston	20	8	12	86	98	.467
15.	Teeguarden/Reid, Boston	17	7	10	77	90	.461
16.	Court/Gunter, Hawaii	20	7	13	85	106	.445
17.	Stuart/Holladay, San Diego	36	12	24	147	186	.441
18.	Reid/Stevens, Boston	6	2	4	24	32	.429
19.	Jones/Fromholtz, Los Angeles	6	2	4	23	32	.418
20.	Stap/Russell, Pittsburgh	10	1	9	39	59	.398
21.	Gunter/Gourlay, Hawaii	8	0	8	33	52	.388
22.	Stap/Gourlay, Hawaii	10	1	9	38	61	.384
23.	Shaw/Tolleson, Phoenix	5	0	5	14	32	.304
24.	Gunter/Michel, Pittsburgh	5	1	4	12	30	.286
25.	Louie/Stap, Hawaii	1	0	1	2	6	.250
26.	Overton/Fox, Cleveland	2	0	2	3	12	.200
27.	Beaven/Siegelman, New York	2	0	2	3	12	.200
28.	Tolleson/Farood, Phoenix	1	0	1	1	6	.143
29.	Beaven/Wade, New York	1	0	1	1	6	.143
30.	Louie/Gourlay, Hawaii	2	0	2	1	2	.077

*WTT Super Star

Mixed Doubles

		SP	SW	SL	GW	GL	GWP
1.	Evert/Roche, Phoenix	0	0	0	1	0	1.000
2.	Tolleson/Roche, Phoenix	2	2	0	12	4	.750
3.	Wade/Mayer, New York	1	1	0	6	2	.750
4.	Stove/Borowiak, Golden Gaters	1	1	0	6	2	.750
5.	Durr/Okker, Golden Gaters	1	1	0	6	2	.750
6.	Stap/Nastase, Hawaii	1	1	0	6	3	.667
7.	Court/Nastase, Hawaii	6	6	0	41	26	.612
8.	Stove/Lucas, Golden Gaters	1	1	0	6	4	.600
*9.	Kiyomura/Ruffels, Indiana	14	12	2	82	55	.599
10.	King/Dent, New York	14	10	4	79	54	.594
11.	Casals/Pasarell, Los Angeles	1	1	0	7	5	.583
12.	Stuart/Hagey, San Diego	4	3	1	22	16	.579
13.	King/Mayer, New York	12	8	4	69	52	.570
14.	Shaw/Pattison, Phoenix	2	2	0	13	10	.565
15.	Gourlay/Buchholz, Hawaii	1	1	0	9	7	.563
16.	Teeguarden/Estep, Boston	4	2	2	23	18	.561
17.	Jones/Lutz, Los Angeles	2	2	0	14	11	.560
18.	Durr/McMillan, Golden Gaters	29	19	10	156	123	.559
19.	Goolagong/Cox, Pittsburgh	10	7	3	54	45	.545
20.	Casals/Lutz, Los Angeles	13	7	6	68	58	.540
21.	Stap/Mitton, Pittsburgh	3	1	2	16	14	.533
22.	Casals/Ralston, Los Angeles	14	8	6	71	63	.530
23.	Stevens/Estep, Boston	35	22	13	184	163	.530
24.	Wade/Dent, New York	10	5	5	48	43	.527
25.	Shaw/Roche, Phoenix	17	10	7	91	84	.520
26.	Court/Davidson, Hawaii	17	10	7	81	75	.519
27.	Casals/V. Amritraj, Los Angeles	7	3	4	36	37	.493
28.	Stove/McMillan, Golden Gaters	11	5	6	54	56	.491
29.	Gourlay/Nastase, Hawaii	5	2	3	24	25	.490
30.	Russell/Cox, Pittsburgh	23	10	13	115	120	.489
31.	Kiyomura/Ball, Indiana	25	11	14	124	131	.486
32.	Shaw/Walts, Phoenix	15	6	9	72	77	.483
33.	Stuart/Case, San Diego	32	14	18	153	168	.477
34.	Overton/Gildemeister, Cleveland	21	12	9	96	107	.473
35.	Russell/Mitton, Pittsburgh	3	1	2	15	17	.469
36.	Tolleson/Walts, Phoenix	4	1	3	20	23	.465
37.	Fox/Rahim, Cleveland	7	3	4	32	37	.464
38.	Overton/Riessen, Cleveland	3	1	2	12	14	.462
39.	Michel/Cox, Pittsburgh	3	1	2	11	14	.440

40.	Gourlay/Davidson, Hawaii	13	5	8	52	68	.433
41.	Guerrant/Ruffels, Indiana	1	0	1	5	7	.417
42.	Meyer/Ball, Indiana	1	0	1	5	7	.417
43.	Tolleson/Cheney, Phoenix	1	0	1	5	7	.417
44.	Jones/Pasarell, Los Angeles	1	0	1	5	7	.417
45.	Goolagong/Gerulaitis, Pittsburgh	1	0	1	4	6	.400
46.	Navratilova/Rahim, Cleveland	1	0	1	4	6	.400
47.	Meyer/Ruffels, Indiana	1	0	1	4	6	.400
48.	Reid/Estep, Boston	1	0	1	4	6	.400
49.	Fromholtz/Lutz, Los Angeles	1	0	1	4	6	.400

*WTT Super Star

Individual Records

MEN:

		SINGLES		DOUBLES		MIXED		TOTALS	
		GW-GL	PCT	GW-GL	PCT	GW-GL	PCT	GW-GL	PCT
John Alexander	LA-1974	—		129-159	.488	76-88	.463	205-247	.454
	BOS-1976	203-224	.475	215-215	.500	—	—	418-439	.488
	TOTALS	203-224	.475	344-374	.479	76-88	.463	623-686	.476
Anand Amritraj	SD-1975	—		132-159	.453	76-88	.463	208-247	.457
	LA-1976	—		8-7	.533	—		8-7	.533
	TOTALS	—		140-166	.456	76-88	.463	216-254	.460
Ashok Amritraj	LA-1976	1-6	.143	—		—		1-6	.143
Vijay Amritraj	SD-1975	180-158	.532	129-154	.456	6-3	.667	315-315	.500
	LA-1976	93-98	.487	123-91	.575	36-37	.493	252-226	.527
	TOTALS	273-256	.516	252-245	.507	42-40	.512	567-541	.512
John Andrews	SD-1975	28-26	.519	50-57	.467	26-30	.464	104-113	.479
Jeff Austin	DEN-1974	—		37-34	.521	90-107	.457	127-141	.474
	PHX-1975	14-22	.389	88-106	.454	146-174	.456	248-302	.451
	TOTALS	14-22	.389	125-140	.472	236-281	.456	375-443	.458
Syd Ball	IND-1976	—		122-138	.469	134-150	.472	256-288	.471
Roy Barth	IND-1975	9-15	.375	23-27	.460	84-104	.447	116-146	.443
Gerald Battrick	PITT-1974	6-2	.750	133-138	.490	128-120	.516	267-260	.507
Mike Belkin	FLA-1974	13-26	.333	14-21	.400	15-14	.517	42-61	.408
Byron Bertram	BALT-1974	23-30	.433	43-65	.398	—		66-95	.410
Dick Bohrnstedt	GG-1974	132-178	.425	151-153	.496	7-18	.280	290-349	.454
	GG-1975	9-9	.500	15-13	.536	103-126	.450	127-148	.462
	TOTALS	141-187	.430	166-166	.500	110-144	.433	417-497	.456
Jeff Borowiak	GG-1976	19-16	.543	—		6-2	.750	25-18	.581
Bill Bowrey	HOU-1974	—		35-39	.472	71-64	.525	106-103	.507
Butch Buchholz	CHI-1974	100-104	.490	86-96	.472	22-20	.523	208-220	.486
	HAW-1975	149-168	.470	169-208	.448	15-20	.429	333-396	.457
	HAW-1976	18-29	.383	84-137	.380	10-13	.435	112-179	.447
	TOTALS	267-301	.470	339-441	.435	47-53	.470	653-795	.451
Don Candy	BALT-1974	—		—		13-18	.419	13-18	.419
Bob Carmichael	BALT-1974	126-130	.492	147-168	.466	153-134	.533	426-432	.496

		SINGLES		DOUBLES		MIXED		TOTALS	
		GW-GL	PCT	GW-GL	PCT	GW-GL	PCT	GW-GL	PCT
Ross Case	HAW-1974	171-211	.447	132-130	.503	27-24	.529	330-365	.475
	LA-1975	37-57	.394	225-222	.503	37-24	.607	299-303	.497
	SD-1976	26-18	.591	194-186	.511	171-204	.456	391-408	.489
	TOTALS	234-286	.450	551-538	.506	235-252	.483	1020-1076	.48
J.B. Chanfreau	LA-1974	—		63-86	.422	20-21	.487	83-107	.437
Brian Cheney	PHX-1976	—		17-20	.459	8-13	.381	25-33	.431
Jimmy Connors	BALT-1974	106- 63	.627*	56-50	.528	6-4	.600	168-117	.589
Jeff Cowan	SD-1975	—		4-12	.250	—		4-12	.250
Mark Cox	FLA-1974	28-30	.482	158-150	.512	183-146	.556	369-326	.531
	PITT-1975	115- 89	.564	170-157	.520	54-44	.551	339-290	.539
	PITT-1976	—		172-155	.526	181-185	.495	353-340	.509
	TOTALS	143-119	.546	500-467	.520	418-375	.527	1061- 956	.526
Pat Cramer	LA-1974	—		68-106	.390	19-23	.406	87-129	.403
Doug Crawford	BOS-1974	—		—		13-19	.406	13-19	.406
Ian Crookenden	BALT-1974	—		48-65	.424	8-15	.347	56-80	.412
Owen Davidson	MINN-1974	38-50	.431	227-195	.537	43-46	.483	308-291	.514
	HAW-1975	—		96-98	.495	36-39	.480	132-137	.491
	HAW-1976	—		200-257	.438	133-143	.482	333-400	.454
	TOTALS	38-50	.431	523-550	.487	212-228	.482	773-828	.483
Phil Dent	DET-1974	222-224	.497	172-157	.522	10- 8	.555	404-389	.509
	NY-1976	58-81	.417	225-188	.545	127- 97	.567	410-366	.528
	TOTALS	280-305	.419	397-345	.535	137-105	.566	814-755	.519
Peter Doerner	HOU-1974	—		—		8-9	.470	8-9	.470
Bill Drake	BOS-1975	—		—		20-15	.571	20-15	.571
Cliff Drysdale	FLA-1974	155-148	.511	154-144	.516	12- 5	.705	321-297	.519
	SD-1976	28-27	.509	50-63	.442	5-12	.295	83-102	.449
	TOTALS	183-175	.511	204-207	.496	17-17	.500	404-399	.503
Tom Edelfsen	HAW-1975	9-13	.409	58-80	.420	56-83	.403	123-176	.411
Roy Emerson	GG-1974	90-71	.559	63-57	.525	8-12	.400	161-140	.535
Mike Estep	T/B-1974	7-6	.538	157-137	.534	221-216	.505	378-353	.517
	BOS-1976	—		36-44	.450	211-187	.530	247-231	.517
	TOTALS	7-6	.538	193-181	.516	432-403	.517	625-584	.517
Brian Fairlie	PHIL-1974	105-121	.464	208-199	.511	9-13	.409	321-333	.491
	PHX-1975	96-110	.466	122-103	.542	—		218-213	.506
	TOTALS	201-231	.465	330-302	.522	9-13	.409	539-546	.497
Ian Fletcher	T/B-1974	27-39	.409	47-46	.505	24-32	.428	98-117	.456
John Fort	LA-1974	1-6	.143	—		8-9	.470	9-15	.375
Frank Froehling	FLA-1974	35-43	.448	68-79	.462	66-58	.532	169-180	.484
Vitas Gerulaitus	PITT-1974	17-19	.472	89-53	.517	112-144	.437	218-216	.502
	PITT-1975	115-117	.496	156-157	.498	43-45	.489	314-319	.496
	PITT-1976	175-173	.503	107-125	.461	4-6	.400	286-304	.484
	TOTALS	307-312	.496	352-365	.491	159-195	.449	818-839	.494
Hans Gildemeister	CLV-1976	—		25-25	.500	96-107	.473	121-132	.478
Bob Giltinan	CLV-1975	41-53	.436	80-94	.460	40-48	.455	161-195	.452
	CLV-1976	—		2-4	.333	7-12	.368	9-16	.360
	TOTALS	41-53	.436	82-98	.456	47-60	.439	170-211	.446

Clark Graebner	CLV-1974	—		218-213	.505	178-174	.505	396-387	.505
	CLV-1975	—		166-167	.498	160-149	.518	326-316	.508
	TOTALS	—		384-380	.503	338-323	.511	722-703	.507
Chico Hagay	SD-1976	—		—		22-16	.579	22-16	.579
Bob Hewitt	MINN-1974	190-199	.488	190-156	.549	6-4	.600	386-359	.518
	BOS-1975	88-99	.471	231-194	.544	42-29	.592	361-322	.529
	BOS-1976	—		—		2-6	.250	2-6	.250
	TOTALS	·278-298	.483	421-350	.546	50-39	.562	749-687	.522
Rod Laver	SD-1976	188-158	.543	198-193	.506	—		386-351	.524
Tom Leonard	SD-1975	—		6-2	.750	7-6	.538	13- 8	.619
Bill Lloyd	MINN-1974	11-19	.366	49-53	.480	218-207	.512	278-279	.499
John Lucas	GG-1976	7-10	.412	4-6	.400	9-10	.474	20-26	.435
Bob Lutz	LA-1975	131-134	.494	26-25	.510	29-26	.527	186-185	.501
	LA-1976	95-84	.531	186-173	.518	86-75	.534	367-332	.525
	TOTALS	226-218	.509	212-198	.517	115-101	.532	553-517	.517
Mike Machette	HAW-1974	17-15	.531	86-95	.475	61-60	.504	164-170	.491
	SD/LA-1975	2-6	.250	8-18	.308	10- 8	.556	20-32	.385
	TOTALS	19-21	.475	94-113	.454	71-68	.511	184-202	.477
Barry MacKay	HAW-1974	—		6-12	.333	11- 9	.550	17-21	.447
	HAW-1975	—		—		15-18	.455	15-18	.455
	TOTALS	—		6-12	.333	26-27	.491	32-39	.451
Geoff Masters	LA-1974	85-100	.459	125-121	.508	194-185	.512	404-406	.499
	LA-1975	39-48	.448	197-191	.508	164-152	.519	400-391	.506
	TOTALS	124-148	.456	322-312	.508	358-337	.515	804-797	.502
Sandy Mayer	NY-1974	34-43	.441	59-83	.415	2-6	.250	95-132	.418
	NY-1975	211-202	.511	208-215	.492	—		419-417	.501
	NY-1976	154-114	.575*	237-192	.552	76-60	.559	467-366	.561
	TOTALS	399-359	.526	504-490	.507	78-66	.542	981-915	.517
Bob McKinley	HOU-1974	—		3-6	.333	—		3-6	.333
Frew McMillan	GG-1974	3-6	.500	213-214	.498	156-157	.498	372-377	.497
	GG-1975	—		232-177	.567	103- 83	.554	335-260	.563
	GG-1976	—		223-168	.570	210-179	.540	433-347	.555
	TOTALS	3-6	.500	668-559	.544	469-419	.528	1140- 984	.537
Shushi Menon	SD-1975	5-7	.417	3-6	.333	—		8-13	.381
Bernie Mitton	PITT-1976	47-47	.500	181-166	.527	31-31	.500	259-244	.515
Ray Moore	CLV-1974	45-33	.576	218-213	.505	60-65	.480	323-311	.509
Buster Mottram	PHIL-1974	168-165	.504	35-45	.437	10-18	.357	213-228	.483
J. Mukertea	BALT-1974	—		70-82	.460	—			
Ilie Nastase	HAW-1976	179-176	.504	119-125	.488	71-57	.555	369-358	.508
John Newcombe	HOU-1974	194-133	.593*	231-179	.563	64-60	.516	489-372	.568
	HAW-1975	59-47	.557	103-101	.505	88-68	.564	250-216	.536
	TOTALS	253-180	.584	334-280	.544	152-128	.543	739-588	.557
Tom Okker	T/B-1974	234-161	.592	190-173	.523	—		424-334	.559
	GG-1975	230-202	.532	229-172	.571	—		459-374	.551
	GG-1976	210-186	.530	213-160	.571	6·2	.750	429-348	.552
	TOTALS	674-549	.551	632-505	.556	6-2	.750	1312-1056	.554
Charlie Owens	NY-1974	30-39	.434	83-101	.451	75-89	.457	188-229	.417
	NY-1975	3-12	.200	10- 9	.526	67-67	.500	80-88	.476
	TOTALS	33-51	.393	93-110	.458	142-156	.477	268-317	.458

		SINGLES		DOUBLES		MIXED		TOTALS	
		GW-GL	PCT	GW-GL	PCT	GW-GL	PCT	GW-GL	PCT
Charles Panui	HAW-1974	—		—		27-41	.397	27-41	.397
	HAW-1975	—		—		1-7	.125	1-7	.125
	TOTALS	—		—		28-48	.368	28-48	.368
Charles Pasarell	HAW-1975	20-22	.476	—		5-9	.357	25-31	.446
	LA-1976	—		67-85	.441	12-12	.500	79-97	.449
	TOTALS	20-22	.476	67-85	.441	17-21	.447	104-128	.448
Andrew Pattison	DEN-1974	239-218	.522	249-213	.538	22-29	.431	510-460	.526
	PHX-1975	61-58	.513	65-65	.500	—		126-123	.506
	PHX-1976	171-187	.478	199-190	.512	19-22	.463	389-399	.494
	TOTALS	471-463	.504	513-469	.522	41-51	.477	1025- 982	.511
Nikki Pilic	NY-1974	142-148	.489	136-170	.444	40-41	.493	318-359	.470
Haroon Rahim	CLV-1976	78-91	.462	216-237	.477	65-103	.387	359-431	.454
Dennis Ralston	HAW-1974	23-32	.418	92-111	.453	120-115	.510	235-258	.477
	SD-1975	31-32	.492	56-92	.378	85-90	.486	172-214	.446
	LA-1976	—		69-86	.445	96-93	.508	165-179	.480
	TOTALS	54-64	.450	217-289	.429	301-298	.503	572-651	.468
Whitney Reed	GG-1974	4-6	.400	11-10	.523	55-84	.395	70-100	.412
	GG-1975	—		—		4-7	.364	4-7	.364
	TOTALS	4-6	.400	11-10	.523	59-91	.393	74-107	.409
Raz Reid	BOS-1974	82-84	.493	115-137	.456	67-62	.519	264-283	.483
	BOS-1975	88-112	.440	41-48	.461	56-59	.487	185-219	.460
	TOTALS	170-196	.464	156-185	.457	123-121	.504	449-502	.472
Cliff Richey	CLV-1974	213-204	.510	—		6-1	.897	219-205	.517
	LA-1976	6-3	.667	1-6	.143	—		7-9	.438
	TOTALS	219-207	.514	1-6	.143	6-1	.897	226-214	.514
Marty Riessen	CLV-1975	187-141	.570	182-183	.499	29-26	.527	398-350	.532
	CLV-1976	145-134	.520	207-228	.476	12-14	.462	364-376	.492
	TOTALS	332-275	.547	389-411	.486	41-40	.506	762-726	.512
Tony Roche	DEN-1974	56-48	.538	236-193	.550	171-137	.555	463-378	.551
	PHX-1975	40-37	.519	167-164	.505	52-57	.477	259-258	.501
	PHX-1976	37-35	.514	159-156	.505	104- 88	.542	300-279	.518
	TOTALS	133-120	.526	562-513	.523	327-282	.537	1022- 915	.528
Ken Rosewall	HAW-1976	5-12	.294	6-3	.667	—		11-15	.423
Ray Ruffels	CHI-1974	36-35	.507	13- 9	.590	22-20	.523	71-64	.526
	IND-1975	99-93	.516	204-166	.552	59-61	.492	362-320	.531
	IND-1976	91-111	.450	158-155	.505	91-68	.572	340-334	.504
	TOTALS	226-239	.486	375-330	.532	172-149	.536	773-718	.518
Manuel Santana	NY-1974	23-28	.450	63-76	.453	93-84	.525	179-188	.488
Bill Schoen	SD-1975	—		—		6-4	.600	6-4	.600
Gene Scott	NY-1974	—		7-12	.368	21-28	.428	28-40	.412
Butch Seewagon	DET-1974	5-17	.227	25-35	.416	40-59	.404	70-111	.387
Lendward Simpson	DET-1974	—		—		0-5	.000	0-5	.000
Graham Stilwell	CHI-1974	65-103	.386	98-107	.478	87-108	.446	250-318	.440
Dick Stockton	HOU-1974	99-74	.572	199-146	.576	102-104	.495	400-324	.552
	HAW-1975	9-11	.450	3-6	.333	—		12-17	.414
	TOTALS	108-85	.560	202-152	.571	102-104	.495	412-341	.547

131

Name		SINGLES GW-GL	PCT	DOUBLES GW-GL	PCT	MIXED GW-GL	PCT	TOTALS GW-GL	PCT
Fred Stolle	PHIL-1974	6-7	.461	211-210	.501	275-211	.565	492-428	.535
	NY-1975	3-6	.333	198-206	.489	164-116	.586	365-328	.527
	NY-1976	3-6	.333	24-18	.571	16-34	.320	43-58	.426
	TOTALS	12-19	.387	433-434	.499	455-361	.558	900-814	.525
Allan Stone	DET-1974	9-24	.272	197-192	.506	205-174	.540	411-390	.513
	IND-1975	102-97	.512	227-193	.540	63-68	.481	392-358	.527
	IND-1976	123-123	.500	158-189	.455	—		281-312	.474
	TOTALS	234-244	.490	582-574	.503	268-242	.525	1084-1060	.506
Ken Stuart	SD-1975	—		—		3-12	.200	3-12	.200
Roger Taylor	BOS-1974	149-162	.479	151-171	.468	5-12	.294	305-345	.469
	PHX-1975	—		1-6	.143	6-7	.462	7-13	.350
	TOTALS	149-162	.479	152-177	.462	11-19	.367	312-358	.466
Ion Tiriac	BOS-1974	—		66-77	.461	117-107	.522	183-184	.499
	BOS-1975	22-31	.415	208-172	.547	113-103	.523	343-306	.529
	BOS-1976	—		184-185	.499	6-12	.333	190-197	.491
	TOTALS	22-31	.415	458-434	.513	236-222	.515	716-687	.510
Jerry Van Linge	LA-1974	22-28	.440	—		1-6	.143	23-34	.404
Butch Walts	PHX-1976	5-12	.294	73-78	.483	92-100	.479	170-190	.472
Stephan Warboys	BOS-1974	—		12-15	.444	41-54	.431	53-69	.434
Kim Warwick	CHI-1974	19-25	.431	171-174	.495	110-126	.466	300-325	.480
	PITT-1975	3-6	.333	110-126	.466	135-126	.517	248-258	.490
	TOTALS	22-31	.415	281-300	.484	245-252	.493	548-583	.485

*Season Leader
**Career Leader

WOMEN:

Name		SINGLES GW-GL	PCT	DOUBLES GW-GL	PCT	MIXED GW-GL	PCT	TOTALS GW-GL	PCT
Julie Anthony	PHIL-1974	0-6	.000	202-111	.645	256-205	.555	458-322	.587
Pam Austin	DEN-1974	—		—		32-28	.533	32-28	.533
	PHX-1975	—		—		25-27	.481	25-27	.481
	TOTALS	—		—		57-55	.509	57-55	.509
Peaches Bartkowicz	CLV-1974	0-6	.000	105-90	.538	62-39	.613	167-135	.553
Mary Ann Beattie	DET-1974	—		55-43	.461	81-96	.457	136-139	.495
	HAW-1975	—		4-6	.400	1-6	.143	5-12	.294
	TOTALS	—		59-49	.546	82-102	.446	141-151	.483
Lindsey Beaven	NY-1976	—		4-18	.182	—		4-18	.182
Fiorelia Bonicelli	NY-1974	—		1-12	.076	27-32	.457	28-44	.389
Pat Bostrom	BOS-1974	1-6	.143	154-157	.495	148-164	.474	303-327	.481
	IND-1975	1-6	.143	123-147	.456	90-115	.439	214-268	.444
	TOTALS	2-12	.143	277-304	.471	238-279	.460	517-595	.465
Leslie Bowrey	HOU-1974	42-46	.477	82-77	.515	86-78	.524	210-201	.511
Maria Bueno	FLA-1974	15-25	.375	2-6	.250	13-13	.500	30-44	.405

		SINGLES		DOUBLES		MIXED		TOTALS	
		GW-GL	PCT	GW-GL	PCT	GW-GL	PCT	GW-GL	PCT
Rosie Casals	DET-1974	271-173	.610	204-169	.546	9-8	.529	484-350	.580
	LA-1975	209-145	.590	130-116	.528	105- 87	.547	444-348	.561
	LA-1976	67-66	.504	175-185	.486	182-163	.528	424-414	.506
	TOTALS	547-384	.588	509-470	.520	296-258	.534	1352-1112	.548
Joyce Champaigne	HAW-1975	—		—		3-6	.333	3-6	.333
Margaret Court	HAW-1975	131-126	.510	144-164	.468	8-8	.500	283-298	.487
	HAW-1976	14-16	.467	101-123	.451	122-101	.547	237-240	.497
	TOTALS	145-142	.505	245-287	.461	130-109	.544	520-538	.491
Brigitte Cuypers	HAW-1974	91-117	.437	14-32	.304	10-19	.344	115-168	.406
	HAW/SD-1975	55-105	.344	79-115	.407	90-87	.508	224-307	.422
	TOTALS	146-222	.397	93-147	.388	100-106	.485	339-475	.416
Heather Dalgren	HAW-1975	—		—		9-15	.375	9-15	.375
Cynthia Doerner	HOU-1974	—		7-13	.350	7-13	.350	14-26	.350
Barbara Downs	CHI-1974	18-22	.450	3-12	.200	2-6	.250	23-40	.365
Laura Dupont	CLV-1974	32-47	.405	120-139	.463	53-85	.384	205-271	.431
	CLV-1975	3-10	.231	29-38	.433	65-79	.451	97-127	.433
	TOTALS	35-57	.380	149-177	.457	118-164	.418	302-398	.431
Francoise Durr	DEN-1974	251-208	.546	209-163	.562	14-16	.466	474-387	.550
	PHX-1975	201-181	.526	216-185	.539	—		417-366	.533
	GG-1976	61-70	.466	226-167	.575	162-125	.564	449-362	.554
	TOTALS	513-459	.528	651-515	.558	176-141	.559	1340-1115	.546
Sue Eastman	CHI-1974	—		—		41-45	.476	41-45	.476
Lynn Epstein	FLA-1974	1-6	.143	—		—		1-6	.143
Chris Evert	PHX-1976	226- 97	.700	205-170	.547	1-0	.000	432-267	.618
Donna Fales	FLA-1974	—		12-25	.324	44-41	.517	56-66	.459
Lele Forood	PHX-1976	—		1-6	.143	—		1-6	.143
Pat Faulkner	DET-1974	—		—		0-5	.000	0-5	.000
Isabel Fernandez	PITT-1974	36-46	.439	8-7	.533	87-100	.465	131-153	.461
Laurie Fleming	FLA-1974	4-30	.117	132-174	.431	167-141	.542	303-345	.468
Rayni Fox	PITT-1975	—		29-36	.446	95-95	.500	124-131	.486
	CLV-1976	—		3-12	.200	—		3-12	.200
	TOTALS	—		32-48	.400	95-95	.500	127-143	.470
Tory Fretz	PHIL-1974	—		44-30	.594	28-18	.608	72-48	.600
Dianne Fromholtz	LA-1976	131-136	.491	69-77	.473	4-6	.400	204-219	.482
Donna Ganz	FLA-1974	—		4-6	.400	2-6	.250	6-12	.333
Evonne Goolagong	PITT-1974	240-167	.589	227-138	.621	12- 5	.705	479-310	.607
	PITT-1975	227-132	.632	215-152	.586	7-6	.538	449-290	.608
	PITT-1976	215-121	.640	153-127	.546	58-51	.532	* 426-299	.588
	TOTALS	682-420	.619	595-417	.588	77-62	.544	1354- 899	.601
Raquel Giscafre	GG-1976	—		10-11	.476	—		10-11	.476
Helen Gourlay	HOU-1974	66-65	.503	99-127	.438	112-111	.502	277-303	.478
	HAW/SD-1975	7-12	.368	167-215	.437	130-128	.504	304-355	.461
	HAW-1976	2-6	.250	88-142	.383	85-100	.459	175-248	.414
	TOTALS	75-83	.475	354-484	.422	327-339	.491	756-906	.455
Carol Graebner	PITT/NY-1974	—		39-73	.348	25-26	.490	64-99	.393

Name	Team-Year	W-L	Pct	W-L	Pct	W-L	Pct	W-L	Pct
Mona Guerrant	MINN-1974	35-46	.432	190-167	.532	76-70	.520	301-283	.515
	NY-1975	—		183-112	.620	118- 90	.567	301-202	.598
	IND-1976	153-180	.459	229-180	.560	5-7	.417	387-367	.513
	TOTALS	188-226	.454	602-459	.567	199-167	.544	989-852	.537
Nancy (Gunter) Richey	CLV-1974	229-162	.585	148-164	.471	28-33	.459	405-359	.530
	PITT-1975	13-10	.565	6-12	.333	—		19-22	.463
	PITT/HAW-1976	150-172	.466	130-188	.409	—		280-360	.438
	TOTALS	392-344	.533	284-364	.438	28-33	.459	704-741	.487
Mary Hamilton	HAW-1975	—		—		0-3	.000	0-3	.000
Kerry Harris	DET-1974	5-12	.294	149-126	.541	165-137	.546	319-275	.537
Kathy Harter	LA-1974	5-11	.312	185-186	.498	15-19	.441	205-216	.487
	LA-1975	—		119-123	.492	70-58	.547	189-181	.511
	TOTALS	5-11	.312	304-309	.496	85-77	.525	394-397	.498
Terry Holladay	MINN-1974	—		—		25-27	.480	25-27	.480
	SD-1976	170-228	.427	147-186	.441	—		317-414	.437
	TOTALS	170-228	.427	147-186	.441	25-27	.480	342-441	.437
Joyce Hume	BALT-1974	37-92	.286	206-159	.564	53-61	.464	296-312	.487
Leslie Hunt	GG-1974	201-196	.506	175-163	.517	11-12	.478	387-371	.511
	SD-1975	116-147	.442	146-183	.444	32-36	.471	294-366	.445
	TOTALS	317-343	.480	321-346	.481	43-48	.473	681-737	.480
Stephanie Johnson	DEN-1974	—		18-28	.391	26-43	.376	44-71	.383
Ann Jones	MINN-1974	222-183	.548	17-14	.548	131-124	.513	370-321	.535
	CLV-1975	118-143	.452	170-204	.455	29-27	.518	317-374	.459
	LA-1976	—		152-172	.469	19-18	.514	171-190	.474
	TOTALS	340-326	.511	339-390	.465	179-169	.514	858-885	.492
Billie Jean King	PHIL-1974	318-181	.637	246-141	.635	4-6	.400	568-328	.634
	NY-1975	161- 90	.641	215-134	.617	105- 87	.547	481-311	.607
	NY-1976	80-50	.615	220-178	.553	148-106	.583	448-334	.573
	TOTALS	559-321	.635	681-453	.601	257-199	.564	1497- 973	.606
Ann Kiyomura	HAW-1974	3-12	.200	111-140	.442	118-112	.513	232-264	.468
	GG-1975	1-4	.200	196-177	.525	73-82	.471	270-263	.507
	IND-1976	7-9	.438	235-183	.562	206-186	.526	448-378	.542
	TOTALS	11-25	.306	542-500	.520	397-380	.511	950-905	.512
Ilana Kloss	GG-1974	12-20	.375	200-196	.505	162-149	.520	374-365	.506
	GG-1975	7-18	.280	178-155	.535	43-60	.417	228-233	.495
	TOTALS	19-38	.333	378-351	.519	205-209	.495	602-598	.502
Karen Krantzcke	HOU-1974	121-135	.472	176-191	.479	41-36	.532	338-362	.483
Kathy Kuykendall	PHIL/BALT-1974	64-119	.349	—		11-25	.305	75-144	.342
	HAW-1975	75-103	.421	47-82	.385	51-60	.459	173-245	.414
	TOTALS	139-222	.385	47-82	.385	62-85	.422	248-389	.389
Kate Latham	GG-1975	—		—		1-4	.200	1-4	.200
Marcie Louie	CHI-1974	41-51	.445	2-6	.250	23-32	.418	66-89	.426
	HAW-1976	33-42	.440	3-18	.143	—		36-60	.375
	TOTALS	74-93	.443	5-24	.172	23-32	.418	102-149	.406
Ceci Martinez	NY-1974	—		1-12	.076	21-28	.428	22-40	.355
Carrie Meyer	IND-1975	118-157	.430	123-147	.456	59-51	.536	300-355	.458
	IND-1976	20-47	.299	6-3	.667	9-13	.409	35-63	.357
	TOTALS	138-204	.404	129-150	.462	68-64	.515	335-418	.445

		SINGLES		DOUBLES		MIXED		TOTALS	
		GW-GL	PCT	GW-GL	PCT	GW-GL	PCT	GW-GL	PCT
Peggy Michel	PITT-1974	7-5	.583	224-138	.618	126-141	.471	357-284	.557
	PITT-1975	8-9	.471	216-143	.602	130-114	.533	354-266	.571
	PITT-1976	—		75-87	.463	11-14	.440	86-101	.460
	TOTALS	15-14	.517	515-368	.583	267-269	.498	797-651	.550
Audrey Morse	BALT-1974	—		—		10-19	.344	10-19	.344
Betsy Nagelsen	NY-1975	—		—		7-15	.318	7-15	.318
Martina Navratilova	CLV-1976	227-198	.534	222-184	.547	4-6	.400	453-388	.539
Janet Newberry	BOS-1974	13-21	.382	105-115	.477	62-56	.525	180-192	.484
Janet O'Neill	T/B-1974	22-50	.305	12-48	.200	108-108	.500	142-206	.408
Wendy Overton	T/B-1974	156-186	.456	108-177	.378	95-88	.519	359-451	.443
	IND-1975	52-78	.400	122-156	.439	57-67	.460	231-301	.434
	CLV-1976	—		225-196	.534	108-121	.472	333-317	.512
	TOTALS	208-264	.441	455-529	.462	260-276	.485	923-1069	.463
Kristie Pigeon	HAW-1974	5-12	.294	14-15	.483	16-23	.410	35-50	.412
	HAW-1975	—		14-12	.538	9-13	.409	23-25	.479
	TOTALS	5-12	.294	28-27	.509	25-36	.410	58-75	.436
Marita Redondo	LA-1974	198-205	.491	—		8-9	.470	206-214	.490
	SD-1975	3-12	.200	6-7	.462	7-5	.583	16-33	.327
	TOTALS	201-217	.449	6-7	.462	15-14	.517	222-247	.473
Kerry Reid	BOS-1974	222-205	.519	65-58	.528	23-25	.479	310-288	.518
	BOS-1975	162-154	.513	98-130	.430	19-11	.633	279-295	.486
	BOS-1976	115-142	.447	101-122	.453	4-6	.400	220-270	.449
	TOTALS	499-501	.499	264-310	.460	46-42	.573	809-853	.487
Laura Rossouw	T/B-1974	15-30	.333	118-201	.369	42-52	.446	175-283	.382
JoAnn Russell	PITT-1976	—		129-129	.500	130-137	.487	259-266	.493
Kristien Shaw	DEN-1974	24-40	.375	207-171	.547	211-186	.531	442-397	.527
	PHX-1975	6-7	.462	239-191	.556	173-198	.466	418-396	.514
	PHX-1976	11-18	.379	219-202	.520	176-171	.507	406-391	.509
	TOTALS	41-65	.387	665-564	.541	560-555	.502	1266-1184	.517
Linda Siegelman	NY-1976	—		—		3-12	.200	3-12	.200
Sue Stap	CHI-1974	177-183	.491	158-185	.457	11-14	.440	346-382	.475
	CLV-1975	60-66	.476	111-136	.449	130-105	.553	301-307	.495
	PITT/HAW-1976	5-20	.200	79-126	.385	22-17	.564	106-163	.394
	TOTALS	242-269	.474	348-447	.438	163-136	.545	753-852	.469
Greer Stevens	BOS-1975	51-48	.515	98-101	.492	29-17	.630	178-166	.517
	BOS-1976	38-57	.400	110-130	.458	48-43	.527	196-230	.460
	TOTALS	89-105	.459	208-231	.474	77-60	.562	374-396	.486
Betty Stove	BALT-1974	51-85	.375	206-159	.564	163-147	.525	420-391	.518
	GG-1975	195-177	.524	52-60	.464	93-70	.571	340-307	.526
	GG-1976	118-161	.423	236-178	.570	66-62	.520	420-401	.512
	TOTALS	364-423	.463	494-397	.554	322-279	.536	1180-1099	.518
Bettyann Stuart	FLA-1974	191-183	.512	138-125	.440	50-22	.694	379-330	.535
	LA-1975	10-25	.285	190-185	.507	55-57	.491	255-267	.486
	SD-1976	3-12	.200	187-223	.456	175-184	.487	365-419	.466
	TOTALS	204-220	.481	515-533	.491	280-263	.516	999-1016	.496
Karen Susman	LA-1974	—		185-186	.498	219-216	.503	404-402	.501
Francis Taylor	BOS-1974	4-6	.400	—		—		4-6	.400
Pam Teeguarden	NY-1974	118-127	.481	68-116	.369	131-116	.530	317-359	.469
	BOS-1975	23-32	.418	163-188	.464	23-18	.561	209-238	.468
	TOTALS	141-159	.470	231-304	.432	154-134	.535	526-597	.468

Player	Team-Year								
Pat Thomas	CLV-1974	—		4-6	.400	4-6	.400	8-12	.400
Margo Tiff	CLV-1975	—		—		1-6	.143	1-6	.143
Stephanie Tolleson	PHX-1975	1-6	.143	13-6	.684	6-13	.316	20-25	.444
	PHX-1976	6-12	.333	15-38	.283	37-34	.521	58-84	.408
	TOTALS	7-18	.280	28-44	.389	43-47	.478	78-109	.417
Denise Triolo	GG-1974	—		25-33	.431	50-98	.337	75-131	.368
Francis Troll	BOS/SD-1975	—		6-4	.600	4-6	.400	10-10	.500
Wendy Turnbull	MINN-1974	—		207-181	.533	35-36	.492	242-217	.527
	BOS-1975	4-6	.400	117-119	.496	123-106	.537	244-231	.514
	TOTALS	4-6	.400	324-300	.519	158-142	.527	473-448	.514
Judy Vincent	HAW-1974	—		—		6-2	.750	6-2	.750
Andrea Voikos	BOS-1974	—		—		10-9	.526	10-9	.526
Virginia Wade	NY-1974	113-93	.548	93-102	.476	8-12	.400	214-207	.508
	NY-1975	77-69	.527	106-70	.602	54-55	.551	237-183	.564
	NY-1976	146-129	.531	221-184	.546	54-45	.545	421-358	.540
	TOTALS	336-308	.522	420-356	.541	116-101	.535	872-748	.538
Sharon Walsh	NY-1974	7-12	.368	81-102	.442	34-52	.395	122-166	.424
Winnie Woolridge	CLV-1974	—		34-59	.365	30-23	.566	64-82	.438
Janet Young	CHI-1974	2-12	.143	158-185	.460	166-183	.475	326-380	.462
	SD-1975	—		155-204	.432	101-123	.445	256-327	.439
	SD-1976	—		40-37	.519	—		40-37	.519
	TOTALS	2-12	.143	353-426	.453	267-306	.466	622-744	.455
Val Ziegenfuss	HAW-1974	91-132	.408	135-175	.435	96-93	.507	322-400	.446
	BOS/CLV-1975	13-21	.429	125-160	.439	96-113	.459	234-296	.442
	TOTALS	104-153	.405	260-335	.437	192-206	.482	556-694	.445

WTT: 1977 and Beyond

After three years in Major Wingfield's Garden, the weed known as WTT was no longer weak and ugly. On the contrary, it had become a prominent member of that botanical community and one that an increasing number of people were finding attractive. Some even spoke of the day in the not too distant future when the weed would be the garden's chief attraction.

In 1977, the one hundredth anniversary of Wimbledon, the sport's cornerstone event, World Team Tennis entered its fourth season. After a shaky beginning, the league was thriving and its potential for future growth was unlimited. In its brief history it had proved to be a vehicle for unprecedented mass tennis spectatorship. This was a particularly impressive achievement, because unlike new leagues in other professional sports, WTT had to create its own following since there existed no established tennis league from which to draw support.

Along the way WTT met, and successfully survived countless obstacles that such an ambitious and radical enterprise was bound to confront. And each victory brought further acceptance for the league as it sought to become a legitimate theater of tennis.

This does not mean that WTT's battle for acceptance is over. It is not. The league still finds itself on the receiving end of an occasional well-aimed potshot.

As recently as December 1976, for instance, the Women's International Professional Tennis Council, aka the Women's Pro Council, rejected a proposal to include WTT in the 1977 Colgate International

Series. The Series links major tournaments throughout the world with a point system leading to bonus prizes of $600,000 for the top women players. In addition, the top eight players in the final point standings will be eligible to compete in the lucrative Colgate International Series Championships in October 1977.

Since the vast majority of top women players participate in WTT four months out of the year, the move to bar WTT from the Series obviously will hinder their chances in the point standings. Therefore, the decision of the Women's Pro Council may be interpreted as something less than supportive of WTT. Colgate, sponsor of the Series, was not against including WTT, nor was the WTA, which has three representatives on the Council. Why then was the league snubbed?

Well, besides the three WTA reps, the Women's Pro Council has three members chosen by the ILTF. The ILTF also has the deciding vote when matters before the Council reach an impasse. When a deadlock occurs, Derek Hardwick, President of the Council is empowered to cast the tiebreaking ballot. Incidentally, Mr. Harwick is the President of the ILTF.

Typically, however, WTT just shrugged off the slap in the face administered by the Women's Pro Council, and turned to the business at hand, preparing for the 1977 season. With the addition of the Soviet team in January, the 1977 WTT lineup was complete. A schedule was drawn up, and the annual player draft was conducted. The usual stream of optimistic projections and predictions were being issued by WTT headquarters, only this time no one was laughing. The anticipated attendance figure of 1.4 million in 1977 seemed realistic, or maybe even slightly conservative, and corporate sponsorship promised to surpass the combined total the league had attracted in its first two years of operation.

WTT will explore new markets, most notably in the Pacific Northwest, and will return to an original WTT city, Philadelphia, for the first time since 1974. The fourth WTT season will also bring a number of personnel changes. With Pittsburgh out of action, the Triangles' roster was scattered. Evonne Goolagong was picked up by the Golden Gaters, but she will probably sit out the 1977 season after the birth of her first child in the spring. Another three-year Triangles' vet, Vitas Gerulaitis, signed with the Indiana Loves. Billie Jean King spent most of the winter recuperating from a knee operation, her third, but she will once again bring her impressive talent to the New York Apples.

Bjorn Borg, the 1976 Wimbledon men's singles champion, will make his WTT debut as a member of the Cleveland Nets, and Chris Evert, the number one female player in the world, will be back for a second year with the Phoenix Racquets.

But what lies beyond 1977?

There are some who believe that the entry of the Soviet team is the first step towards the day when countries all over the world will field national teams and WTT will be a truly global league seen by millions.

Until then, however, we can only be certain of two things: that World Team Tennis will remain predictably unpredictable, and that it will be around for us to enjoy for a long, long time.

Photo credits:

Bissell/Lukor Fotographie: p. 66 (right), 67

California Photo Service: p. 89

Todd Friedman/WTT: p. 26 (top left), 36 (center and bottom, 43 (right), 44-59, 66 (left), 82, 86, 91, 102

Dina Makarova: p. 42

The author wishes to thank WTT and all the individual WTT teams for supplying photographs for this book.

Illustrations:

Plate from Walter Wingfield, *The Game of Sphairistike or Lawn Tennis*, 5th edition, 1876. Photo: British Museum. p. 3

Print published by the centenary celebrations of the Leamington Lawn Tennis Club. Courtesy Tom Todd. Photo: David Rudkin. p. 4

Drawing of Sister Mary Mummy by Frank Ansley, p. 69

About the author

Greg Hoffman is a former associate editor of *womenSports* magazine, whose work has been published in *Tennis Illustrated, Creem, The New York Times,* and *Catholic Digest.* He has also been the editor of *Tenniswomen,* The Virginia Slims national program, and *Super Tiebreaker,* the World Team Tennis national program.

He has written comedy material for Phyllis Diller and one of his well-known "Sister Mary Mummy" articles had been selected for inclusion in *Best Sports Stories 1977.*

Mr. Hoffman, who is currently working on a tennis book with Billie Jean King and Charles Schulz, lives in the San Francisco Bay Area with his wife and seven-year-old son.